English Unlimited

B1 **Pre-intermediate**
Coursebook with e-Portfolio

Alex Tilbury, Theresa Clementson, Leslie Anne Hendra & David Rea
Course consultant: Adrian Doff

CAMBRIDGE
UNIVERSITY PRESS

Acknowledgements

The authors would like to thank all the team at CUP for their ideas, support and commitment to *English Unlimited*, in particular their editors Karen Momber, Greg Sibley and Keith Sands, and David Lawton for his work on the cover and page design. They'd also like to thank Adrian Doff for his consistently encouraging and remarkably detailed feedback; and Dave Willis, Jane Willis, Alison Sharpe and Sue Ullstein for their ideas and inspiration in the early days of this project.

Thanks are also due to Michael Stuart Clark, Dariusz Klimkowicz, Monica Koorichh and Li Mills for particular ideas and contributions.

Alex Tilbury would like to dedicate his work on *English Unlimited* to Geoffrey William Tilbury, Carol Tilbury and Sławek Smolorz, with love and thanks.

David Rea would like to thank the students, teachers, trainers and staff at IH Kraków, IH Heliopolis, IH Buenos Aires, IH Paris and IH London for all the support, development and fun over the years. He'd also like to thank Emma McLachlan: the most beautiful woman in the world.

Leslie Anne Hendra would like to thank her four long-time students and friends in Japan: Junko Terajima, Eiko Kanai, Akiko Tsuzuki and Akiko Ohno. With much appreciation for all the wonderful time we spent together.

Theresa Clementson would like to thank Anthony, Sam and Megan for their ideas, support and unwavering confidence, and Cristina Rimini for her help and advice on all matters TEFL over the years.

The authors and publishers would like to thank the following teachers for invaluable feedback they provided when reviewing draft material:
Howard Smith, Merryn Grimley (UK); María de los Ángeles Vélez Guzmán (Mexico); Justyna Kubica (Poland); Gill Hamilton (Spain); Martin Goosey (Korea); Catherine Land (Czech Republic); Iris Grallert, Donna Liersch (Germany); Rachel Connabeer (Italy); Jamelea Nader (Japan); Amanda Gamble (Turkey); and the various members of the Cambridge Adult Panel.

The authors and publishers are also grateful to the following contributors:
Design and page make-up: Stephanie White at Kamae Design
Picture research: Hilary Luckcock
Photography: Gareth Boden
Audio recordings: John Green at Audio Workshop and id-Audio, London

The authors and publishers would like to thank all of those who took part in the authentic recording sessions, especially:

Annie Gentil, Alba Higgins, David Warwick, Susanne Neubert, Siew Wan Chai, Xi Yen Tan, Paula Porroni, Natalie Krol, Leonardo Solano, Megan Rivers-Moore, Manuel Arroyo-Kalin, Pham Thi Thanh An, Andrew Reid, Richa Bansal, Masha Sutton, Seung Yang, Tom Boyd, Fran Disken, Astrid Gonzales-Rabade, Anri Iwasaki, Annie Gentil, Martin Huarte-Espinosa, Ivan Gladstone, Nuria Gonzales-Rabade.

The authors and publishers acknowledge the following sources of copyright material and are grateful for the permissions granted. While every effort has been made, it has not always been possible to identify the sources of all the material used, or to trace all copyright holders. If any omissions are brought to our notice, we will be happy to include the appropriate acknowledgements on reprinting.

With thanks to the WOMADelaide Foundation and writer David Sly for the extract on p11; Ruben Gonzalez, www.OlympicMotivation.com, for the text on p13; Judi Bevan for the text on p27; Melissa Plaut for the text on p36 taken from: http://newyorkhack.blogspot.com/2006/08/cow-catcher.html. Reproduced by permission of Melissa Plaut; Microcredit Summit Campaign for the extracts on pp45, 124. Reproduced by permission of Microcredit Summit Campaign; Mark Glaser for the text on p110 taken from: http://www.pbs.org/mediashift/2006/03/open-source-reportingliving-your-life-online086.html. Copyright PBS 2006; Content copyright © Dr.Nandita Iyer for the text on p116; *The Metro* for the article 'The Cycle Washer' by Sarah Hills on p124, © *The Metro*.

The publisher has used its best endeavours to ensure that the URLs for external websites referred to in this book are correct and active at the time of going to press. However, the publisher has no responsibility for the websites and can make no guarantee that a site will remain live or that the content is or will remain appropriate.

The publishers are grateful to the following for permission to reproduce copyright photographs and material:

Key: l = left, c = centre, r = right, t = top, b = bottom

Alamy Images/John Sylvester for p7(tc), /©JupiterImages/Comstock for p7(tl), /©Blend Images for p7(tc), /©OJO Images Ltd for p7(tr), /© OJO Images Ltd for p8(tl), /©Photo Resource Hawaii for p12(bl), /©Studio9 for p14(tr), /©Radius Images for p18(tl), /©Radius Images for p18(tc), /©Alex Segre for p18(bl), /©Jenny Matthews for p18(br), /©Radius Images for p20(t), /©Radius Images for p20(b), /©Dave Penman for p26(l), /©Peter Horree for p26(c), /©Matt Griggs for p26(r), /©Graham Corney for p27(l), /©Itani Images for p27(ltc), /©Mira for p27(lbc), /©Blend Images for p31(c), /©Steve Teague for p32(H), /©LOOK Die Bildagentur der Fotografen GmbH for p35, /© LOOK Die Bildagentur der Fotografen GmbH for p40(c), /©JTB Photo for p46(tr), /©imagebroker for p48(t), /©A T Willett for p52(t background), /©imagebroker for p52(tr), /©uli nusko for p52(tcr), /©Robert Read for p52(tc), /©Richard Naude for p56(tr), /©Rupert Horrox/Sylvia Cordaiy Photos Ltd for p71, /©Pictures Colour Library for p63, /©Andre

Jenny for p64(t), /©Mark Dyball for p67(b), /©INTERFOTO Pressebildagentur for p69(t), /©INSADCO Photography for p70(B), /©40260.com for p70(bl), /©Image State for p74(A), /©Gary Cook for p79(t), /©Sunday Photo Europe a.s. for p79(b), /©Jeff Greenberg for p80, /©Ian Shaw for p81, /©View Stock for p82(b), /©Iain Masterston for p84(t), /©RedCopsticks.com LLC for p84(b), /©Roussel Bernard for p85(t), /©UpperCut Images for p87(tr), /©David Young-Wolff for p87(b), /©Guillen Photography for p95, /©Ashley Cooper for p99(b), /©croftsphoto for p102(tl), /©Blend Images for p106(bl), /©Elmtree Images for p118(l), /©Roy Lawe for p118(c), /©Hornbil Images for p118(r), /©Image Source Black for p119(bl), /©Digital Vision for p120, /©imagebroker for p142(cheese), /©Andrew Twort for p142(cream), /©foodfolio for p142(salad), /©Jeffrey Blackler for p142(sauces), /©Andre Jenny for p142(spices), /©mediablitzimages (UK) Ltd for p142(vegetables), /©B & Y Photography for p142(spaghetti), /©foodfolio for p142(bake), /©Edd Westmacott for p142(boil), /©Red Fred for p142(fry), /©foodfolio for p142(roast); Alex Gadsden for p50(r); Beinbecke Rare Book & Manuscript Library, Yale University for p68(l); Bob Lestina for p45; Bopha Devi, Docklands, Australia for p28(tc); Corbis/©Dan Forer/Beateworks for p7(br), /©LWA-Dann Tardif for p8(tr), /©Jim Craigmyle for p8(b), /©Studio Eye for p30(c), /©Bjoern Sigurdsoen/epa for p44, /©Jonny le Fortune/zefa for p46(tl), /©image 100 for p47, /©The Irish Image Collection for p56(tl), /©Corbis Premium RF for p74(C), /©Corbis Super RF for p74(D), /©Paul Almasy for p92(l), /©Peter Turnley for p102(tr), /©Bettmann for p103(b), /©Studio Eye for p142(grill); DK Images for p142(stir), /©Howard Shooter for p32G, /©Dave King for p142(shake); Egyptian Museum, Cairo for pp68(r), 73; Emporis GmbH for p90(tr); Fondation Le Corbusier for pp 92 (cl, cr, r); Getty Images/©Stone for p10(tcl), /©Altrendo Images for p10(tr), /©Image Bank for p18(bc), /©Gulf Images for p21, /©Photolibrary for p24(r), /©imagewerks for p46(bl), /©Timothy A Clary/AFP for p50(l), /©Harald Sund for p60(b), /©Paul Quayle for p66(tr), /©PNC for p66(tr), /©Alan Becker for p66(br), /©Stephen Hoeck for p70(bcr), /©Narinder Nanu/AFP for p93, /©Aurora for p100(l), /©Denis Poroy/AFP for p100(r), /©Steve Smith for p115, /©Mike Powell for p114(t); istockphoto/©Arkady Chubykin for p52(br), /©Mummu Media for p74(E); Dr Nandita Iyer for p116; PA Photos/AP Photo/Diane Bondareff for p36(l); Panos/©Tim A Hetherington for p64(b); Photolibrary/©OJO Images Ltd for p18(tr), /©Hans-Peter Merten for p28(tl), /©PhotoDisc for p31(t), /©Robert Lawson for p32(E), /©PhotoDisc for p66(bl), /©image100 for p74(B), /©Jon Arnold RF for p82(t), /©OJO Images for p83, /©Richard Glover for p90(tl), /©Warwick Kent for p90(b), /©Juan Carlos Munoz for p104, /©Robert Harding Travel for p106(br), /©fancy for p109, /©Atlantide SNC for p111(t), /©Brand X for p126(t), /©PhotoDisc for p126(b); Pictures Colour Library/©David Tomlinson for p40(t); Punchstock/©Valueline for p7(bcr), /©Glowimages for p31(b), /©Valueline for p48(br), /©Corbis for p52(tcl), /©photosindia for p52(cr), /©Glowimages for p85(b), /©GoGo Images for p87(tl), /©Digital Vision for p102(cl), /©Cultura for p119(br), /©Comstock for p142(toast); Random House Inc for p36(r); Rex Features for p27(lb), /©Geoff Robinson for p33, /©Sipa Press for p60(t), /©Everett Collection for p60(c), /©Sky Magazine for p112(c); Ruben Gonzalez for p12(tl, tr); Science Museum for p112(t); Shutterstock/©David P Lewis for p9, /©Lana Langlois for p10(tcr), /©Smit for p32(A), /©spe for p32(B), /©Sandra Caldwell for p32(C), /©Sandra Caldwell for p32(D), /©HP_photo for p32(F), /©Stephen Coburn for p40(r), /©Margo for p52(tl), /©Ramzi Hachicho for p54(tr), /©Benis Arapovic for p54(bl), /©Rene Jansa for p55, /©Carsten Reisinger for p58(b), /©Ivana Rauski for p70(A), /©grzym for p70(C), /©Tootles for p70(C), /©Sergey Titov for p70(D), /Juriah Mosin for p75, /©MaxFX for p97, /©SF Photo for p99(t), /©Lee Torens for p106(tr), /©serg64 for p112(b), /©ultimathule for p142(basil), /©vinicius Tupinamba for p142(chicken), /©Joe Gough for p142(curry), /©Jan Hopgood for p142(fruit), /©Valda for p142(herbs), /©Joe Gough for p142(lasagne), /©luchschen for p142(mushrooms), /©stoupa for p142(strawberries), /©viktor1 for p142(bread), /©ZTS for p142(cake), /©ZTS for p142(cucumber), /©Sarune Zurbaite for p142(ice cream), /©Olga Lyubkina for p142(oil), /©ncn18 for p142(olives), /©Juha-Pekka Kervinen for p142(pasta), /©Anton Gvozdikov for p142(a pear), /©Robert Redelowski for p142(potatoes), /©Kentoh for p142(prawns), /©Tobik for p142(rice), /©Stuart Monk for p142(salmon), /©Chin Kit Sen for p142(soup), /©Joe Gough for p142(steak), /©Robyn Mackenzie for p142(tomatoes), /©Elke Dennis for p142(chop), /©3445128471 for p142(cut), /©iker canikligil for p142(pour); Stock Food UK for p32(tr,br); The Terem Quartet for p11(r); Topfoto/©Fortean for p68(c); www.judybevan.com for p27(r); www.sekwaman.co.za for p12(br); www.womadelaide.com for p11(l).

We have been unable to trace the copyright holder of the photographs on pp58(tl,tr), 69(b) and 124 and would welcome any information enabling us to do so.

The photograph on 28(tr) was kindly taken by an employee of the Melbourne Office, Cambridge University Press.

The following photographs were taken on commission by Gareth Boden for CUP:
7(bcl), 16, 22, 24(l), 28(bl), 42(l, r), 43, 48(bl), 54(tl), 56(cr), 62, 76(A, B, C, D), 78

We are grateful to the following for their help with the commissioned photography:
Fitzwilliam Museum, Cambridge; Greens Health & Fitness, Cambridge; Greg Sibley; Legal Moves, Hertford; Linda Matthews; Stephen Perse 6th Form College, Cambridge; The Lounge, Hertford; Thomas Cook, Cambridge.

Illustrations by Derek Bacon, Kathy Baxendale, Tom Croft, Mark Duffin, Kamae Design, Julian Mosedale, Mark Preston, Nigel Sanderson, Sean Simms.

Content

	Goals	Language	Skills	Explore

How to use this coursebook

Every unit of this book is divided into sections, with clear, practical **goals** for learning.

The first four pages of the unit help you build your language skills and knowledge. These pages include speaking, listening, reading, writing, grammar, vocabulary and pronunciation activities. They are followed by a **Target activity** which will help you put together what you have learned.

The **Explore** section of the unit begins with a **Keyword**, which looks at one of the most common and useful words in English. It also includes either an **Across cultures** or an **Independent learning** section, and then an **Explore speaking** or **Explore writing** task. The Explore section gives you extra language and skills work, all aiming to help you become a better communicator in English and a more effective learner.

The **Look again** section takes another look at the target language for the unit, helping you to review and extend your learning.
Sometimes you will also find this recycling symbol with the goals, to show when a particular goal is not new but is recycling language that you have met before.

This symbol shows you when you can hear and practise the correct pronunciation of key language, using the audio DVD-ROM.

The **e-Portfolio** DVD-ROM contains useful reference material for all the units, as well as self-assessment to help you test your own learning, and Wordcards to help you test your vocabulary learning.

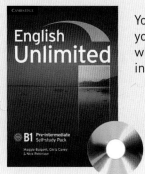

You can do more practice by yourself using the **Self-study Pack**, which includes a workbook and interactive DVD-ROM.

The DVD-ROM contains video and over 300 interactive activities.

Intro goals
◎ introduce and talk about yourself
◎ talk about needs, wants and reasons

Me and my life

I'm from Ottawa

1 Introduce yourself to your group.

Hi, my name's Kate Mori. I'm from Ottawa in Canada.

the Rideau Canal, Ottawa

Kate Mori

2 a Look at the pictures from Kate's life. What can you guess about her:

    1 family?   2 work?   3 free time?

b 🔊 **1.1** Listen to check your ideas.

Your life

3 Complete Kate's sentences. 🔊 **1.1** Listen again to check.

1 I live with *my husband, Masao.*	5 I speak … 8 I like …
2 We have …	6 I'm studying … 9 I play …
3 I'm a …	7 I'm interested in … 10 I go …
4 I work …	

4 Add more words to each group.

family members	jobs	languages	study subjects	sports and hobbies
husband	teacher	English	art history	tennis

5 a Think of five things to tell other students about yourself.

b Talk to each other in groups.

Ela's from Poland. She speaks Polish, English and Spanish.

6 How much can you remember about the people in your group?

7

I really want to …

Kate from Canada

Sun-Hi from South Korea

Kemal from Turkey

Kate, Kemal and Sun-Hi are all learning languages.

LISTENING

1   a **1.2** Can you remember what language Kate is learning?
Why do you think she's learning it? Listen to check.

   b **1.2** Listen again. Does Kate learn at home or go to a class? Why?

2   a **1.3** Now listen to Kemal and Sun-Hi.

   1   What languages are they learning?
   2   Who's learning for work? Who's learning for fun?

   b **1.3** Listen again. What exactly does each person want to do in the language?

3   Read the scripts on p143 to check your answers in 1 and 2.

VOCABULARY

Needs, wants and reasons

4   Who says these things: Kate, Kemal or Sun-Hi?

   1   I need English for my work. *Sun-Hi*
   2   I sometimes need English for my studies.
   3   I don't need English for travel.
   4   I need to practise my writing.
   5   One day I want to watch Spanish films.
   6   I really want to talk with my husband's family.
   7   I'd like to have a real conversation with them.
   8   I'd really like to go to Spain.

5 Complete these sentences with because or so.

1 I'm learning Japanese *because* I want to talk with my husband's family.
2 I didn't want to stop studying, _____ I started going to classes.
3 I'm learning Spanish _____ I like it.
4 I have a job with an international company, _____ I need English for my work.

6 a Why are you learning English? Think about why you need it and what you'd like to do.

b Talk together. Which reasons are the most common and the most interesting?

> I need English for work because I travel a lot.

> I'd like to watch American films, so I need to improve my listening.

SPEAKING

7 a Read 1–8. Write questions.

Do you want to move to another city or town?

Find someone who:
1 wants to move to another city or town.
2 would like to change jobs.
3 always needs a coffee first thing in the morning.
4 likes modern art.
5 wants to run in a marathon.
6 would like to have more free time.
7 is interested in motorbikes.
8 goes to night school.

b Make two more questions for the people in your class.

8 a Talk to different people. Ask each other questions and use *because* or *so* to give reasons.

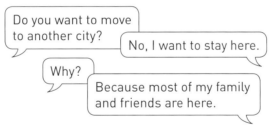

> Do you want to move to another city?

> No, I want to stay here.

> Why?

> Because most of my family and friends are here.

b In pairs, tell each other what you learned about the people in your class.

Self-assessment

Can you do these things in English? Circle a number on each line. 1 = I can't do this, 5 = I can do this well.

◎ introduce and talk about yourself	1 2 3 4 5
◎ talk about needs, wants and reasons	1 2 3 4 5

1 Play

1.1 goals
- talk about music
- talk about what to do in your free time

Local music

LISTENING

Natalie talks about music in Trinidad and Tobago, where she grew up.

1 Talk together.

1 Do you listen to music a lot?
2 What types of music do you like?
3 Can you play any instruments?

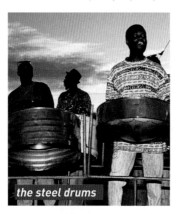

the steel drums

the piano

the guitar

2 **1.4** Listen to Natalie and answer the questions.

1 Do people in Trinidad and Tobago only listen to local music, or music from around the world?
2 Which instruments in the pictures does Natalie talk about?

3 a Which instrument does Natalie play now? Which doesn't she play? Why?

b **1.4** Listen again to check.

VOCABULARY

Talking about music

4 a Natalie mentions these types of music. Can you think of any more?

Cuban music, reggae, classical, calypso, salsa, rumba ...

b What types of music are popular where you live?

5 Match 1–7 with a–g and complete the sentences from Natalie's interview.

1 I learned how to play the steel drum when	a calypso.
2 I would love to be able to	b play classical piano.
3 I was brought up to	c Cuban music.
4 Nowadays I play more	d I was a little girl.
5 We have our own instrument called	e Latin America.
6 We have a local music called	f play it again.
7 Calypso is similar to music from	g the steel drum.

6 Write four or five sentences about some of these things. Use the highlighted expressions from 5.

- music in your country
- a special instrument in your country
- a type of music you like
- music in your childhood
- music in your life now
- something you'd like to learn

SPEAKING

7 Talk to each other about music in your country and in your life. Ask questions to find out more.

I learned how to play the guitar when I was a teenager.

Were you in a band?

Music around the world

READING AND LISTENING

1 Read the online programme for WOMADelaide on Sunday. Do you know any of the performers? Which would you most like to see?

WOMADelaide — BOTANIC PARK, ADELAIDE SUNDAY 12.00 – 6.00

WOMAD (World of Music, Arts and Dance) organises international music festivals in over twenty countries.

At WOMADelaide, you can enjoy the magical sounds of the planet in the sunshine with friends and family. (Kids under 12 are free.) Come for a night, a day, or for the whole three days.

Cesaria Evora – Cape Verde Cesaria Evora's beautiful songs are sung in Creole Portuguese and originate from traditional Portuguese and Brazilian music.

Toumani Diabate's Symmetric Orchestra – Mali More than any other kora player, Toumani Diabate has brought the unique 21-string West African harp to people around the world.

Mista Savona – Australia This 13-piece group – including some of Jamaica's best singers together with leading Australian musicians – brings a huge and exciting reggae sound to the stage.

The Beautiful Girls – Australia Singer-songwriter-guitarist Mat McHugh started The Beautiful Girls in 2002, but the band has changed a lot since then. Their music takes in hip-hop and reggae, soul and pop.

Terem Quartet – Russia Putting new life into Russian folk music, the Terem Quartet's performances are full of fun and incredible musical energy.

Terem Quartet

TIMES AND STAGES. * FULL LINE-UP. * SITE MAP.

2 **1.5** Listen to two friends at work, Cameron and John, talking about the programme. Which performers do they talk about? Which do they both want to see?

VOCABULARY
Deciding what to do

3 a Complete the sentences from the conversation with words from the box.

> see   have a look   good   idea   ~~go~~   get   into

1 JOHN   Do you want to _**go**__?
  CAMERON Sure, if we can get tickets for a day or a night.

2 J Why don't we _____ online?
  c OK, hang on a minute.

3 J Mista Savona looks interesting.
  c Hm, I'm not really _____ reggae.

4 J What do you think about this? The Terem Quartet?
  c The folk? Yeah, that sounds _____ .

5 J Do you want me to _____ if there are any tickets?
  c Good _____ .

6 J Maybe we could _____ a group together.
  c Yeah, it would be a good laugh.

b **1.5** Listen again to check. **P**

4 Work in pairs. Take turns to say the first lines in 1–6 and remember the responses.

SPEAKING

5 a Work alone and choose:

1 two performers from the programme that look interesting.
2 two performers you don't want to see.

b In groups, decide:

1 one performer you'd all like to see.
2 who will book the tickets.
3 where to meet.

6 Tell the class what you decided. Which are the most popular performers in the class? Which are the least popular?

An unusual athlete

1.2 goals
⊙ talk about past events and present activities
⊙ talk about sport and exercise

READING

1 Read the introduction to an interview. What's unusual about Ruben?

An interview with Ruben Gonzalez

At school, Argentina's Ruben Gonzalez was not a natural athlete. However, at the age of 21, he started doing the Olympic sport of luge and, four years later, he represented Argentina at the Calgary Winter Olympics. How did he do it?

▲ *Ruben today*

▲ *Ruben at the 2002 Winter Olympics*

2 Read the interview with Ruben on p13 and answer the questions.

1 Why did Ruben decide to become an Olympic athlete?
2 Why did he choose the luge?
3 How many Winter Olympics was he in?
4 What's his job now?

3 Read the interview again. Why is luge a difficult sport? Find three reasons.

4 What do you think about Ruben? What do you think about what he's done?

GRAMMAR

Present simple, past simple, present progressive

5 Complete 1–3 in the table with the correct time expression from the box.

> at the moment   ~~sometimes~~   in 1988

6 Now complete 4–9 with are, do, didn't, don't, 'm not, did.

present simple	past simple	present progressive
⊕ I still practise on the luge ¹*sometimes* .	I went to the Olympics ² _____ .	I'm making a film ³ _____ .
⊘ How often ⁴ _____ you practise?	When ⁵ _____ you go to the Olympics?	What ⁶ _____ you doing at the moment?
⊖ I ⁷ _____ practise at weekends.	I ⁸ _____ go in 1998.	I ⁹ _____ doing anything.

7 a Complete the questions with the correct form of the verb in (brackets).

1 What sport _*did*_ Ruben _*play*_ at school? (play)
2 Why _____ he _____ the luge? (choose)
3 When _____ luge athletes usually _____ training? (start)
4 How fast _____ a luge _____ ? (go)
5 How often _____ he _____ ? (practise)
6 What _____ he _____ these days? (do)

Grammar reference and practice, p132

b Write two more questions to ask a partner about Ruben.

c How much can you remember? Ask and answer all the questions.

SPEAKING

8 a Look at the photos. What can you guess about the people?

b Work in A/B pairs. A, read about Michelle on p122. B, read about Vincent on p128. Follow the instructions.

c Tell each other about Michelle and Vincent.

Michelle Sung Wie

Vincent Mantsoe

Interviewer So, Ruben, how did you get into the luge?

Ruben Well, at school, I couldn't jump high or run fast. I played football but I wasn't very good. It was really sad! But when I was ten, I saw the Olympics on TV for the first time and I loved it. And later, when I was 21, I saw Scott Hamilton win an Olympic medal in figure skating. Scott's about 155 cm tall and weighs about 50 kilos, and he gave me hope. I thought: if that little guy can do it, I can do it too. So I decided to be an Olympic champion – but I had to find a sport. It's true, I'm not a great athlete, but I never give up. I try again and again. So I chose the luge because people get hurt a lot, people often break bones – ninety percent of them give up. And I thought, well, I don't give up, so I have a chance.

Interviewer Most Olympic luge athletes start training at 12. You started at 21, but you've competed in three Olympics.

Ruben Yes, I started in 1984. I went to the Winter Olympics in Calgary in 1988 and in Albertville in 1992. Then, nearly ten years later, my old coach phoned me up and said "Argentina needs you!" So at age 39, I competed in the 2002 Salt Lake City Winter Olympics.

Interviewer What's it like to luge down a mountain at 90 miles an hour?

Ruben Well, at that speed, you don't have time to think. The luge is very sensitive. If you hiccup, you can crash. And when you finish, you have to sit up and stop the luge by putting your feet on the ice. It takes a couple of hundred metres to stop because you finish the run at about 80 miles an hour. I still practise on the luge sometimes and I'm frightened on every run.

Interviewer And what do you do these days?

Ruben I'm a motivational speaker. I talk about my experiences and how to be successful. I'm making a film about success at the moment. We're interviewing a lot of business people, philosophers, athletes, Hollywood people. It's very interesting.

Physical activities

A
B
C
D

E
F
G
H

I

VOCABULARY

Sports and exercise

1 a Match the activities with the pictures A–I.

> aerobics   hockey   karate   running   skiing
> swimming   tennis   volleyball   yoga

b Match the activities with the verbs 1–3.

1   I play *hockey*   2   I do …   3   I go …

c Can you think of more activities for verbs 1–3?

PRONUNCIATION

Word stress

2 a How many syllables are there in the words in 1a? Where's the stress? Put the words in groups.

Oo ¹	Ooo ²	oOo ³
hockey		

b 🔊 **1.6** Listen to check. ℗

SPEAKING

3 In groups, ask and answer the questions. Find out more.

1   What activities do you do?
2   What do you watch?
3   What did you do when you were younger?

> When I was at college, I did aerobics.
>> Did you like it?

Target activity

Talk about an interest

1.3 goals
◎ talk about past events and present activities ♻
◎ talk about your interests and how they started

Li from England

TASK LISTENING

1 Which of these things are you interested in? Why? Talk together.

fashion   books   motorbikes   cars   sports   computers   cooking   travel
art   history   music   photography   science   cinema   politics

2 🔈 **1.7** Listen to Li talking about her interest in motorbikes. Where does she like riding her motorbike?

3 a Can you remember what Li says about:

1   when she was a child and a teenager?
2   why she decided to start riding a motorbike?
3   her motorbike lessons?
4   what she likes about being on a motorbike?

b 🔈 **1.7** Listen again to check.

TASK VOCABULARY

Talking about interests

4 Make six sentences from the interview with Li. Which are about the past? Which are about now?

1 It started when	a learn something new.
2 I really got into	b going fast.
3 I really wanted to	c I was a kid.
4 The great thing about it is,	d motorbikes when I was a teenager.
5 I'm not interested in	e it doesn't take very long to learn.
6 For me,	f speed isn't important.

TASK

5 a Choose something you're really interested in. Think about these questions.

1   When and how did your interest start?
2   How did you feel about it when you started?
3   How do you feel about it now? Why do you like it?
4   How much time does it take? When do you do it? Where?

I really got into cooking when I was a teenager

b Tell each other about your interests. Ask questions to find out more.

6 Would you like to try any of the things you talked about?

Keyword *so*

1 We use *so* before a result, like this:

> My first boyfriend had a really nice bike, so we went riding in the countryside a lot. Unit 1

Add *so* to the correct place in each sentence.

1 I thought, well, I don't give up ∧ I have a chance. Unit 1
2 A steel drum's about a metre high I couldn't really travel with it. Unit 1
3 I have a job with a large international company I need English for my work. Intro unit
4 Masao's interested in art too we usually go to galleries together. Intro unit

2 a What important decisions have you made in the last five years? Write three sentences with *so*.

I wanted a better job, so I started studying at the local college.

> What did you study?

b Listen to each other's sentences. Ask questions to find out more.

3 Make four conversations and then practise in pairs. Take turns to say 1–4 and remember a–d.

1 Do you need to work late tonight?
2 Do you think it'll rain tomorrow?
3 What's the capital of Morocco? Is it Rabat?
4 Do you think the bank's open now?

a Yes, I think so, but Casablanca's much bigger.
b I'm really tired but yes, I suppose so / I guess so.
c I hope so. This weather's too hot for me.
d No, I don't think so. They usually close at four.

4 a Write three questions for a partner about these topics.
Use: Do you think ... ?

> Do you think chocolate is good for you?
>
> I hope so. I eat lots of it!

• food and drink • sport • music • the weather • free time

b Ask and answer the questions. Try to use the expressions in 3.

Across cultures Culture shock

1 a What do you think happens when people move to a new country or culture? Make three sentences.

1 At first
2 After a few days or weeks
3 After a while

a life is difficult and you miss your home.
b you start living normally.
c you think everything is great.

b Read the article to check. Do you agree with the ideas?

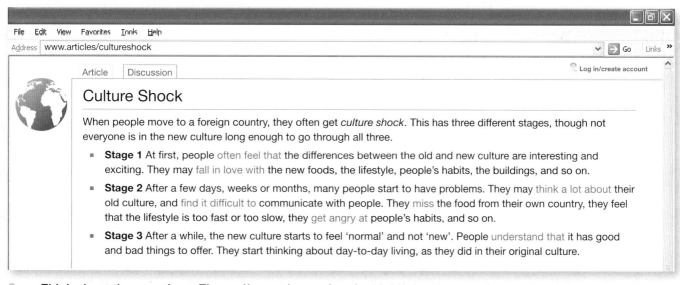

Culture Shock

When people move to a foreign country, they often get *culture shock*. This has three different stages, though not everyone is in the new culture long enough to go through all three.

- **Stage 1** At first, people often feel that the differences between the old and new culture are interesting and exciting. They may fall in love with the new foods, the lifestyle, people's habits, the buildings, and so on.

- **Stage 2** After a few days, weeks or months, many people start to have problems. They may think a lot about their old culture, and find it difficult to communicate with people. They miss the food from their own country, they feel that the lifestyle is too fast or too slow, they get angry at people's habits, and so on.

- **Stage 3** After a while, the new culture starts to feel 'normal' and not 'new'. People understand that it has good and bad things to offer. They start thinking about day-to-day living, as they did in their original culture.

2 Think about the questions. Then talk together, using the highlighted expressions in the article to help you.

1 Have you (or people you know) ever had culture shock? What happened?
2 What things do people usually like when they come to your country? What things can be difficult for them?
3 Have you ever gone to live, work or study in a new place? Would you like to?
4 What things were new for you? How did you feel about them? Did you get used to them?

Goal

© write messages of request and invitation to different people

1 Look at the photo. What's wrong with Cameron? How do you think he feels?

2 a Read the emails.

1 What will Cameron do for the next few days? Why?
2 What are the names of: his friends? his client?
3 What does he arrange to do next week?

b Which emails are more formal? Which are less formal?

3 a What expressions do Cameron, Marc and Pam use to begin and end their emails? Make two lists.

Beginning (x4): _Dear Marc_ , ...
Ending (x5):   _Regards, Cameron Clarke_ ...

b Which expressions from 3a would you use when writing to these people? Compare your ideas.

- someone in your family • a friend
- your manager • a client
- someone you don't know

4 a Cover the emails. Can you complete the sentences with these expressions?

> ~~Any time~~   drop by   changing our appointment
> give me a call   take a few days off
> If so   over lunch

Requests

1 Would you mind _____ to Monday or Tuesday next week? _Any time_ is fine.
2 When you see John, could you tell him to _____?
3 Is it all right if I _____ tomorrow, or would you prefer to be alone?

Invitations

4 Would you like to join me at Chez Michel at one o'clock? We could talk about the project _____.
5 Do you want to meet up this evening – barbecue maybe? _____ let me know.
6 I have to _____. How about dinner next week?

b Look at the emails to check.

5 Write short emails for these situations.

1 Invite a friend to meet you somewhere. Give the date, time and place.
2 Cancel an appointment with a client. Give the reason, suggest a new time, and invite her / him to lunch.

6 Exchange emails with a partner. Write a short reply to each one.

7 Look at all your emails together. Do you think they have the correct style?

Dear Marc,
I'm very sorry but I have to cancel our appointment for today. I'm not well. Would you mind changing our appointment to Monday or Tuesday next week? Any time is fine.
Regards,
Cameron Clarke

Hello Cameron,
I'm sorry to hear you're not feeling well. Tuesday next week is fine with me. Would you like to join me at Chez Michel at one o'clock? We could talk about the project over lunch. Get well soon.
Best wishes,
Marc

Hi Cameron,
Do you want to meet up this evening – barbecue maybe? If so, let me know. John and Jen are coming too.
Love, Pam

Delete   Reply   Reply All   Forward   Print

Pam,
Really sorry but I woke up this morning with a cold and feel terrible. I have to take a few days off. How about dinner next week?
Cameron.

PS When you see John, could you tell him to give me a call?

You poor thing! Yes, next week will be good. Is it all right if I drop by tomorrow, or would you prefer to be alone? Take care, P :-)

1 Look again ♻

Review

1 **a** Work together. How many words or expressions can you think of:

1 connected with music? *jazz, instrument ...*
2 for sports and exercise? *swimming, yoga ...*

b 🎧 **1.8** Listen to eight instructions. Write down your answers – but don't write them in order.

c Look at each other's answers. Can you guess what they mean?

> Wrestling ... Do you like watching wrestling on TV?
>
> No, I hate it!

GRAMMAR Question patterns

2 **a** Put the words in order. Write the questions in the table.

1 like do What you doing in the evening?
2 Can ride you a motorbike?
3 did Where go you to school?
4 reading you Are anything interesting at the moment?
5 you would What places like to visit in future?

Question word	Auxiliary verb	Subject	Verb	
1 *What*	*do*	*you*	*like*	*doing in the evening?*
2 –	*Can*	...	...	...

b Write two more questions to ask a partner. Then ask and answer all the questions.

CAN YOU REMEMBER? Intro unit – Needs, wants

3 **a** Complete the conversations with 'd like, want, need.

1 A I can't find my bank card.
  B I think you _____ to phone the bank.
2 A Hello. Can I get you something?
  B Yes, I _____ some cake and a coffee, please.
3 A Shall we go out tonight?
  B No, I _____ / _____ to stay at home. There's a good film on TV.

b Write sentences about things you'd like, want or need to do:

- after this lesson
- tomorrow
- next weekend
- next week
- next year

c Listen to each other's sentences. Give more information.

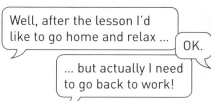

> Well, after the lesson I'd like to go home and relax ...
>
> OK.
>
> ... but actually I need to go back to work!

Extension

SPELLING AND SOUNDS *or, wor-*

4 **a** 🎧 **1.9** Listen and repeat the words with or and wor-.

or with stress /ɔː/	*or* without stress /ə/	*wor-* /wɜː/
sport born	motorbike doctor	work

b Add these words to the correct group. Practise saying them.

forget morning word
orchestra visitor world

c 🎧 **1.10** Spellcheck. Close your book. Listen to ten words with or and wor- and write them down.

d Look at the script on p144 to check your spelling.

NOTICE Extreme adjectives

5 **a** Find the adjectives in this unit which mean:

1 really good, special: m*agical* , u_____e, i_____e.
  (the festival programme on p11)
2 really nice: l_____y.
  (Natalie's script on p143)
3 really good, great: a_____g
  (Cameron and John's conversation on p143)
4 really interesting: f_____g
5 really frightening: t_____g
6 really bad: t_____e
  (the interview with Li on p143–4)

b Think about how to describe some things and people you really like or don't like, for example:

- a musician
- a book
- a TV programme
- a sportsperson
- a film
- a politician
- a place
- an activity

c Tell each other your ideas. Do you agree?

Self-assessment

Can you do these things in English? Circle a number on each line. 1 = I can't do this, 5 = I can do this well.

⊚ talk about music	1	2	3	4	5
⊚ talk about what to do in your free time	1	2	3	4	5
⊚ talk about sport and exercise	1	2	3	4	5
⊚ talk about past events and present activities	1	2	3	4	5
⊚ talk about your interests and how they started	1	2	3	4	5
⊚ write messages of request and invitation to different people	1	2	3	4	5

- For Wordcards, reference and saving your work » e-Portfolio
- For more practice » Self-study Pack, Unit 1

2.1 goals
◉ talk about personal experience
◉ talk about your studies

Work and studies

Lifelong learning

LISTENING

1 **Ask and answer the questions.**

1 At what age do people in your country usually do these things?
  • start school • go to college or university • do exams
  • do military service • start work • retire
2 What do you think are the best ages to do them?

2 **Read the introduction to a radio programme. Is this true of people where you live?**

In today's programme, we'll be taking a look at lifelong learning. In the past, people went to school and maybe university, then they got a job and that was it. Today, however, all that is changing. Many people are continuing to study all their lives and some are going back to school or university when they are much older.

Luis

Pierre

Margaret

3 **🔊 1.11 Listen to interviews with three students, Luis, Pierre and Margaret.**

1 Match them with pictures A–C.
2 Who:
  a started studying after they retired?
  b works and studies at the same time?
  c went to college after working for 20 years?

Ⓐ

Ⓑ

Ⓒ

4 **a** Can you remember the answers to these questions?

Luis	1	What does he do?	2	What are his plans for the future?
Pierre	3	Why didn't he like school?	4	Why does he enjoy his studies now?
Margaret	5	Why did she join the U3A?	6	How is the U3A different from other universities?

b 🔊 1.11 Listen again to check.

5 **Do you know anyone with similar stories to Luis, Pierre or Margaret? Talk together.**

VOCABULARY
Studying

6 **a** Who mentions these subjects? What do they say about them?

Spanish IT skills archaeology history maths science music art

b In groups, add more subjects to the list. Then compare as a class.

geography, French ...

7 a Complete the sentences from the interviews with words or expressions from the box.

exams
a degree
a thesis
an IT skills course
colleges
~~a doctorate~~
courses
degrees
School

1 I'm doing *a doctorate* in archaeology.
2 I'm writing _____ on my work in the Amazon.
3 I passed my _____ – just!
4 I wanted to do _____ in art.
5 I applied to some _____ .
6 I got into the _____ of Art and Design in Limoges.
7 We don't do exams or get _____ .
8 I've done _____ in music, local history and Spanish.
9 Last week I signed up for _____ .

b Which words in the box in 7a can go with these verbs? do get pass / fail

do a degree, do a doctorate ...

8 Write five sentences about your past or present studies. Use the expressions in 7a.

SPEAKING

9 Listen to each other's sentences. Ask questions to find out more.

> Last year I did a course in marketing.

> Where did you do it?

I've done ...

GRAMMAR

Present perfect 1 – for experience

1 Look at the sentences from the interview with Pierre and answer the questions.

1 I've always enjoyed art.   2 I didn't like a lot of subjects at school.

In which sentence is he talking about: a only the past? b his whole life up to now?

2 a Complete the sentences with have, has, 've, haven't, hasn't.

have

haven't
have

have / has + past participle	
❓ What kind of courses _____ you done? ➕ I've done courses in music, local history and Spanish. ➖ I choose things I _____ studied before. ➖ I _____ never been very good with computers.	Has she ever studied Spanish? Yes, she _____ . has No, she _____ . hasn't

b 🔊 1.12 Listen to check. ℗

3 Complete the questions with the past participles of the verbs in (brackets).

1 What subjects have you always *enjoyed*? (enjoy)
2 What subjects have you always _____ good at? (be) been
3 What's the most useful subject you've ever _____? (study) studied
4 Who's the best teacher you've ever _____? (have) had
5 Have you ever _____ a course in your free time? (do) done
6 Have you ever _____ a thesis or a very long essay? (write) written
7 Have you _____ a lot of exams in your life? (do) done
8 What's the most difficult exam you've ever _____? (pass) passed

Grammar reference and practice, p133

You can look up irregular past participles on p160, *Irregular verbs*.

PRONUNCIATION

Sentence stress

4 a 🔊 1.13 We stress the most important words in a sentence (often question words, nouns, verbs, adjectives and adverbs). Listen to these questions from 3 and practise.

1 What subjects have you always enjoyed?
2 What subjects have you always been good at?

b Look at the other questions in 3. Decide which words should be stressed and underline them. 🔊 1.14 Then listen and compare.

SPEAKING

5 Ask and answer the questions in 3. Ask questions to find out more.

> I've always loved maths.

> Why? Did you have good teachers at school?

A great place to work?

2.2 goals
⊚ talk about personal experience
⊚ talk about your work

SPEAKING

1 **a** Use the work quiz to interview each other. Give reasons for your answers.

The work quiz

What would be your ideal job? Would you prefer to:

1 (a) work for a big company?   (b) work for a small company?
   (c) be self-employed?

2 (a) have a full-time job?   (b) have a part-time job?
   (c) work whenever you want?

3 (a) work in an office?   (b) work outdoors?   (c) work at home?

4 (a) work alone?   (b) work with the same people every day?
   (c) often work with different people?

5 (a) have a well-paid job?   (b) have an interesting job?
   (c) have a job which helps other people?

b For each question 1–5, what's the most common answer in the class? Are your reasons the same?

READING

2 Read four web postings by people who work for CSP, a company which designs and sells computer software. Who's generally happy at CSP? Who's not happy?

File Edit View Favorites Tools Help

Address www.theworkplace/chatroom   Go Links »

The Workplace > chat

1 Posted by: Marco

I've worked here since 2008 when I left college and I quite like it. I work in the IT department and there's a nice atmosphere. Everyone's easy to work with, friendly – it's a bit like a family really. I'm always busy but we have flexible working hours: sometimes I'm here from 7 to 3, sometimes from 10 to 6. That's good when you've been out the night before! The pay's good too. <u>View 2 replies to this comment</u>

2 Posted by: noname99

I've only worked here for a couple of months but I already hate it. The people in IT never seem to do any work. There's one young guy who's always late, and that can be really difficult. The management isn't very good either. They don't listen to you and they're often not here or too busy to talk. So basically, it's a terrible place to work and I'm looking for a new job. <u>View 3 replies to this comment</u>

3 Posted by: Lauren101

I've been with the sales team at CSP for three months and it's a great place to work. My boss is the best – she's never here, always away on business trips! But seriously, the atmosphere here's pretty relaxed because we often don't have a lot to do, and we probably spend a bit too much time surfing the Internet and having long lunch breaks. The pay's not great, but it's enough for now. <u>View 10 replies to this comment</u>

4 Posted by: Lydia

I started working here about three years ago. The job's interesting but it can be quite stressful because I work with the sales team. They make a lot of mistakes, and then I have to fix them. The pay's not great – I never have any money at the end of the month! But the benefits are OK – I get four weeks' holiday a year and free health care. <u>No replies to this comment</u>

[handwritten notes in left margin:]
1. Lauren
2. Lydia
3. Marco
4. Nouama
5. Laura
6. Marco
7. Nouama
8. Nouama

3 Read the postings again. Who:

1 is in the sales team?
2 sometimes has problems because of the sales team?
3 is in the IT department?
4 isn't happy with the IT department?
5 doesn't have a lot of work?
6 came to CSP after college?
7 wants to leave CSP?
8 doesn't say anything about money?

4 Who do you think would be good to work with? Who could be difficult to work with? Why?

VOCABULARY

Working conditions

[handwritten notes:]
1 f
2 c
3 - b
4 - a
5 - d
6 - e

5 Complete statements 1–6. Then read the postings again to check.

1 We have flexible working hours:
2 The management isn't very good either.
3 The benefits are OK –
4 The pay's not great –
5 It's a terrible place to work
6 There's a nice atmosphere.

a I never have any money at the end of the month!
b I get four weeks' holiday a year and free health care.
c They don't listen to you.
d and I'm looking for a new job.
e Everyone's easy to work with.
f sometimes I'm here from 7 to 3, sometimes from 10 to 6.

SPEAKING

What's your job like?

It's great, because we have flexible working hours ...

6 a Think about how to describe some of these things with the expressions in 5.

1 your job now   2 jobs in your past   3 jobs of people you know

b Talk together.

I've worked here for ...

GRAMMAR

Present perfect 2 – with *for* and *since*

1 Look at the sentences from the postings.

> *Marco*   I've worked here since 2008.
> *Lauren101* I've been with the sales team at CSP for three months.

1 When did Marco and Lauren start working at CSP?
2 Do they work there now?
3 Complete a and b with for and since:

a You can use _____ to say when something started (Monday, last month, 2008).
b You can use _____ with a period of time (a week, three months, five years).

2 a Write four sentences about yourself on a piece of paper. Use the ideas below with for and since. Then give your sentences to your teacher.

I've worked at ...   I've been a ...   I've lived in ...
I've known ...   I've studied ...   I've had my ...

I've worked at my present company for about five years.

Grammar reference and practice, p133

b Listen to each set of sentences. Can you guess who wrote them?

SPEAKING

3 Talk in groups. What can you remember about each other from 2? Ask questions to find out more.

You've been a teacher for five years, right?

No, only two.

Oh, sorry, two years. What do you teach?

Target activity

Have an interview

2.3 goals

◉ talk about personal experience
◉ talk about your studies
◉ talk about your work

Let **Findajob** help you find your dream job. Simply give us your CV and come in for an interview and we'll find the best job for someone with your skills and interests. You'll get experience with some of the world's best organisations and have the freedom to work how you want to. We can find you a job with a permanent or temporary contract and you can work full-time or part-time – the choice is yours!

TASK LISTENING

Lauren Gordon has left CSP and is looking for a new job. She has an interview at the Findajob agency.

1 Read the advert for a job agency.

   1   Do many people use job agencies where you live?
   2   What are the advantages and disadvantages of using a job agency?
   3   Have you or people you know ever used a job agency?

2 **1.15** Listen to part of Lauren's interview. In what order does the interviewer ask about these things?

   ☐ experience in sales   *5*
   1 qualifications in catering   *1*
   ☐ strengths and weaknesses   *6*
   ☐ languages   *4*
   ☐ computer skills   *2*
   ☐ driving licence   *3*

3 **a** Can you remember if these sentences are true or false? Lauren:

   1   brings her CV with her. *true*   *1 - T*
   2   only wants to work in catering.   *2 - F*
   3   has her Food Safety certificate with her.   *3 - F*
   4   speaks some French and Spanish.   *4 - T*
   5   left CSP because she wasn't happy there.   *5 - F*
   6   says she has no weaknesses.   *6 - F*

   b **1.15** Listen again to check.

TASK VOCABULARY

Presenting yourself

1 - f
2 - e
3 - b
4 - g
5 - a
6 - c
7 - d
8 - h

4 **a** What does Lauren say in her interview? Match 1–8 with a–h.

1	I've got experience in	a work for a big company.
2	I'm looking for work in	b Food Safety for Catering.
3	I've got a certificate in	c talking to people, I think.
4	I've been in	d working in a team.
5	I've always wanted to	e any of those areas, really.
6	I'm good at	f sales, administration and catering.
7	I really enjoy	g sales for a year now.
8	I'm not very good at	h working on my own.

   b Look at the script on p144 to check.

   c Use the highlighted expressions in 4a to write five sentences about yourself.

TASK

5 **a** Work in A/B pairs.

   A, you've got an interview with Findajob. Think of answers to questions 1–5.
   B, you're the interviewer. Write two more questions.

   1   What experience have you got?
   2   What kind of work are you looking for?
   3   What qualifications have you got?
   4   What languages can you speak?
   5   What are your strengths and weaknesses?

   b Interview your partner. Then change roles and do the interview again.

6 Were you happy with your interview? Why / Why not? Talk together.

Keyword *for*

1 a Look at the highlighted expressions in sentences 1–4 from this unit. Match them with explanations a–d.

```
1    I've only worked here for a couple of months.
2    Simply give us your CV and come in for an
     interview.
3    You worked for Café Concerto last summer.
4    I'm sure we'll have something for you.
```

a   You can use *for* to give a reason, to answer *Why?*
b   You can use *for* with a time period.
c   You can use *for* to say who receives something.
d   You use *for* after some verbs (*ask, look, wait, work*, etc.).

b Now match more examples from the box with a–d.

```
1    I'm looking for a new job. Unit 2
2    Come for a night, a day, or for the whole
     three days. Unit 1
3    Do you use your bike for getting around,
     getting to work … ? Unit 1
4    Last year I wrote a book for children. Unit 1
5    I need English for my work. Intro unit
```

2 a Which sentence talks about a time period:
a   in the past?   b   in the future?   c   up to now?

1   I've been in sales for a year.
2   Next year, I'm going to work in Brazil for the summer.
3   When I was a student, I went to university in Paris for nine months.

b Write three sentences like 1–3 about you. Then listen to each other's sentences and ask questions to find out more.

3 Put the words in order to make questions. Then ask and answer them in groups.

1   make / your friends / Do you ever / for / things / ?
    Do you ever make things for your friends?
2   your mobile phone / taking photos / for / use / Do you ever / ?
3   organised / someone / Have you ever / a party / for / ?
4   How often / you / for / do / buy tickets / or other events / concerts / ?
5   for / What websites / you / your work / do / use / or studies / ?
6   someone / the last time / for / a present / bought / you / When was / ?

Independent learning Noticing and recording collocations

1 a *Collocations* are words that often go together. Cross out the word that doesn't usually go with the highlighted words.

1   do / ~~make~~ / pass / fail **an exam**
2   a part-time / well-paid / happy / difficult **job**
3   a lunch / breakfast / coffee / cigarette **break**

b Which of the collocations are: adjective + noun?   verb + noun?   noun + noun?

2 Work in three groups. Complete the collocations with words from the postings on p20. Then show them to the other groups.

Group A, find adjectives:	Group B, find verbs:	Group C, find nouns:
a _nice_ atmosphere	_____ mistakes	the _____ department
a _____ place to work	_____ the Internet	the _____ team
a _____ place to work	_____ a break	a _____ trip

3 a Look at three ways of recording collocations. Can you think of more ways?

Studies
go to university
pass an exam
fail an exam
write a thesis

Unit 2
We have flexible working hours.
horario de trabajo es flexible
I get free health care.
asistencia sanitaria gratuita

dancing   running
go — for a walk
home
to university

b Which do you prefer? Choose ways to record the collocations in 1a and 2.

1 a 🔊 **1.16** Listen to the phone call and choose a, b or c.

1 The caller's name is
  a Clare.
  b Lisa Moore.
  c Yusuf Karim.
2 The person he needs to speak to is
  a at lunch.
  b in a meeting.
  c on holiday.
3 The caller leaves his
  a mobile number.
  b home number.
  c home address.
4 He wants Lisa Moore to
  a email him.
  b phone him.
  c send him something.

b Read the conversation to check.

2 a Read the conversation again. Which highlighted expressions:

1 ask someone to slow down? (x1)
2 ask someone to say something again? (x3)
3 ask someone to spell something? (x1)
4 show you understand? (x3)

b 🔊 **1.17** Listen to check. 🅿

3 a Put the words in order to make sentences or questions about taking messages.

1 take you Would me message to like a ?
2 name again What your was please ?
3 would like to tell you What me her ?
4 message give her I'll the .
5 ask you her to I'll contact .

b Read the conversation to check.

4 a Cover the conversation. Role-play a similar conversation in A/B pairs.

A, you're Clare from CSP.
B, you're Yusuf Karim from Findajob (telephone 0412 556 207, email y.karim@findajob.com.au).

Try to use the highlighted **expressions in 2 and 3.**

b Change roles and practise again.

5 a Make two new phone calls in A/B pairs.

A, you work for CSP. Read role card 1 on p126.
B, you work for Findajob. Read role card 2 on p129.
Start the call.

b Change roles.

B, you work for CSP. Read role card 4 on p130.
A, you work for Findajob. Read role card 3 on p126.
Start the call.

Goals

◉ ask people to repeat, spell things and slow down
◉ show you understand
◉ take a phone message

A manager at the Findajob agency calls CSP to ask about their ex-employee, Lauren Gordon.

CLARE	Hello, CSP, Clare speaking. How can I help you?
YUSUF	Oh hello, my name's Yusuf Karim. I'm from the job agency, Findajob. Could I speak to Lisa Moore, please?
CLARE	Certainly. Can I ask you the reason for the call?
YUSUF	Of course. I'm calling about an ex-CSP employee, Lauren Gordon. Lisa Moore was her manager.
CLARE	Thank you. Let me just see if Lisa's available. Hello? I'm afraid she's in a meeting. Can I take a message?
YUSUF	I'm sorry, this line's not very good. **Could you say that again, please?**
CLARE	Yes, of course, I'm sorry. Would you like me to take a message?
YUSUF	Yes, please.
CLARE	Er, **what was your name again, please?**
YUSUF	Yes, it's Yusuf Karim.
CLARE	*Could you spell that for me?*
YUSUF	Yes, it's Yusuf with a Y, Y-U-S-U-F, and Karim is K-A-R-I-M.
CLARE	OK. And what's your telephone number?
YUSUF	I'll give you my mobile number. It's 0412 556 207.
CLARE	Sorry, **can you speak more slowly, please?**
YUSUF	Yes, it's 0412 556 207.
CLARE	**Right.** And has Lisa got your email address?
YUSUF	Er, no. It's y.karim@findajob.com.au.
CLARE	**Sorry, y.karim@ … ?**
YUSUF	Findajob – that's one word – dot com dot au.
CLARE	**OK, so that's** y.karim@findajob.com.au. And what would you like me to tell her?
YUSUF	Well, I'd like to ask her some questions about Lauren Gordon, what was she like as an employee and things. It would be great if she could phone me.
CLARE	OK, I'll give her the message and ask her to contact you.
YUSUF	Thank you. That's very helpful.
CLARE	No problem. Goodbye.

2 Look again ♻

Review

GRAMMAR Present perfect

1 a Read the 'Find someone who' sentences below. Write four more like these for the people in your class.

Find someone who:
- has had the same job for more than two years.
- has always liked the same music.
- has worked for more than three companies.

b Make questions from the sentences, then ask them. Find out more details.

> Have you always liked the same music?

c Talk in groups. What did you find out about other people in the class?

VOCABULARY Working conditions

2 a Use the expressions to complete Fleur's posting. Is she happy in her job?

> flexible working hours   pay   free health care
> ~~easy to work with~~   benefits   management
> atmosphere

Posted by: Fleur89

The job's a bit boring, but the people are
¹*easy to work with* and there's a really good
² _____ in the office. The ³ _____ aren't bad – I
get ⁴ _____ – but the ⁵ _____ is terrible! I haven't
had a rise since I started. We don't have ⁶ _____
– we start at eight in the morning and often work
late. But the ⁷ _____ is quite good. My boss is
great and tells me conditions will get better if I
stay here longer.

b Write a posting like Fleur's about your job or the job of someone you know.

CAN YOU REMEMBER? Unit 1 – Music, sports and exercise

3 a Use verbs from the box to complete the questions.

> done   go (x2)   listen to   play

1 Can you *play* volleyball?
2 Do you ever _____ running?
3 How often do you _____ to concerts?
4 Do you ever _____ classical music?
5 Have you ever _____ yoga?

b Think of two more endings for each question.

1 *Can you play the guitar?*
   Can you play football?

c Ask and answer all the questions in 3a and b.

Extension

SPELLING AND SOUNDS Words with -er, -or, -ar, -our

4 a 🔊 **1.18** You say the endings -er, -or, -ar, -our in the same way, /ə/. Listen and repeat.

-er	-or	-ar	-our
lawyer	visitor	grammar	neighbour

b Complete these words with the correct endings. Practise saying them.

teach*er*   direct___   danc___
act___   sug___   behavi___

c 🔊 **1.19** Spellcheck. Listen to ten more words and write them down.

d Look at the script on p145 to check your spelling.

NOTICE Collocations

5 a Complete the highlighted collocations from the radio interviews with Pierre and Margaret.

> ask   free   got   great   have   IT   ~~left~~   passed

1 I *left* school when I was eighteen. I _____
   my exams – just! – and then I _____ a job.
2 It's a _____ experience, completely different
   from school.
3 I'm a lot older ... so it's easier to _____
   questions, talk to the teachers, things like that.
4 We _____ meetings and talks in members'
   homes.
5 I retired three years ago. I had a lot of _____
   time, and nothing to do.
6 Last week I signed up for an _____ skills
   course.

b Look at script 1.11 on p144 to check.

c Choose three collocations and write questions with them.

Do you have a lot of meetings where you work?

d Ask and answer your questions.

Self-assessment

Can you do these things in English? Circle a number
on each line. 1 = I can't do this, 5 = I can do this well.

⊚ talk about personal experience	1	2	3	4	5
⊚ talk about your studies	1	2	3	4	5
⊚ talk about your work	1	2	3	4	5
⊚ ask people to repeat, spell things and slow down	1	2	3	4	5
⊚ show you understand	1	2	3	4	5
⊚ take a telephone message	1	2	3	4	5

- For Wordcards, reference and saving your work » e-Portfolio
- For more practice » Self-study Pack, Unit 2

3

How's your food?

Supermarkets or small shops?

VOCABULARY

Giving opinions

1 Look at the pictures. In groups, ask and answer the questions.

1 How often do you shop at places like these?
2 In your home, who does the food shopping?

2 Read three people's opinions about supermarkets. Do they like or dislike them? Why?

❝ I think small shops are better. The owners are usually friendly and you can ask them about things. I find supermarkets quite stressful. They're always crowded and noisy. If you ask me, they're only interested in making money, not in their customers. ❞

Jenny, New Zealand

❝ Well, supermarkets are cheap and convenient but I prefer convenience stores. They're fast and modern and sell interesting things. Also, supermarkets bring a lot of their stuff here by plane and that's bad for the environment. They should sell more local food. ❞

Akio, Japan

❝ I go to the market near my flat every day to buy food – things like meat, fish and vegetables. I never buy things like that in the supermarket. I don't think their food is fresh. But I guess they're good for cleaning products, pet food and so on. ❞

Luz, Spain

3 Match the beginnings and endings of the opinions. Then look at 2 to check.

1 I think small shops
2 I find supermarkets
3 If you ask me,
4 They should
5 I don't think their food
6 I guess they're good for

a sell more local food.
b cleaning products and pet food and so on.
c are better.
d is fresh.
e quite stressful.
f they're only interested in making money.

1-c
2-e
3-f
4-g
5-d
6-b

4 a Find the opposites of these adjectives in 2.

> unfriendly *friendly* expensive relaxing inconvenient
> quiet boring empty old-fashioned

b 🔊 1.20 Listen to check. ⓟ

SPEAKING

5 a Think about places where people buy food in your country. What are their good and bad points?

b Listen to each other's opinions in groups. Say if you agree or disagree and give reasons.

> I think supermarkets are only good for people with cars.

> Yes, I agree.

> Well, I don't agree. I think …

Food and you

tinned food

frozen food

fresh fruit and vegetables

ready-made meals

1 Look at the pictures. Which kinds of food do you prefer to buy? Why?

2 Read the article by Judi Bevan. Which paragraphs:

a are about supermarkets now?   c compare shopping in the past and present?
b are about shopping in the past?

In defence of supermarkets

[1] I like supermarkets. I can buy a week's shopping in ninety minutes, giving me time to help my daughter with her homework, or read a good book in the bath.

[2] Supermarkets sell an amazing choice of fresh and frozen food. If I want to spend hours cooking a three-course dinner for friends, I can find all the ingredients I need at my local supermarket. If I choose an Italian meal, there are porcini mushrooms, fresh basil and mozzarella cheese. If I want some other cuisine – Indian, Chinese or French – herbs, spices, sauces and vegetables from every continent are only a few minutes away.

[3] On the other hand, when I'm tired and just want to put together a quick family meal, I can buy a ready-made lasagne or curry, a bag of salad and some fresh fruit – and start eating it ten minutes after I get home.

[4] Thanks to supermarkets, I can now shop all day from early morning to late at night. In some stores I can even shop 24 hours.

[5] When I was a child, my mother didn't have these choices, as she went to three or four depressing little shops every day to buy what she needed. These shops opened from 9 am to 5 pm Monday to Saturday, and they all closed on Thursday afternoons.

[6] The food was not always good, there was almost no choice and the shopkeepers were not very friendly. And at that time, food was very expensive. Cream on strawberries was a luxury, and roast chicken was for special occasions only.

[7] Not many people would say that shopping in their local supermarket on a crowded Saturday morning makes them happy. But it's much, much better than what we had before.

Judi Bevan is a freelance financial journalist, author and broadcaster. Her books include *Trolley Wars – the Battle of the Supermarkets*, published in 2006.

3 Read the article again. Find four reasons why Judi likes supermarkets and four problems with shopping in the past.

4 Judi describes supermarkets in the UK. Which things are true about supermarkets in your country? Which things are different?

5 Add vowels to make food words from the article. Then look at the article to check. Look on p131 to check any words you don't know.

1 bsl *basil*	4 vgtbls	7 strwbrrs	10 lsgn	13 mshrms
2 chs	5 crry	8 hrbs	11 sld	14 crm
3 spcs	6 frt	9 scs	12 chckn	

6 Match the examples from the box with a–d. Think of two more examples each for a–d.

> basil   dessert   lasagne   breakfast

a a meal   b a course   c an ingredient   d a dish

7 In groups, ask and answer the questions. Find out more information.

1 Do you have a favourite kind of food, dish, or meal of the day?
2 What dishes can you, or people you know, cook? What ingredients do you use a lot?
3 Where you live, are there any good places to buy food from other countries?

I never eat mushrooms.

Why not? I love them!

Eating out

3.2 goals
● talk about food and eating ♻
● order a meal in a restaurant

READING AND LISTENING

1 Talk together.

1 How often do you go to cafés or restaurants?
2 Are there any good places to eat near your home?

1 - 3
2 - 1
3 - 2
4 = 1

2 a Read the information from a guide to eating out in Melbourne, Australia. Which restaurant:

1 is owned by a family?
2 has tables outside?

3 is open on Sundays?
4 sometimes has live music?

b Which of these restaurants would you like to go to? Why?

food&drink

1

The Bridge Restaurant

45 Hardware Lane, Melbourne Vic 3000
☎ *03 9600 234*

★★★★☆

The Bridge has a modern dining room serving quality European food. There is also a beautiful terrace for outdoor dining, and live jazz every Friday. Bookings essential. *Open Monday–Friday 12 pm – 10 pm, Saturday 5 pm – 10 pm.*

2

Bopha Devi Docklands

27 Rakaia Way, Docklands Vic 3008
☎ *03 9600 187*

★★★★☆

The new place in Docklands that everyone's talking about. The Bopha Devi Cambodian restaurant combines fantastic food with excellent service. *Open 12 pm – 11 pm. Closed Mondays.*

3

Abla's Lebanese Restaurant

109 Elgin Street, Carlton Vic 3053
☎ *03 9347 006*

★★★★☆

Choose from an exciting menu of Middle Eastern food, then sit back and enjoy the friendly service in this family-owned restaurant. *Open Thursday–Friday 12pm – 3pm, Monday–Saturday 6pm – 11pm*

3 ● **1.21** Listen to Bryan and Lynn talking about the restaurants. Which one do they choose? Why?

4 Read the restaurant menu. Which dishes would you like to try? Look on p131 to check any words you don't know.

Bryan and Lynn are cousins. They want to celebrate Lynn's birthday.

STARTERS
Soup of the day
Pear, apple and cheese salad (v)
Warm olives with oil and bread (v)

MAIN COURSES
Home-made pasta in a tomato and olive sauce (v)
Grilled salmon with potatoes and green salad
Steak in a mushroom sauce with roasted potatoes
Fried rice with mushrooms (v)
Prawns and green vegetables with a fresh cucumber salad

DESSERTS
Warm chocolate cake – with chocolate or vanilla ice cream (v)
Cheese plate with toast (v)
Fresh fruit salad with cream (v)

(v) – suitable for vegetarians

5 ● **1.22** Listen to Lynn and Bryan ordering their meals. Tick (✓) the things they order.

5 10
1 6
9 4
7 8
3 12
11 2

fizzy drinks =
bebidas con gas

VOCABULARY
Ordering a meal

6 a Put the lines of the restaurant conversation in order, 1–12.

Waiter

☐5 OK. And for you, sir?
☐1 Hi, are you ready to order?
☐ All right. Can I get you something to drink?
☐ Fine, and how would you like your steak?
☐ Today it's cream of mushroom soup.
☐ Sure. Sparkling or still?

Customers

☐ Can we have a bottle of water?
☐ Could I have the cheese salad to start ...
  and then the steak?
☐ OK, so I'll have that and the pasta, please.
☐ Medium, please.
☐ Still, please.
☐2 Yes, I think so. What's the soup of the day?

b 🔊 1.22 Listen again to check.

PRONUNCIATION
Schwa /ə/ sound

7 a 🔊 1.23 Words or syllables without stress often have a schwa /ə/ sound. Listen and say the sentence.

Can we have a bottle of water?

b Mark the /ə/ sounds in the rest of the customers' sentences in 6a.

c 🔊 1.24 Listen and read the script on p145 to check. ❿ Practise saying the sentences.

SPEAKING

8 a Look at the menu and decide what you want to order.

b Work in groups of three. Student A, you're the waiter. Students B and C, you're the customers. Order a meal.

c Have two more conversations. Take turns to be the waiter.

Describing a meal

GRAMMAR
Nouns with prepositional phrases

1 Look at sentences 1 and 2. Then circle the nouns and underline the prepositional phrases in 3–6.

1 Soup of the day
2 Warm chocolate cake with ice cream
3 Fresh fruit salad with ice cream
4 Pasta in a tomato and olive sauce
5 Warm olives with oil and bread
6 Steak in a mushroom sauce with roasted potatoes

2 a Put the highlighted phrase in the correct place in each sentence.

1 I'd like to book a table, please. for two
2 My parents cook a big meal every weekend. for nine or ten people
3 Could I have the chicken, please? in garlic sauce
4 That table is free. Why don't we sit there? in the corner
5 Would you like a bottle with your meal? of water
6 The weather was great, so we sat at a table on the terrace
7 There's a good menu and the staff are very friendly. with lots of vegetarian dishes
8 I'll have the salmon, please. with rice

b 🔊 1.25 Listen to check. ❿

Grammar reference and practice, p134

SPEAKING

3 a Think about a meal you had recently.

1 Where did you have the meal:
   in a restaurant or café?   at a party?   at a friend's house?
2 When did you have it? Who with?
3 What did you eat? How was the food?
4 What was the place like?
5 Did you have a good time?

b In groups, describe your meals. Give details.

We went to Abla's. It's a Lebanese restaurant with really friendly staff. We sat at a table in the corner ...

Plan a meal

Manuel from Chile

Susanne from Germany

Sarah from South Africa

Eren from Turkey

TASK LISTENING

1 🔊 **1.26** Four people are planning a barbecue, but some of their friends are vegetarian. What do they decide to do? Listen and choose from 1–4.

1 cook meat and vegetables together
2 cook only meat but make some salads too
3 cook meat and vegetables on different grills
4 cook only vegetables

2 🔊 **1.27** Listen to the second part of the conversation. Tick (✓) the things they need for the salad.

lettuce   black olives   parmesan cheese   olive oil
feta cheese   limes   garlic   tomatoes

TASK VOCABULARY

Making suggestions

3 a Can you remember which six of these suggestions the friends make?

1 How about we organise a barbecue?
2 We could do some pasta.
3 We can put veggies on the barbecue as well.
4 Why don't we get some burgers?
5 Sausages are nice.
6 How about a fruit salad?
7 Perhaps we should make a cake.
8 What about fruit?
9 Melons?

b 🔊 **1.26** 🔊 **1.27** Listen again to check.

TASK

4 a You're going to plan a meal for your group. Work alone and think about these questions.

1 Should you eat inside or outside? Could the meal be in or near your home?
2 What kind of food should you make? How many courses? What about drinks?
3 Who should make the food? How can you help?

b Now think about how to:

1 describe the food.   *Chicken with ...*
2 give opinions.   *I think we should ...*
3 make suggestions.   *How about ... ?*

5 In groups, plan your meal. Make a list of the dishes you decide to make.

6 Read the other groups' lists. Which meals do you think sound the nicest or the most interesting?

Keyword *with*

1 a Match 1–3 with a–c to make three sentences.

1 I've never been very good
2 I work
3 It has a good menu

a with lots of vegetarian dishes. Unit 3
b with the sales team. Unit 2
c with computers. Unit 2

b Which sentence has: a noun + with?   an adjective + with?   a verb + with?

2 Choose the best endings for 1–9.

1 I have an appointment with
2 I've got a problem with
3 I had a meeting with
4 I'm bored with
5 What's wrong with
6 My new flat's nice but I'm not very happy with
7 I'm staying with
8 Steve's going out with
9 The tour of the castle starts with

a Cecile? She looks ill.
b the view.
c a walk around its famous gardens.
d my computer. It won't start up.
e this film. Can we change channels?
f Erika now. They met at a party a month ago.
g the sales team yesterday.
h friends in Honolulu right now. It's wonderful here.
i Dr Jones for two o'clock.

3 a Complete five or six of these sentences with your own ideas.

I'm (not very) good with …   I work with …   I have a meeting with …   I've got a problem with …
I'm bored with …   I'm (not very) happy with …   I sometimes stay with …   My day usually starts with …

b Compare your ideas in groups. Ask questions to find out more.

> Well, at the moment I've got a problem with my car.

> OK. What's wrong with it?

Across cultures Mealtimes

1 🔊 **1.28** Listen to Matt and Carlos talking about mealtimes. Who talks about these things?

breakfast   the evening meal   dinner on Friday evenings   dinner with guests

2 Can you remember who said these things, Matt or Carlos? 🔊 **1.28** Listen again to check.

1 We usually eat together in the evening.
2 Everyone sits around the table and eats and talks.
3 In my family, we all have breakfast at different times.
4 I send my kids to wash their hands before dinner.
5 My mum says *bon appétit* before we start eating.
6 We usually have a quick meal in front of the TV.

3 a Talk together.

1 What time do you usually have meals? Are meals quick or do they take a long time?
2 Do you eat at the same time as other people? Do you eat in the same room?
3 Do you say or do anything before you begin a meal?
4 What do you do while you're eating? (talk? watch TV? smoke? something else?)
5 If you talk, what do you usually talk about?
6 Where you live, do you think food and mealtimes are a very important part of:
    a family life?   b social life?   c work or business life?

b Now think about these questions and talk again.

1 Are the things in 3a the same or different in other places you know?
2 Have you ever had a meal in someone's home in another country? What was it like?

Matt

Carlos

1 a Look at the pictures of two snacks and items A–H. Which items do you think you need for bruschetta and which for spiced nuts?

Warm spiced nuts

Tomato and cheese bruschetta

b Read the recipe for bruschetta to check.

Tomato and cheese bruschetta

2 medium tomatoes, chopped
100g mozzarella cheese, chopped
2–3 basil leaves
40 ml extra virgin olive oil
salt, pepper
4 slices of good white bread
1 clove of garlic, peeled

Chop the tomatoes and mozzarella and put them in a bowl. Add the basil, oil, salt and pepper. Stir, then leave for 20 minutes to an hour. Toast the bread until golden brown, then put on a plate. Cut the garlic clove in half and rub over each piece of toast. Put a quarter of the tomato mixture on each slice and serve.

2 a Which of these verbs can you find in the recipe for bruschetta?

chop cut pour shake serve stir

You can look up the words on p131.

b In pairs, take turns to mime and guess the verbs for preparing.

3 What kinds of foods do you cook in these ways? Talk together.

bake boil fry grill roast toast

Look on p131 to check any words you don't know.

> I sometimes bake cakes.
>> I never bake bread!

4 Read the recipe for warm spiced nuts. Choose the correct verbs.

Warm spiced nuts

200g mixed nuts
40ml olive oil
a little salt
10ml chopped fresh rosemary
5ml chopped dried chillies

Put the nuts, oil and salt in a bowl. [1] Chop / Shake the fresh rosemary and dried chillies and add to the bowl. [2] Cut / Stir all the ingredients, then pour onto a baking tray. [3] Bake / Boil at 180°C for 15 to 20 minutes, shaking once. [4] Pour / Stir the nuts onto kitchen paper and then into a dish. [5] Shake / Serve warm.

5 Read both recipes again.

1 Which snack do you think is the easiest to make?
2 Would you like to try these snacks? Why? / Why not?

6 a Think of a snack or some other quick dish that you know how to make.

b Write the ingredients for your recipe.

c Write the instructions for your recipe.

7 Look at each other's recipes. Ask and answer the questions.

1 Would you like to try them?
2 Can you understand all the instructions?

3 Look again ♻

Review

VOCABULARY Opinions

1 a Put the words in order to make sentences.

1 are better than fresh ones frozen vegetables I think .
2 seven days a week should open shops I don't think .
3 should buy everyone If you ask me, local food .
4 expensive restaurants I find quite stressful .
5 ready-made meals very good for you I don't think are .

b Talk about the opinions. Do you agree with them?

VOCABULARY Ordering a meal

2 a As a class make a café menu. Suggest your favourite dishes. Include:

starters   main dishes   desserts   drinks

Then think about what you'd like to order.

b Work in groups of three: one waiter, two customers. Order a meal. Take turns to be the waiter.

> Hi, are you ready to order?
>> Yes, I'd like the bruschetta, please.

CAN YOU REMEMBER? Unit 2 – Studying, Working conditions

3 a Work in two teams, A and B.

A, how many expressions about studying can you remember?
Make a list: *IT skills, do a degree ...*
B, how many expressions about working conditions can you remember?
Make a list: *pay, working hours ...*

b Look back at unit 2 to check.
A, look on p19. B, look on p21.

c Follow the instructions for the quiz.

1 Choose five expressions to test the other teams.
2 Write sentences with gaps.
3 Take turns to read your sentences to the other teams.
4 Guess the words. You win a point for every correct word, and a bonus point if you can spell it.

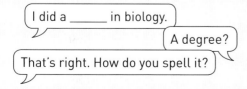

> I did a _____ in biology.
>> A degree?
> That's right. How do you spell it?

Extension

SPELLING AND SOUNDS *oi, oy*

4 a ● 1.29 You say oi and oy in the same way: /ɔɪ/. Listen, then say the words.

enjoy   employee   noisy   boil

b Complete the rules with oi or oy.

1 We usually write _____ before a consonant.
2 We usually write _____ before a vowel or at the end of a word.

c ● 1.30 Spellcheck. Listen to eight words and write them down.

d Look at the script on p146 to check your spelling.

NOTICE Making sentences stronger / weaker

5 a Look at these sentences from Judi Bevan's article, *In Defence of Supermarkets*. Decide where the missing words go in each sentence. Then look back at the article on p27 to check.

1 I can find ↓ the ingredients I need at my local supermarket.   all
2 ... vegetables from every continent are a few minutes away.   only
3 In some stores I can shop 24 hours.   even
4 The food was not good ...   always
5 ... there was no choice,   almost
6 ... and the shopkeepers were not friendly.   very
7 And at that time, food was expensive.   very
8 But it's much better than what we had before.   much

b Cover the highlighted words. Can you remember the complete sentences 1–8?

Self-assessment

Can you do these things in English? Circle a number on each line. 1 = I can't do this, 5 = I can do this well.

◉ give opinions	1	2	3	4	5
◉ talk about food and eating	1	2	3	4	5
◉ order a meal in a restaurant	1	2	3	4	5
◉ make suggestions	1	2	3	4	5
◉ give and understand written instructions	1	2	3	4	5

• For Wordcards, reference and saving your work » e-Portfolio
• For more practice » Self-study Pack, Unit 3

Encounters

Taxi!

VOCABULARY
Taxis

1 Ask and answer the questions together.

1 How often do you use taxis in your own city? What do you use them for?
2 What about when you're travelling?
3 When was your last trip by taxi? Where did you go?

2 a Read the questions. Match the highlighted expressions with A–F in the pictures.

1 When was the last time you phoned for a taxi or got a taxi at a taxi rank?
2 How much is the minimum fare for a taxi in your city?
3 What's the maximum number of passengers a taxi can usually take?
4 Do taxis in your city always use a meter? What about in other cities you know?
5 Do you usually ask the driver to keep the change?
6 Do you ever ask for a receipt at the end of a journey?

b 🔊 1.31 Listen to check. ❿

SPEAKING

3 Ask and answer the questions together. Find out more.

> The last time I got a taxi at a taxi rank was two weeks ago.

> Really? Where was that?

> It was outside the train station. It was raining and ...

Two journeys

Tony is a taxi driver in Vancouver, Canada.

1 **1.32** Listen to Tony's conversations with two passengers, first Nicola and then Dan.

1 Who wants to go to:
   a a bank? b a hotel? c the airport?

a - Dan
b - Nic
c - Dan

2 Who asks Tony:
   a for a receipt? b to wait? c how much the journey will cost?

a - Dan
b - Dan
c - Nicola

2 a Can you remember if these sentences are true or false?

1 It's Nicola's first time in Canada. F
2 She wants to go to a hotel. ✓
3 Dan goes to the bank to get some money. F
4 He's going on a business trip. ✓
5 It costs more than $30 from the bank to the airport. ✓

b **1.32** Listen again to check.

3 Do you ever chat with people you meet in these situations? What do you talk about?

in a taxi on a plane / bus / train waiting for a bus sharing a table in a café

1 - c
2 - a
3 - d
4 - b

5 - f
6 - h
7 - e
8 - g

4 a Match what the passengers say 1–8 with the driver's replies a–h.

The start of a journey
1 How much is it to the city centre?
2 Can you take me to the Park Inn?
3 I'd like to go to the airport, please.
4 Can I put my case in the back?

a The Park Inn on Broadway, right?
b I'll do that for you.
c It's usually about thirty, thirty-five dollars.
d OK. Which terminal?

The end of a journey
5 Could you wait here for five minutes?
6 How much is it?
7 Just make it thirty-five dollars.
8 And can I have a receipt, please?

e Thanks very much ... And here's your change, fifteen dollars.
f Well, OK, but can you pay me first?
g Sure ... Here you are.
h Thirty-one fifty, please.

b Cover 1–8 and look at a–h. Can you remember what the passengers say?

5 a Mark the stressed syllables in these sentences.

1 How much is it to the city centre?
2 Can you take me to the Park Inn?
3 I'd like to go to the airport, please.
4 Can I put my case in the back?
5 And can I have a receipt, please?

b Remember that words or syllables without stress often have a schwa /ə/ sound. Mark the /ə/ sounds in the sentences in 5a.

1 How much is it to the city centre?

c **1.33** Listen and read the script on p146 to check. **P** Practise saying the sentences.

How much is it to Broad Street?

Usually about six dollars.

OK. Can you take me to the OSP building, please?

6 a You're going to take a taxi. Work alone and think about these questions.

1 Where are you?
2 Where do you want to go?
3 What's the reason for your journey?
4 What will you chat about with the driver? (the weather, the traffic, your job ...)

b Take turns to be the passenger and taxi driver. Have conversations with three parts:

the start of your journey → a short chat → the end of your journey

c Change pairs and have two more conversations.

Hack

4.2 goals
⊚ describe past events
⊚ tell a story

Melissa Plaut is one of only 400 women among New York's 40,000 taxi drivers. "I started driving a cab after losing my boring office job," says Melissa. "I didn't want to work in an office again, so I decided to get my cab licence." She started a blog about her experiences as a taxi driver, newyorkhack. blogspot.com, which quickly became popular. She's also written a book called *Hack*. In New York, hack is slang for taxi, or taxi driver.

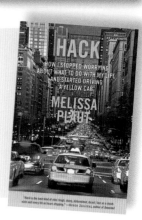

READING

1 Read the information about Melissa Plaut, a New York taxi driver.

1 How did Melissa become a taxi driver?
2 Where can you read about her experiences as a driver?

2 a You're going to read a true story from Melissa's blog. Look at these words and expressions from the story and guess what happened.

a Canadian man   the airport   a wallet   credit card
phoned   shopping   fifty dollars   laughed

b Read the story to check your ideas.

www.newyorkhack.blogspot.com

During rush hour, a Canadian man and his teenage son got in the cab and asked me to take them to La Guardia airport. They were going back to Canada. We had a nice conversation together and when they got out, they gave me a good tip.

When my next passenger got in, he handed me a wallet and said he found it on the back seat. I immediately knew it belonged to the Canadian man. It contained a driving license and a credit card, nothing much else.

Now, I liked the Canadian guy, so I found the 800 number on the back of the credit card and phoned the company. I explained what happened and gave them my number. After about half an hour, the Canadian guy called and asked me to go back to the airport and return the wallet. So I turned off my cab light and I started for the airport. Five or six people tried to stop me as I was driving through the city, but I didn't stop. I was doing a good thing!

Forty minutes later, I arrived at La Guardia. The guy was standing outside the terminal building and looking pretty stressed. I gave back the wallet and told him that I only did a little shopping with his credit card! Just a joke. He was so happy, he just laughed. "You're my favourite New Yorker ever," he said. Then he handed me fifty dollars and ran back into the airport. The whole thing – plus the fifty dollars! – really made my night.

3 Read the story again. Answer the questions in groups.

1 Why do you think Melissa liked the Canadian man?
2 How did the Canadian man know Melissa's phone number?
3 Why do you think the Canadian man was looking stressed when Melissa saw him?
4 Why did the Canadian man laugh?
5 How did Melissa feel at the end of the story? Why, do you think?

4 What do you think are the good and bad points about being a taxi driver? Talk together.

Handwritten notes (top right):
1 - During
2 - When
3 - After
4 - As
5 - Later
6 - Then

Telling a story

After as During
later Then When

Handwritten note: Algo q pasa al = t → Periodo de t

1 a Cover the blog. Use the words in the box to complete the sentences from the story.

1 _____ rush hour, a Canadian man and his teenage son got in the cab and …
2 _____ my next passenger got in, he handed me a wallet and …
3 _____ about half an hour, the Canadian guy called and …
4 Five or six people tried to stop me _____ I was driving through the city, but …
5 Forty minutes _____, I arrived at La Guardia. The guy was …
6 "You're my favourite New Yorker ever," he said. _____ he handed me fifty dollars and …

b Look at the story again to check.

2 Cover the story. In pairs, tell the whole story using the sentences in 1a for help.

3 a Look at the beginning of Melissa's story. Then choose a or b.

past simple

> … a Canadian man and his teenage son got in the cab and asked me to take them to La Guardia airport. They were going back to Canada.

past progressive

When Melissa met the Canadian man and his son:
a their journey to Canada was finished.
b they were in the middle of their journey to Canada.

b Circle the correct words.

1 Use the past simple / progressive to talk about a finished action.
2 Use the past simple / progressive to say an action was in progress in the past.

4 a Complete the sentences with was, were, wasn't, weren't.

was / were + -ing

was
wasn't

❓ What _____ he doing?
➕ He was standing outside the terminal.
➖ He _____ looking very happy.

were
weren't

❓ _____ they going back to Canada?
✅ Yes, they were.
❌ No, they _____.

b 🔊 1.34 Listen to check. ℗ Do we say was and were with a schwa /ə/ in:

a questions and positive sentences, or
b negative sentences and short answers?

5 a Look at three pictures from the start of a story. Use the best form, the past simple or the past progressive, to complete the paragraph.

The Ten-Dollar Bill

One sunny morning a man ¹_____ (walk) through the city on his way to work. He ²_____ (wear) a smart suit and tie and ³_____ (talk) on his phone. Suddenly, the sun ⁴_____ (go) in and it ⁵_____ (start) raining heavily. The man ⁶_____ (see) a taxi and ⁷_____ (start) running towards it. As he ⁸_____ (run), a $10 bill ⁹_____ (fall) from his pocket onto the ground, but he didn't notice. He ¹⁰_____ (get) into the cab, ¹¹_____ (shut) the door, and the cab ¹²_____ (drive) away.

Handwritten notes (right):
10 · got
11 · shut
12 · drove

Grammar reference and practice, p134

b 🔊 1.35 Listen to check. ℗

Handwritten notes (left):
1 · was walking
2 · was wearing
3 · was talking
4 · went
5 · started
6 · saw
7 · started
8 · was running
felt

6 a In pairs, look at the pictures from the rest of the story on p123. Plan how to tell the rest of the story. Think about how to do these things.

• describe the events in the story • link the events together
• describe people, places and the weather • add extra information

b Practise telling your story together.

7 Listen to each other's stories. What are the differences between them?

Tell stories about memorable meetings

4.3 goals
- describe past events ♻
- tell a travel anecdote

Osman　　Bernd

Annie　　Lukas

TASK LISTENING

1 a The people in the pictures have just met each other. Where are they? Do you think they're having a good time together?

b 🎧 **1.36** Listen to Osman's and Annie's stories. Check your ideas.

2 a Which sentence in each pair is about Osman and Bernd? Which is about Annie and Lukas?

1 - OB — AL
2 - OB — AL
3 - AL - OB
4 - AL - OB
5 - OB - AL

1	a They met in Germany.	b They met in France.
2	a They were going to the US on business.	b They had French lessons together.
3	a They met one or two years ago.	b They met a long time ago.
4	a They met a few times.	b They only met once.
5	a They're not in contact now.	b Now they're pen friends.

b 🎧 **1.36** Listen again to check.

TASK VOCABULARY

Starting a story

3 a Make sentences for starting a story.

1 b
2 c
3 a
4 e
5 d
6 i
7 h
8 g
9 j
10 f

1	I was	a	for a little restaurant.	6	I was	f	for a train.
2	I was living	b	in France.	7	It was	g	in a shop.
3	I was looking	c	in Frankfurt.	8	I was working	h	summer.
4	I was on my way	d	my brother.	9	I was travelling	i	to the USA.
5	I was visiting	e	to a conference.	10	I was waiting	j	with two friends.

b Look at 1–10 again. Think of more ways to complete each sentence.

TASK

4 a Think of a time in your life when you met someone interesting. Think about these questions.

1　Where were you? When was it?
2　What were you doing?
3　What was the person like?
4　What did you talk about?
5　Did you spend much time together?
6　Are you in contact now?

b Tell each other about the people you met.

Keyword *back*

verbs with *back*

1 **a** Read the sentences. How do the two highlighted expressions differ in meaning?

> a I'd like to go to the airport, please. Unit 4
> b The Canadian guy called and asked me to go back to the airport. Unit 4

b Add *back* to the correct place in each sentence.

> 1 Could you wait? I'll be in five minutes. Unit 4
> 2 … a Canadian man and his son were going to Canada. Unit 4
> 3 I gave the wallet and told him I only did a *little* shopping! Unit 4
> 4 He handed me fifty dollars and ran into the airport. Unit 4

back (opposite of *front*)

2 Which highlighted expressions refer to:

a a motorbike?   b a car?   c a credit card?

> 1 Can I put my case in the back? Unit 4
> 2 He handed me a wallet and said he found it on the back seat. Unit 4
> 3 I found the number on the back and phoned the company. Unit 4
> 4 I really wanted to ride it, not sit on the back! Unit 1

3 **a** Complete the questions with the words and expressions in the box.

> a shop   car   home   how quickly   old   the next day   travelled   wardrobe

1 Have you ever flown to a different country and come back *the next day*?
2 Have you ever been back to your _____ school or college?
3 When someone texts you, _____ do you text them back? What about emails?
4 When was the last time you took something back to _____? What was it?
5 What's the first thing you do when you get back _____ after a day at work or college?
6 Do you know anyone who's _____ on the back of an elephant?
7 Have you ever spent the night on the back seat of a _____?
8 What things do you keep in the back of your _____?

b Ask and answer the questions together.

> Well, a few months ago I took a pair of jeans back to a shop.

> Oh. Why?

Independent learning English outside the classroom

Astrid from Mexico

Tom from England

Masha from Russia

1 **a** ◆ 1.37 Listen to three people talking about how they learn languages outside the classroom. Which things A–E does each person talk about?

b ◆ 1.37 How do they use the things in the pictures? Listen again and make notes.

Astrid – read children's books

c What do you think about their ideas? Why? Talk together.

2 **a** Can you think of more ways of learning English outside the classroom? Make a list of your ideas. Think about listening, speaking, reading and writing.

b Compare with the list on p123.

3 Talk together. Which of the ideas for learning outside the classroom:

1 do you do now?   2 do you like / not like?   3 would you like to try?

Tony

Valérie

1 **a** ●1.38 Listen to a conversation between Tony and Valérie.

1   Why's Valérie in Vancouver?
2   What does she do?

b Do you think they have a friendly conversation? Why? / Why not?

2   Read the conversation.

1   How many questions does Tony ask?
2   Which highlighted expressions in the text are used:
   a   to show interest? *So ...*
   b   to add extra information? *Actually, ...*
3   Underline the extra information Valérie gives in her answers.

3 **a** In pairs, write the next five lines of Valérie and Tony's conversation.

b Compare your conversations with another pair. Were your ideas the same or different?

4 **a** Think of four questions for starting a conversation. Use the expressions in A below or your own ideas.

b In A/B pairs, use your questions to start conversations. Then continue the conversations.

A	Are you interested in ... ?		Do you like ... ?
	What's your favourite ... ?		Have you seen ... ?
	Have you ever been to ... ?		Where do you ... ?
	Are you going to ... ?		Have you got ... ?

↓

B Answer the question. Give some extra information.

↓   ↑

A Listen carefully to what your partner says. Ask another question.

5   Tell another partner about the conversations you had.

1   What did you talk about?
2   What was your most interesting conversation?

VALÉRIE	Good morning, can you take me to the Holiday Inn, please?
TONY	Sure. Which one?
VALÉRIE	The one on Broadway, please.
TONY	So, what brings you to Vancouver?
VALÉRIE	I have some old friends here. **Actually,** <u>we were at university together</u>.
TONY	So it's not your first time here?
VALÉRIE	Oh, no. I visit every three or four months.
TONY	Right. So you like it here?
VALÉRIE	Yes. In fact, I'd really like to live here.
TONY	Oh, yeah? Where do you live?
VALÉRIE	In Montreal. Well, actually, I've got a small business there.
TONY	Really? What do you do?
VALÉRIE	I own a couple of restaurants.

Do you like football?

Yes. Actually, I play for a team at work.

So where do you play?

Review

VOCABULARY Getting a taxi

1 a Put the words in 1–8 in the correct order.

1 is centre much it city How the to ?
2 you Can the take Park Inn to me ?
3 like to station to the please I'd go .
4 suitcases the I my put in Can back ?
5 five Could for minutes here you wait ?
6 it much is How ?
7 Just thirty it make dollars .
8 Can a have receipt I please ?

b In pairs, take turns to say 1–8 and think of answers.

GRAMMAR The past progressive

2 a Choose a time from yesterday. Make sure you all choose a different time.

b Find out what different people were doing at the time you chose. Make notes.

> What were you doing at 9.30 in the evening?

> Hm ... I think I was having a shower.

c Choose one of the people in your class. Make sure you all choose a different person.

d Find out from the others what your person did yesterday. Make notes.

> What can you tell me about Jakub?

> Well, at 9.30 pm he was having a shower.

e In groups, tell each other what your people did yesterday. Who had the most interesting day?

> In the morning, Jakub drove to work. He had a meeting and ...

CAN YOU REMEMBER? Unit 3 – Ordering a meal

3 a Complete the restaurant conversation.

WAITER   Hi, are you ¹_____ to order?
CUSTOMER Yes. What's the soup of the ²_____ ?
WAITER   It's vegetable soup ³_____ fresh herbs.
CUSTOMER That sounds nice. I'll ⁴_____ that and the fish, please.
WAITER   All right. And for you, sir?
CUSTOMER ⁵_____ I have the green salad to start and then the steak?
WAITER   Yes, and ⁶_____ would you like your steak?
CUSTOMER ⁷_____ , please.
WAITER   And can I ⁸_____ you something to drink?
CUSTOMER Can we have a bottle ⁹_____ water, please?
WAITER   Of course. ¹⁰_____ or still?
CUSTOMER Still, please.
WAITER   OK, thanks very much.

b Practise in groups of three. Change the food and drink to make new conversations.

Extension

SPELLING AND SOUNDS gh

4 a ● 1.39 gh is usually silent. Listen, then say the words.

right   night   frightening   eight   neighbours
bought   through   straight

b ● 1.40 In a few words, gh is pronounced /f/ or /g/. Listen, then say the words.

/f/   enough   laugh
/g/   yoghurt   spaghetti

c ● 1.41 Spellcheck. Close your book. Listen to ten words with gh and write them down.

d Look at the script on p147 to check your spelling.

NOTICE find

5 a Look at the sentences from this unit. Which highlighted expression describes a feeling or an opinion? Which describe an action?

1 ... when my next passenger got in, he handed me a wallet and said he found it on the back seat.
2 I liked the Canadian guy, so I found the number on the back of the credit card and phoned the company.
3 When I was learning French ... I liked reading children's books. I found it very useful because the sentences are very simple.

b Ask and answer the questions in groups.

1 Have you ever found something on the street, in a taxi, etc.? What was it? What did you do?
2 What was the last thing you lost? Did you ever find it?
3 What situations or things do you find: stressful? boring? fascinating? terrifying? funny? inconvenient?

> I find travelling stressful.

> Why? I usually find it really interesting.

Self-assessment

Can you do these things in English? Circle a number on each line. 1 = I can't do this, 5 = I can do this well.

◉ use a taxi	1	2	3	4	5
◉ tell a story	1	2	3	4	5
◉ tell a travel anecdote	1	2	3	4	5
◉ describe past events	1	2	3	4	5
◉ show interest in a conversation	1	2	3	4	5
◉ develop a conversation by asking questions and giving longer answers	1	2	3	4	5

• For Wordcards, reference and saving your work » e-Portfolio
• For more practice » Self-study Pack, Unit 4

5

Money

5.1 goals
◎ change money
◎ understand instructions on a cash machine
◎ pay for things in different places

Money matters

 **A**
 **B**
 **C** **D** **E**
 **F**

VOCABULARY
Money

1 **a** Read the questions. Match the highlighted words and expressions with the things in pictures A–F.

1 How many different coins and notes are there in your country? What pictures do they have on them?
2 How often do you use a cash machine or go into a bank? What do you do at each place?
3 When you go shopping, how do you prefer to pay? (in cash? by card? another way?)
4 How do you usually pay bills? Do you ever use the Internet for paying bills, banking or shopping?

b 🔊 **2.1** Listen to check. ℗

2 Ask and answer the questions together.

LISTENING

3 🔊 **2.2** Thiago's flying from France to Scotland. Before his flight, he changes some money in the airport. Listen to Thiago's conversation.

1 How much money does he change?
2 How much does he get?

4 **a** Match the questions and answers. Which questions does Thiago ask? Which does the assistant ask?

1 Do you have Scottish pounds?   a No problem. Are twenties OK?
2 Can I change these euros, please?   b Of course.
3 That's a hundred and eighty euros, yes?   c No, we don't.
4 Sorry, do you have any smaller notes?   d Yes, that's right.

b 🔊 **2.2** Listen again to check.

SPEAKING

5 **a** How many different currencies can you think of? *euros, pounds ...*

b You're going to change money at a bureau de change. Decide:

• which currency you want to change, and how much
• which currency you want to get

c Have conversations in different pairs. Take turns to be the customer and assistant.

READING

6 Thiago uses a cash machine in Glasgow, Scotland.
Put the screens A–E on p43 in order. Then answer the questions.

1 Which buttons on screen A, 1–6, can you press if you want to:
    a get some money?
    b change your PIN number?
    c know how much money you have?
2 Find words or expressions in screens A–E that mean:
    a choose   b question   c how much

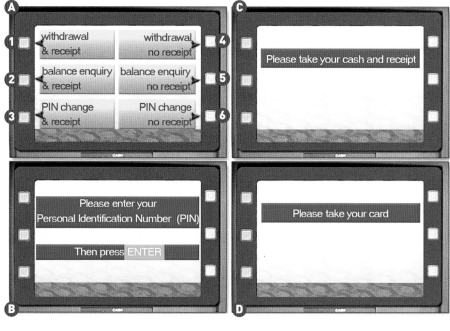

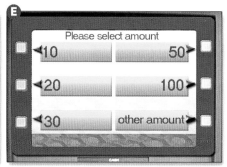

How would you like to pay?

LISTENING

1 **2.3** Listen to three conversations with Thiago in Glasgow. In each conversation:

a Where is he?
  1 a bus station   3 a shop
  2 a museum   4 a restaurant
b Does he pay in cash or by card?

2 **2.3** Listen again and complete the information.

Conversation 1 Thiago buys some _____ They cost _____
The assistant asks him if he'd like a _____
Conversation 2 The waitress asks Thiago to type in his PIN and press _____
She gives him a _____
Conversation 3 The receptionist asks to see a _____ His ticket costs _____
He pays with a £ _____ note.

VOCABULARY
Paying for things

3 **a** Which of these questions does Thiago ask?

1 Anything else?
2 How much‿is that?
3 Can‿I pay by card?
4 Would you like‿a bag?
5 Could‿I have the bill?
6 How would you like to pay?
7 Do you take cards?
8 Can‿I see your student card?
9 Do you have‿anything smaller?

b Think of ways to answer all the questions. Then compare your ideas with the script on p147.

PRONUNCIATION
Linking consonants and vowels 1

4 **2.4** Listen to questions 1–9. Notice how consonant and vowel sounds link (‿). Does a consonant or a vowel come:

1 at the end of the first word?   2 at the start of the next word?

5 In pairs, practise asking the questions and giving different answers. **P**

SPEAKING

6 **a** Work in A/B pairs.

A, look at your role cards on p123.
B, look at your role cards on p129.

Hello, can I help you?
Yes, do you have ...

b Have two conversations.

Microcredit

READING

1 Why do people borrow money from banks? Make a list of reasons.

to buy a home ...

2 Complete the sentences with these words.

credit   interest   a loan   repayments

1 I borrowed some money from the bank. → I got _____ / _____ from the bank.
2 Now I pay money to the bank every month. → I make _____ every month.
3 Borrowing the money costs seven percent a year. → I pay seven percent _____ a year.

3 a What do you think *microcredit* is? Is it credit for:

1 people without much money?
2 buying computer software?
3 the education of children?

b Read the article to check.

A new kind of banking?

✦ In 1976, Muhammed Yunus, a Bangladeshi professor of economics, started Grameen Bank. Grameen gives small loans – usually no more than US$100 – to very poor people who can't get credit from normal banks. This kind of credit is called *microcredit*.

✦ Most of Grameen's customers live in villages in the Bangladeshi countryside. 97 percent of them are women. They use the credit to start small businesses and make money for their families. For example, they make furniture, repair clothes, or buy animals for milk.

✦ Customers usually have to make repayments every week for twelve months. They pay about 16 percent interest a year. Grameen says that 98 percent of its customers make all their repayments.

✦ People who want a loan from Grameen have to make groups of five people, called loan circles. The people in the circle meet regularly to talk about their ideas and help each other. If someone in the group doesn't make their repayments, no one in the group can get credit in the future. However, if everyone makes their repayments, they can get bigger loans.

✦ In 2007, Grameen Bank had over seven million customers in nearly eighty thousand villages. There are now more than seven thousand other microcredit organisations around the world, including in Europe and the United States.

✦ Professor Yunus and Grameen Bank won the Nobel Peace Prize in December 2006.

4 Read the article again. What are these numbers in the text?

100   97   12   16   98   5   7,000,000   80,000   7,000

SPEAKING

5 Talk together.

1 Why do you think most of Grameen's customers are women?
2 Why do you think Professor Yunus got the Nobel Peace Prize? Do you think he was a good choice?

READING

6 a You're going to find out about two people who used microcredit to start businesses. They make the things in the pictures. What would you like to find out? In pairs, write two questions.

Where are the people from?

b Try to find the answers to your questions. Student A, read Alice's story on this page. Student B, read Rukmani's story on p124.

http://www.microcreditsummit.org/stories/alice.htm

BORROWER SUCCESS STORIES
MICROCREDIT SUMMIT CAMPAIGN

When Alice Pallewela got married, she and her husband went to live in Yodagama, a tiny farming village in the west of Sri Lanka.

"My husband works for the government, but his pay isn't enough for both of us," explains Alice. "I needed to make some money, so I decided to sell sweets. I've always loved sweets, and there weren't any sweet shops in Yodagama."

Alice started her business with a loan of US$100. She makes a few different kinds of sweets, all with local ingredients. She now employs six young women, and her sweets have an excellent reputation.

SPEAKING

7 Tell each other about Alice and Rukmani. Whose story do you find the most interesting? Why?

You have to …

GRAMMAR
have to, can

1 a Look at the grammar table. Circle the correct expressions in sentences 1–4.

have to	can
1 Grameen's customers have to / don't have to make groups of five people. 2 They have to / don't have to be women.	3 They can / can't usually get credit from normal banks. 4 They can / can't get bigger loans if they make all their repayments.
_____ they have to be women? Yes, they _____. No, they _____.	_____ they get credit from normal banks? Yes, they _____. No, they _____.

b Answer the questions.

1 Which highlighted expression means that something is:
   a possible? b not possible? c necessary? d not necessary?
2 Which highlighted expression has a similar meaning to:
   a *need to*? b *don't need to*?

c Complete the questions and short answers in the table with *can*, *can't*, *do*, *don't*.

2 ● 2.5 Listen to sentences 1–4. Notice how we say *can* /kən/ and *to* /tə/ with a schwa /ə/. ●

3 Work alone. Change these sentences so they're true for your country.

1 You can't get married until you're 21.
2 You can't drink alcohol.
3 Everyone over 18 has to vote.
4 You don't have to serve in the army.
5 You have to go to school until you're 17.
6 You can drive a car when you're 15.
7 You don't have to carry an ID card.
8 You can smoke when you're 16.

Grammar reference and practice, p135

SPEAKING

4 Compare your sentences in groups. Then ask and answer the questions.

1 If you're from the same country, do you agree?
2 Are there any laws you'd like to change? Why? How would you change them?
3 What do you know about laws in other countries?

I've heard that in the US, you can drive when you're fourteen.

Yes, but not everywhere.

Give advice to a visitor

5.3 goals
- talk about rules and obligations ♻
- give advice

1 a Look at the pictures and read the situations. Which things, 1–6, do you think you should do? Which things shouldn't you do?

Visiting a home in Canada
1 before the visit, ask if you can bring something
2 take a gift to the hosts
3 wear shoes in their home

Having a hot spring bath in Japan
4 wash yourself before you get into the water
5 get out of the water from time to time and rest
6 make a lot of noise

b Listen to Megan and Yukio and check your ideas. Do you find any of the rules surprising?

Megan from Canada   Yukio from Japan

2 What advice did Megan and Yukio give? Match 1–7 with a–g.

1 You should probably ask ahead of time
2 Maybe you can bring a
3 Don't wear
4 You have to wash
5 After that, you can get into
6 The water's quite hot, so you shouldn't stay in it
7 You can't make

a your shoes inside.
b if you can bring something with you.
c too long.
d off all the soap, so you are really clean.
e a lot of noise.
f the hot spring.
g bottle of wine, or maybe some flowers, something like that.

3 a Choose three things that are useful to tell a visitor about your country. Use these or your own ideas.

- visiting a religious building, e.g. a church, a mosque, a temple …
- using a library, public transport, ski slopes, …
- going to a wedding, someone's house for dinner, a restaurant, …

b You're going to tell someone about the three things. Think about the advice you want to give.

You have to …   You can't …   You should probably …   Don't …

c Listen to each other's advice and ask questions to find out more. If you're from the same country, do you agree?

> When you go to a mosque, there are a few rules. You have to …

Keyword *it*

Three uses of *it*

1 **a** Read the information and answer the questions.

You can use it to talk about:

A things, places and ideas you've mentioned already.

> The water's quite hot so you shouldn't stay in it too long.

B times and dates.

> It was July and I was looking forward to my holiday.

C the weather and temperature.

> It was really nice weather so you could eat outside.

1 What does it refer to in sentence A?
2 Can you think of five more expressions to replace the underlined words?
   a times and dates: It was 1998. *my birthday*
   b the weather: It was rainy. *hot and sunny*

b You're going to talk about an important day from your life. Think about these questions.

When was it? What happened? Why was it important? What was the weather like? How did you feel?

c Tell each other about your important days. Ask questions to find out more.

> It was a summer day in 2005. It was important because it was the day I got married!

Expressions with *it*

2 **a** Complete the conversations with expressions from the box. ● 2.7 Then listen to check. ℗

> Don't worry about it   I'll think about it
> It depends   ~~It doesn't really matter~~
> It's up to you   That's it

1 A When can we meet? Tomorrow? Sunday?
  B *It doesn't really matter* . I'm free all weekend.
2 A I'm sorry I'm late! Where's the meeting?
  B _____ . The meeting hasn't started yet.
3 A Do you like parties?
  B _____ . Generally yes, but not when there are too many people.
4 A Do you want to come to the cinema tonight?
  B Mm, I'm not sure I have time. _____ , OK?
5 A Have we got any food at home?
  B Not really ... we've got some milk in the fridge. _____ .
6 A What time do I have to start work?
  B _____ . But you have to be here eight hours a day.

b Work in pairs. Take turns to start conversations 1–6 and remember the responses.

Across cultures Money

1 Complete the statements with verbs from the box.

> borrow   cost   give   earn   lend   pay (x3)

1 If you need a big loan, you should _____ from your family if you can.
2 If you _____ money to a friend, you shouldn't ask for interest.
3 Parents should _____ some money to their children every week.
4 Adults who live with their parents should _____ rent.
5 You shouldn't talk about how much you _____ .
6 You shouldn't ask people how much their home _____ .
7 If a man and a woman go to a café, the man should always _____ the bill.
8 If you invite friends to a restaurant, you should _____ for all the food and drink.

2 **a** ● 2.8 Listen to Hayley and John. Which statement, 1–8, do they talk about?

b ● 2.8 Listen again. Who agrees with the statement? Who disagrees with it? Why?

c Read the script on p148 to check.

3 Think about these questions. Then ask and answer them together.

1 What do you think about statements 1–8? Why?
2 Where you live, what do most people think? Do they have the same ideas as you?
3 What do people think in other regions or countries that you know?

Hayley from the USA

John from the UK

1 a Imagine you're going to visit a friend who lives in another country. What things would you ask your friend about before you go? Make a list.

the weather, clothes ...

b Read Thiago's email to Chris, who lives and works in Cairo. Which things on your list does he ask about?

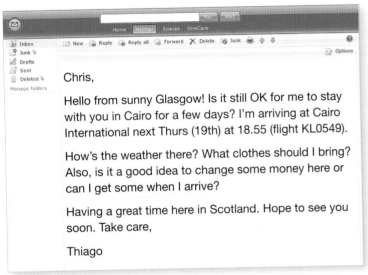

Chris,

Hello from sunny Glasgow! Is it still OK for me to stay with you in Cairo for a few days? I'm arriving at Cairo International next Thurs (19th) at 18.55 (flight KL0549).

How's the weather there? What clothes should I bring? Also, is it a good idea to change some money here or can I get some when I arrive?

Having a great time here in Scotland. Hope to see you soon. Take care,

Thiago

2 Read Chris's reply. Does he answer all Thiago's questions?

Hi Thiago,

Of course it's still OK, no problem. Really looking forward to seeing you!

I'm working when you arrive, so I can't meet you at the airport, sorry. You'll have to find your way to my flat. Take a taxi but remember to agree on a price first. It should be about thirty pounds (Egyptian). I think you've got the address of my flat, right? I'll be at home by the time you arrive.

It's pretty hot here, so make sure you bring plenty of light clothes. You'll need to cover your arms and legs in some parts of the city, so trousers and long-sleeved shirts are good. Also, yes, it's a good idea to change some money before you come. You're arriving Thursday evening and it can be difficult to change money on Fridays here. About a hundred Egyptian pounds should do it.

Another thing is, don't forget to bring a guidebook! I've only been here a couple of months and don't know the city very well yet, so I'm hoping we can explore the city together.

That's everything, I think. If you have any problems, give me a call on my mobile (+2012 530 95 49). See you at my place on Thursday night!

Chris

Goal

© write an email or letter giving advice to a visitor

Thiago is planning to visit his friend Chris in Cairo.

3 a Cover the emails. Can you remember Thiago's questions and Chris's advice?

Asking for advice
1   What ... should I bring?
2   Is it a good idea to change ... ?
Giving advice
3   You'll have to find your way to ...
4   Remember to agree on ...
5   Make sure you bring plenty of ...
6   You'll need to cover your ...
7   It's a good idea to change ...
8   Don't forget to bring a ...

b Read the emails again to check.

4 Complete the sentences. Use the words in (brackets) and different expressions from 3a.

1   There are lots of insects so ... (buy / insect spray)
2   You can't get into the country without the right visa so ... (get / tourist visa)
3   The museums have discounts for students, so ... (bring / student card)
4   The weather here's freezing, so ... (pack / warm clothes)
5   It's a really long train journey, so ... (bring / good book)

5 a Plan an email or letter to a friend who's going to visit you.

1   Which topics do you want to talk about? Use this list and your own ideas.
    the weather   clothes   money   transport   where to meet   phone numbers
2   What do you want to say about each topic?
3   How many paragraphs will you write?
4   What will you say in each paragraph?
5   How will you start and finish your email or letter?

b Write your email or letter. Write about 100 words.

6 Read each other's emails or letters. Is there anything else you'd like to know about? Ask questions to find out.

Review

GRAMMAR can, have to

1 a In pairs, decide on the rules for a library. Complete the sentences with: can, can't, have to or don't have to.

 1 You _____ pay to join the library.
 2 You _____ borrow more than six books.
 3 You _____ keep books for up to three weeks.
 4 You _____ pay a fine if you keep books too long.
 5 You _____ borrow dictionaries.
 6 You _____ keep quiet in the library.

b Work alone. Think of the rules and advice for two places. Use can, can't, have to or don't have to.

c In groups, listen to the rules and advice. Can you guess the places?

> Usually you don't have to buy a ticket. You can bring your own food. You shouldn't leave any rubbish …

> Is it a park?

VOCABULARY Giving advice

2 a Work in pairs. For each situation, think of advice for a friend. Use your own ideas.

 1 I'm going on holiday to Paris but I don't speak any French.
 2 My manager wants me to work this weekend but friends are coming to stay with me.
 3 I promised to meet a friend tonight but I feel too tired now.
 4 I really want to stop smoking but I can't.

b Listen to each other's advice. Who has the best ideas?

> We'd tell our friend: You should talk to your manager. Explain that your friends …

CAN YOU REMEMBER? Unit 4 – Getting a taxi

3 a Match the sentences 1–6 with the responses a–f.

 1 How much is it to the city centre?
 2 Can you take me to the Park Inn?
 3 Could you wait here for five minutes? I just have to get some papers.
 4 The Royal Bank on Howe Street, please.
 5 Just make it thirty-five dollars.
 6 And can I have a receipt, please?

 a Sure … here you are. Have a safe trip now.
 b OK.
 c Thanks very much … And here's your change, fifteen dollars.
 d The Park Inn on Broadway, right?
 e That depends on the traffic.
 f Well, OK, but can you pay me first?

b Practise taxi conversations in pairs. Change the underlined parts of the sentences in 3a.

Extension

SPELLING AND SOUNDS -tion, -ssion, -cian

4 a ● 2.9 You say the endings -tion, -ssion, -cian in the same way, /ʃən/. Listen and say the words. Notice how the stress always goes before the ending.

 conver•sation expr•ession mus•ician

b Practise saying these words with the correct sound and stress.

 politician station discussion reception electrician pronunciation

c ● 2.10 Spellcheck. Close your books. Listen to ten words and write them down.

d Look at the script on p148 to check your spelling.

NOTICE Vague language

5 a What can you remember about the Grameen bank? Complete the sentences with the numbers.

> seven thousand seven million
> 16 eighty thousand 100

 1 Grameen gives small loans – usually no more than US$_____.
 2 They pay about _____ percent interest a year.
 3 In 2007, Grameen Bank had over _____ customers in nearly _____ villages.
 4 There are now more than _____ other microcredit organisations around the world.

b Look at the article on p44 to check.

c ● 2.11 Listen to eight questions and write down your answers – but don't write them in order. Use the expressions in 5a. No more than three.

d Look at each other's answers. Can you guess what they mean? Ask questions to find out more.

> OK, 'No more than three' … is that how much tea or coffee you drink?

Self-assessment

Can you do these things in English? Circle a number on each line. 1 = I can't do this, 5 = I can do this well.

◎ change money	1	2	3	4	5
◎ understand instructions on a cash machine	1	2	3	4	5
◎ pay for things in different places	1	2	3	4	5
◎ talk about rules and obligations	1	2	3	4	5
◎ give advice	1	2	3	4	5
◎ write an email or letter giving advice to a visitor	1	2	3	4	5

• For Wordcards, reference and saving your work » e-Portfolio
• For more practice » Self-study Pack, Unit 5

6 Energy

Burning calories

 A
 B
 C
 D
 E
 F

VOCABULARY
Household chores

1 a What chores can you see in each picture?

> cleaning the windows   doing the cooking   doing the dusting
> doing the ironing   making the bed   doing the vacuuming

b 2.12 Listen to check. ℗ Can you think of more chores?

SPEAKING

2 Talk together.

1 Who does the different chores in your home?
2 Which chores do you like the most? Which don't you like? Why?

3 a Which three chores in 1 do you think use the most energy?

b Read the fact file from a magazine to check your ideas.

Daily chores may do you more good than going to the gym

Doing the vacuuming may be a better way to keep fit than swimming or cycling, according to new research. This is great news for all of us who don't like going to the gym! Here's how some household chores compare to more traditional ways of keeping fit.

	calories an hour
Vacuuming	320
Swimming (20 metres a minute)	270
Walking (5 kilometres per hour)	260
Cycling (10 kilometres per hour)	240
Yoga	230
Ironing	203
Cooking	180
Making beds	180
Cleaning windows	150
Dusting	150

READING

4 a Look at the photos showing two unusual ways to burn calories. What do you think are the advantages of each way?

b Check your ideas in pairs. A, read the article about Manuel Pedro below. B, read the article about Alex Gadsden on p124.

Manuel Pedro on his treadmill in the office.

Alex Gadsden on his cycle washer outside.

The treadmill

When Manuel Pedro's daughter looked at him one morning and said "Wow, you're fat!", he knew it was time to lose some weight. The trouble was, he didn't have time to do any exercise.

"I work in an office all day and when I get home in the evening, I generally just want to sit down and relax. At the weekend I normally do things with my kids, so I just don't have time to go to the gym or go for a run."

However, one day, his wife suggested buying a treadmill and walking on it while he worked.

"I thought she was crazy at first," he says. "But then I thought, why not?"

So the forty-year-old bought a cheap treadmill and put it in the corner of his office. He fixed his laptop to it and began walking and working at the same time.

"At first, I found it hard to type and walk at the same time. I got really stressed and sometimes only did it once or twice a week. I also looked really stupid in a shirt and tie on a treadmill. My colleagues thought it was really funny."

However, soon Manuel got better at working while he walked, and started to feel healthier. After a while he was doing several hours' walking every morning.

"I have a lot more energy now," says the office manager. "When I get to the office, I get straight on the treadmill and check my emails. I do three hours a day at the moment. Every week I do ten minutes' more walking. I've lost a lot of weight. My wife can't stop smiling."

[handwritten notes in margin:]
1 - His wife has the idea
2 - 3 hours a day

5 a Read your article again and answer the questions about Manuel or Alex.

1   Who had the idea?
2   How much time does he spend doing exercise at the moment?
3   What's his morning routine now?
4   How has it changed his life?

b Ask and answer the questions about each other's articles.

6   What do you think about the ideas in the articles?

I tend to …

VOCABULARY

Talking about habits

1 a Which sentences from the articles are about Manuel? Which are about Alex?

1   Then I generally have breakfast and a shower.
2   He normally cycles for 25 minutes to wash the clothes.
3   After a while he was doing several hours' walking every morning.
4   Every week I do ten minutes' more walking.
5   I got really stressed and sometimes only did it once or twice a week.
6   I do three hours a day at the moment.
7   I tend to get up at around six-thirty now and get straight on the cycle washer.
8   The 29-year-old now starts each day with a 45-minute cycle ride.

[handwritten notes in margin:]
1. A
2 - A
3 - M
4 - M
5 - M
6 - M
7 - A
8 - A

b Which highlighted words or expressions from 1–8:

1   mean usually? (x3)
2   say how often you do things? (x3)
3   say how long or when you do things? (x2)

2   Write six sentences about your habits – four true, and two false. Use these topics and your own ideas.

- in the morning   • when you get up   • in the evening
- after your work/studies   • before you go to sleep   • meals, food and drink
- sports and exercise   • household chores

SPEAKING

3 a Listen to each other's sentences. Can you guess which are false?

b Find out more about each other's habits. Do you do the same or different things?

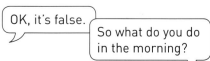

I start each day with two or three cups of coffee.

But you don't like coffee!

OK, it's false.

So what do you do in the morning?

Well, I …

Extreme weather

VOCABULARY

Weather

1 a Read the weather fact file. Find the highlighted words in the pictures. What's the most surprising fact for you?

b Have you experienced these kinds of weather? Which ones occur in your country or region?

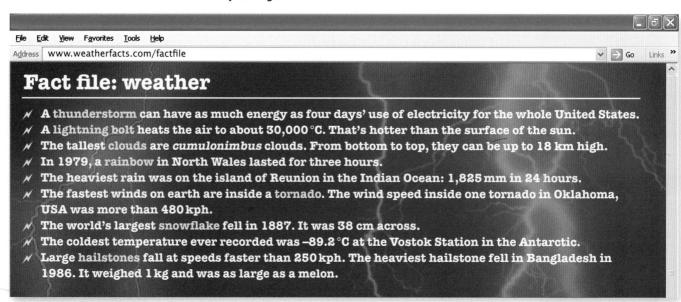

File Edit View Favorites Tools Help

Address www.weatherfacts.com/factfile   ⌄ ➡ Go Links »

Fact file: weather

- A thunderstorm can have as much energy as four days' use of electricity for the whole United States.
- A lightning bolt heats the air to about 30,000 °C. That's hotter than the surface of the sun.
- The tallest clouds are *cumulonimbus* clouds. From bottom to top, they can be up to 18 km high.
- In 1979, a rainbow in North Wales lasted for three hours.
- The heaviest rain was on the island of Reunion in the Indian Ocean: 1,825 mm in 24 hours.
- The fastest winds on earth are inside a tornado. The wind speed inside one tornado in Oklahoma, USA was more than 480 kph.
- The world's largest snowflake fell in 1887. It was 38 cm across.
- The coldest temperature ever recorded was –89.2 °C at the Vostok Station in the Antarctic.
- Large hailstones fall at speeds faster than 250 kph. The heaviest hailstone fell in Bangladesh in 1986. It weighed 1 kg and was as large as a melon.

LISTENING

2 a What problems do you think people can have when the weather's really hot, or really cold?

b •2.13 Listen to Jeevan and Vasily talking about the weather where they live.

1 What kinds of weather do they talk about?
2 Who talks about these things?

- afternoons • driving • air conditioning
- clothes • drinks • temperature • tourists

3 a Can you remember what Jeevan and Vasily say about the things in 2b? Talk together.

b •2.13 Listen again to check.

4 What do you do when the weather's really hot or cold? Do you like this kind of weather?

Jeevan from Kolkata

Vasily from Moscow

It isn't as cold as …

1 a What are the comparatives and superlatives of the adjectives in the table?

One syllable	Two syllables ending in -y	Two or more syllables	Irregular
cold hot large	heavy	careful important	good bad far

colder, the coldest

b Use words from 1a to complete the sentences from the talks and the fact file.

Comparatives and superlatives	as … as …
You have to be _____ on the roads. That's _____ than the surface of the sun. The _____ hailstone fell in Bangladesh in 1986. The _____ thing is to drink a lot.	It weighed 1 kg and was as _____ as a melon. It isn't as _____ as Siberia.

c **2.14** Listen to check. ℗

2 Look at sentences 1–5. Which highlighted expression(s) means:

a big difference?   a small difference?   exactly the same?

1   It's usually –5 to –10 °C but it can get a lot colder.
2   People prefer to go to much hotter countries.
3   You should be a bit more careful in the hot sun.
4   Moscow is almost as cold as Siberia.
5   Helsinki is just as cold as Moscow.

3 Complete the paragraph about Pakistan with these adjectives in the correct form.

large   big   frightening   hot   cold (x2)   heavy

(handwritten notes: 2 - hottest   6 - big   3 - heaviest   4 - coldest   5 - colder   7 - frightening)

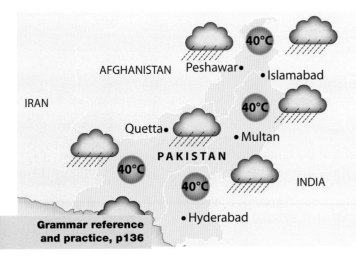

AFGHANISTAN Peshawar• 40°C •Islamabad

IRAN

Quetta• 40°C •Multan

PAKISTAN

40°C

40°C INDIA

•Hyderabad

Grammar reference and practice, p136

When I was little, I lived in Lahore in Pakistan. It's the second ¹ *largest* city in Pakistan after Karachi. The weather in Lahore is extreme during the summer. The ² _____ months are May, June and July, when temperatures can rise to 40–45 °C. The ³ _____ rainfall is in July and August during the monsoon. The ⁴ _____ months are December, January and February, but it doesn't often get ⁵ _____ than 9 °C. What I remember most clearly is the hail. Hailstones almost as ⁶ _____ as tennis balls would hit our house. They could break windows and damage cars. However, the ⁷ _____ moments were the dust storms, when the sky turned black in the middle of the day.

4 a When a word ends in -er or -est, the stress stays on the same syllable. Say these words.

hot → hotter → the hottest   heavy → heavier → the heaviest

b Practise saying the comparatives and superlatives in 1a with the correct stress.

5 a Think about these things in your country or another country you know. Make notes.

- climate and seasons • extreme weather and storms
- oceans or seas • rivers and lakes • mountains

wettest – January and February
longest river – the Nile

b Compare your ideas in groups. If you're from the same country, do you agree?

In Dubai, the wettest months are January and February.

Actually, I think it's just as wet in December.

Do a survey

Sally

Sports Plus is planning to open a new fitness centre. They're doing a survey of local people's habits and preferences.

6.3 goals
- ◎ talk about present habits ♻
- ◎ make comparisons ♻
- ◎ express preferences

TASK LISTENING

1 Is there a fitness centre near where you live? What can you do there? Do you ever use it?

2   ● **2.15** Listen to the interview with Sally.

1   What does Sally think of the fitness centre she visits? *pq acaba en* (s)?
2   How often does she go there?
3   How long does she spend there?
4   What does she usually do?

TASK VOCABULARY

Expressing preferences

3 a Can you remember what Sally says? Complete the sentences with words from the box.

| a nicer pool   facilities   showers   women-only classes   changing rooms   pool |

1   The _____'s OK, but it could be bigger.
2   I'd prefer _____ as well.
3   The _____ could definitely be better.
4   I don't mind the _____.
5   I'd much rather have private _____.
6   I'd rather have _____ than a sauna.

b   ● **2.15** Listen again to check.

4 Cover the sentences and look at the things in the box. Try to remember what Sally says.

TASK

decide to + inf.

5 a You <u>decide</u> to open a new business. In groups, choose one of the following or your own idea.
pueŝt6

- a fitness centre   • a music shop   • a café or restaurant   • a market stall

b Before you open your business, you want to know about people's habits and preferences. Design a questionnaire with six questions. Think about these things.

- the kind of products / facilities / service   • location
- hours   • special features   • other ideas

*Do you ... ?   Where ... ?   When ... ?   Are you interested in ... ?   How often ... ?
How long ... ?   What do you ... ?   Do you prefer ... ?*

> How often do you go to a sports centre?

>> Well, I go swimming once a week.

6 Use your questionnaire to interview people from other groups. Talk to three different people each.

7 a Go back to your group and compare your results. What kind of service would most people like?

b Tell the class about your decisions.

Keyword *do*

1 Put the highlighted collocations with do into three groups:

a work and studies   b chores   c sports and exercise

> 1 Doing the vacuuming may be a better way to keep fit than swimming. Unit 6
> 2 These days we have to do our jobs *and* do exercise to stay healthy! Unit 6
> 3 In your home, who does the food shopping? Unit 3
> 4 I hated doing exams and tests and so on. Unit 2
> 5 I've done courses in music, local history and Spanish. Unit 2
> 6 I do a lot of work in the rainforest, in the Central Amazon. Unit 2
> 7 When I was at college, I did aerobics. Unit 1

2 a Make questions with the collocations in 1.

Have you ever ... ? How often do you ... ? When was the last time you ... ?

Have you ever done yoga?

b Ask and answer the questions together.

3 a Continue sentences 1–6 with a–f.

do + a bit of/a lot of/some + activity
1 I did a bit of singing when I was younger.
2 I'm doing a lot of reading at the moment.
3 When I'm stressed I do some yoga.
do + something/anything/everything
4 I did something really stupid last week.
5 I didn't do anything last night.
6 I have to do everything when my wife is away.

a I left my key in the door!
b The cleaning, the ironing, all the chores.
c The exercise really calms me down.
d I'm half-way through a 500-page book.
e I was really into it.
f I just came home and went to bed.

b Write three more sentences about what you do.

I did a bit of karate when I was at school.

c In groups, read out your sentences. Ask questions to find out more.

Independent learning Reading the phonemic script

1 a Look at the dictionary entry for *routine*. How do you say it?

b Work in pairs. How do you say these sounds?

/b/ /f/ /m/ /θ/ /s/ /j/ /e/ /iː/ /ɪ/ /æ/ /ɔː/ /ʊ/

c Check with the chart on p159.

> routine /ruːˈtiːn/ *noun* the things that you do every day at the same time: *a daily routine*

2 a Match the symbols 1–8 with the highlighted sounds in words a–h. Use the chart to help you.

b ⟨2.16⟩ Listen to check. ℗

3 a In pairs, read the words 1–10.

1 /dʒɪm/
2 /ˈθʌn.də.stɔːm/
3 /ˈsaɪklɪŋ/
4 /tʃɔːrz/
5 /klaʊdz/
6 /ˈkliː.nɪŋ/
7 /ˈreɪn.bəʊ/
8 /ˈvæk.juːmɪŋ/
9 /tɔːˈneɪ.dəʊ/
10 /ˈwɔː.kɪŋ/

b ⟨2.17⟩ Listen to check.

1 /iː/	a her
2 /ʃ/	b stay
3 /ʌ/	c shopping
4 /e/	d current
5 /eə/	e best
6 /dʒ/	f energy
7 /eɪ/	g hair
8 /ɜː/	h free

a café

a newsagent

a fitness centre

1 🔊 **2.18** Listen to three conversations. Match them with the pictures.

2 **a** You can be more polite by speaking less directly. Which sentences are less direct, a or b?

1 a Would you mind answering some questions?
   b Can you answer some questions?
2 a It could be better.
   b It's bad.

b Look at the conversations. Find and <u>underline</u> the expressions that are less direct than these.

Requests
1 Can you answer a few questions?
2 Can you change this ten for me?
3 Can you tell me a bit more?
Refusing requests
4 No, I don't want to.
5 No, I don't need anything.
Opinions
6 The pool is dirty.
7 The staff aren't interested.
8 It's boring.
9 I'm not interested in football.

c 🔊 **2.19** Listen to check. ℗

3 Make these expressions less direct using the words in (brackets). Then compare your answers.

1 My parents are old-fashioned. (a bit)
   My parents are a bit old-fashioned.
2 We're not hungry. (really)
3 Ronnie and Clara are unhappy. (don't seem)
4 I hate bananas. (really like)
5 George is stupid sometimes. (clever)
6 Can you wait for five minutes? (Would you mind)
7 Can you be quiet, please? (Do you think)
8 Can you help me with my bags? (I wonder if)

4 **a** 🔊 **2.20** Listen to a phone conversation between André and Sue. Do you think it sounds polite?

b Look at the script on p149. In pairs, write a more polite version of the conversation. Practise it.

c Listen to each other's conversations. Do you think they sound polite?

❶

BILL	Would you mind answering a few questions, please? It won't take long.
SHEILA	Er, yes, that's OK.
BILL	Thank you. Are you happy with the fitness centre generally?
SHEILA	Erm, well, it could be better.
BILL	Oh. I see. Do you think you could tell me a bit more?
SHEILA	Well, to be honest, the pool isn't always very clean. And the staff don't seem very interested.
BILL	Oh dear. Well, I'll definitely tell the manager.

❷

BEN	Hi. I wonder if you could change this ten for me. I need some coins for the ticket machine.
CLODAGH	Sorry, but I'd rather not. People are always asking me for change.
BEN	Oh.
CLODAGH	Perhaps you'd like to buy something?
BEN	Erm, no, not really.

❸

PHIL	Here's your drink. Sorry it took so long.
CATHERINE	So, what do you think of the game?
PHIL	Um, it's a bit boring.
CATHERINE	Boring?
PHIL	Well, you know I'm not really interested in football.
CATHERINE	So should we go? The second half starts in two minutes.
PHIL	No, you stay here. I'll do some shopping, then come back in an hour, OK?
CATHERINE	Well, OK. See you later.

Review

VOCABULARY Weather

1 **a** Work in teams. Complete these weather words with vowels. Who can finish first?

rn thndrstrm lghtnng snwflk trnd
rnbw hlstns wnd clds tmprtr

b How did you feel about different kinds of weather when you were a child?

> When I was a child, I was afraid of lightning.

> Really? I thought it was exciting.

GRAMMAR Comparing things

2 **a** Order the words in these questions.

1 life / in the past / Do you think / than / is easier now ?
2 it's better for children / Do you think / or / to play computer games / to read ?
3 cheerful / Who's / person you know / the most ?
4 better kinds of / than in the past / Do people have / entertainment ?
5 for you / the best place / What's / to relax ?
6 been to / the most exhausting event / What's / you've ever ?

b Ask and answer the questions. Give examples and reasons.

CAN YOU REMEMBER? Unit 5 – Paying for things

3 **a** Put the sentences of the conversation in order.

☐	ASSISTANT	Anything else?
☐	THIAGO	Next door? OK.
☐	ASSISTANT	Eight postcards. That comes to six pounds forty, please.
☐	THIAGO	No, that's all, thanks. How much is that?
☐	ASSISTANT	I'm afraid not, no. There's a cash machine just –
1	THIAGO	I'll take these postcards, please. And do you have any maps?
☐	THIAGO	No, it's OK, I've got some cash, I think.
☐	ASSISTANT	I'm sorry, we don't have any maps at the moment. You could try next door.
☐	ASSISTANT	Thank you. And that's 60 pence change.
☐	THIAGO	Can I pay by card?

b Practise in pairs, changing the underlined expressions. Take turns to be Thiago and the shop assistant.

Extension

SPELLING AND SOUNDS -able and -ible

4 **a** ⊙ **2.21** These two adjective endings sound the same, /əbl/. Read and listen.

comfortable available possible sensible

b Complete these words to make endings with -ible or -able.

terr__ble fashion__ble imposs__ble
horr__ble memor__ble enjoy__ble

c ⊙ **2.22** Spellcheck. Close your book. Listen to ten words and write them down.

d Look at the script on p149 to check your spelling.

NOTICE Abbreviations

5 **a** Match these words with abbreviations from the weather fact file on p52.

1	millimetre	a	km
2	degrees (Celsius)	b	°C
3	kilometres per hour	c	cm
4	centimetre	d	mm
5	kilometre	e	kg
6	kilo (kilogram)	f	kph

b Can you remember what these figures are about? Talk together, then read to check.

1	38 cm	4	480 kph	6	–89.2 °C
2	18 km	5	1,825 mm	7	1 kg
3	30,000 °C				

> I think 38 cm was the largest snowflake. It was 38 cm across.

c Talk together. Do you know, or can you guess:

1 how tall you are?
2 what the speed limit is for cars in your country?
3 how far it is from your home to the nearest airport?
4 what the temperature was on the hottest and coldest days you've had this year?
5 how much you weighed when you were born?

Self-assessment

Can you do these things in English? Circle a number on each line. 1 = I can't do this, 5 = I can do this well.

◉ talk about present habits	1	2	3	4	5
◉ talk about weather	1	2	3	4	5
◉ make comparisons	1	2	3	4	5
◉ express preferences	1	2	3	4	5
◉ speak more politely by being less direct	1	2	3	4	5

• For Wordcards, reference and saving your work » e-Portfolio
• For more practice » Self-study Pack, Unit 6

City life

Urbanisation

Sheikh Zayed Road in Dubai, 1991

Sheikh Zayed Road in Dubai, 2005

READING

1 Look at the pictures. What changes can you see?

2 Read the introduction to the article about urbanisation. Why do you think so many people around the world are going to live in cities?

www.viewpoint.com/urbanworld

Viewpoint – The urban world in 2050

In 1900, just 13 per cent of the world's people lived in cities. In 2008, the number passed 50 per cent for the first time in history. By 2050, the number will be about 70 per cent. The urban population in Asia and Africa will double, and there will be nearly 30 "megacities" – cities with more than 10 million people. So what will life be like for people in the cities of the future? Professor of human geography Ben Rhodes describes his vision of the urban world in 2050.

Professor Ben Rhodes

[1] Life in cities will be very different from how it is today. Energy, especially oil, will be very expensive, so many people will probably work at home, or have their workplaces close to where they live. There'll be less traffic on the roads, and it'll be easier for people to be close to their families. For these reasons cities won't have just one centre where everyone goes to work and shop. Instead, we'll probably see cities with many different centres.

[2] It will be difficult to provide enough water, gas and electricity for really big cities, so these will probably stop growing. Many people from the countryside will move to smaller cities of 500,000 people or less. Transport over long distances will be a lot more expensive than it is now, so people will have to use food and energy from the countryside around their cities.

They'll use local materials for building, and perhaps traditional styles of architecture too.

[3] The thing I really worry about is that energy may become too expensive for many people. In the end we might have two groups of people: a rich group which can afford energy and lives in clean, green areas, and a bigger, poorer group which can't afford it and has to live in the more polluted parts of the city. This might lead to serious political problems.

[4] As we all know, cities near the sea will probably experience some extra problems. As temperatures around the world go up, sea levels will rise and many places will have problems with flooding. Some cities will be OK, some may even find that the change in the climate is good for them, but others will need help. We really need to start planning for this now.

1 d
2 a
3 c
4 b

3 Read the rest of the article. In which paragraph 1–4 does Professor Rhodes talk about these topics?

a Cities and the countryside
b Cities near the sea
c Energy, money and politics
d Working and living in cities

4 Read the article again. What reasons does Professor Rhodes give for these predictions?

1 Cities will have many centres.
2 Big cities will stop growing.
3 Buildings will use local materials.
4 There might be political problems.
5 Some cities near the sea will need help.

5 In groups, ask and answer the questions.

1 How do you feel about the changes Professor Rhodes describes? Which are good and which are bad?
2 Do you disagree with anything Professor Rhodes says? Why?

VOCABULARY

The environment

6 Cover the article and use the words and expressions from the box to complete the sentences. Then check in the article.

> clean, green   climate   flooding   gas   oil
> polluted   sea levels   traffic   transport

1 Energy, especially _____ , will be very expensive.
2 There'll be less _____ on the roads.
3 It will be difficult to provide enough water, _____ and electricity for really big cities.
4 _____ over long distances will be a lot more expensive.
5 We might have two groups of people: a rich group which lives in _____ areas ...
6 ... and a poorer group which has to live in the more _____ parts of the city.
7 As temperatures around the world go up, _____ will rise and many places will have problems with _____ .
8 Some cities may find that the change in _____ is good for them, but others will need help.

SPEAKING

7 Ask and answer the questions.

1 Do you think the climate is changing around the world? What about where you live?
2 Which places in your country or city:

- have the worst traffic?   • sometimes have problems with flooding?
- have the most popular green areas?   • are the most polluted?
- might have problems if sea levels go up?

Making predictions

GRAMMAR

will, might, may

1 Read sentences 1–5. Then complete the grammar table with the highlighted words.

1 There'll be less traffic on the roads.
2 Cities won't have just one centre.
3 Big cities will probably stop growing.
4 Energy may become too expensive.
5 This might create two groups of people.

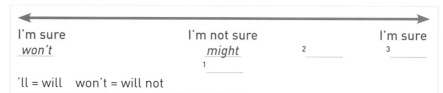

I'm sure	I'm not sure		I'm sure
won't	*might*	2 _____	3 _____
	1 _____		

'll = will   won't = will not

2 What do you think the world will be like in 2050? Make sentences with the words.

1 people / have / free time
2 families / have / children
3 children / study / home
4 people / use / cash / shops
5 food / expensive
6 people / do / exercise
7 English / important
8 people / happier

People will probably have less free time.

Grammar reference and practice, p137

SPEAKING

3 a Think of three more predictions about life in 2050.

b Compare all your predictions from 2 and 3a in groups. Talk about your ideas.

If you're interested in art ...

READING

1 Look at the photos in the website for tourists. What do you know about Amsterdam?

2 Now read the entries. Which place would you most like to visit? Why?

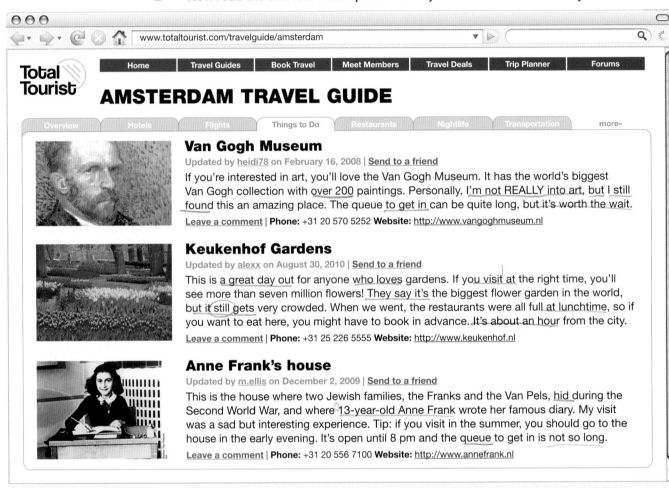

Total Tourist

| Home | Travel Guides | Book Travel | Meet Members | Travel Deals | Trip Planner | Forums |

www.totaltourist.com/travelguide/amsterdam

AMSTERDAM TRAVEL GUIDE

Overview | Hotels | Flights | **Things to Do** | Restaurants | Nightlife | Transportation | more»

Van Gogh Museum
Updated by heidi78 on February 16, 2008 | Send to a friend

If you're interested in art, you'll love the Van Gogh Museum. It has the world's biggest Van Gogh collection with over 200 paintings. Personally, I'm not REALLY into art, but I still found this an amazing place. The queue to get in can be quite long, but it's worth the wait.

Leave a comment | **Phone:** +31 20 570 5252 **Website:** http://www.vangoghmuseum.nl

Keukenhof Gardens
Updated by alexx on August 30, 2010 | Send to a friend

This is a great day out for anyone who loves gardens. If you visit at the right time, you'll see more than seven million flowers! They say it's the biggest flower garden in the world, but it still gets very crowded. When we went, the restaurants were all full at lunchtime, so if you want to eat here, you might have to book in advance. It's about an hour from the city.

Leave a comment | **Phone:** +31 25 226 5555 **Website:** http://www.keukenhof.nl

Anne Frank's house
Updated by m.ellis on December 2, 2009 | Send to a friend

This is the house where two Jewish families, the Franks and the Van Pels, hid during the Second World War, and where 13-year-old Anne Frank wrote her famous diary. My visit was a sad but interesting experience. Tip: if you visit in the summer, you should go to the house in the early evening. It's open until 8 pm and the queue to get in is not so long.

Leave a comment | **Phone:** +31 20 556 7100 **Website:** http://www.annefrank.nl

GRAMMAR
Real conditionals

3 Complete the sentences from the website with words from the box.

'll (x2)   might   should

If + present,	will / might / should + infinitive
1 If you're interested in art,	you _____ love the Van Gogh Museum.
2 If you visit at the right time,	you _____ see more than seven million flowers.
3 If you want to eat here,	you _____ have to book in advance.
4 If you visit in the summer,	you _____ go to the house in the early evening.

4 Write recommendations for visitors to your country.

1 If you're interested in sightseeing, you'll love ...
2 If you want to do some shopping, you should go ...
3 If you enjoy trying new food, you might like ...
4 If you like the countryside, you'll ...
5 If you come in the winter, you should ...
6 If you like sports, you might ...
7 If you're interested in ...
8 If ...

Grammar reference and practice, p137

SPEAKING

5 Listen to each other's recommendations. Which ones would you like to try? If you're from the same country, do you agree?

Getting directions

LISTENING

1 **2.23** Listen to Lizzy's conversation in the tourist office and answer the questions.

    1 Where does she want to go?   2 How far is it?

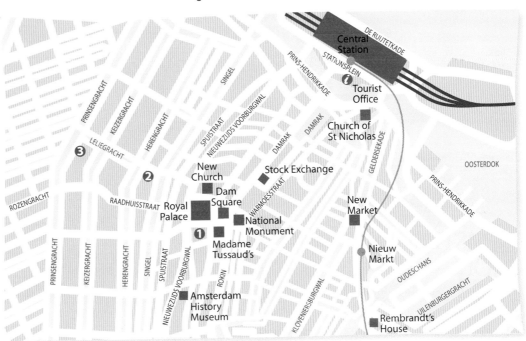

2 **2.23** Find the tourist office on the map and then listen again. Where's Anne Frank's house: 1, 2 or 3?

VOCABULARY
Giving directions

3 **a** Use the map to put the directions in order, 1–8.

Ask   How can I get to Anne Frank's house?

Start   We're next to the main train station.

    ☐ Go along Raadhuisstraat for about five hundred metres.
    2 Go down the big street. It's called Damrak.
    1 Go out of here and turn left.
    ↓ ☐ Turn right and go past the palace.
    ☐ When you get to the canal called Prinsengracht, turn right.
    ☐ If you continue along Damrak, you'll come to the Dam.
    3 You'll go past a big building on your left, the Beurs.
    ☐ You'll see the National Monument on your left and the Royal Palace on your right.

Finish   The house is by the canal.

b Check in the script on p149. Then cover 3a, look at the map and give directions to Anne Frank's house.

PRONUNCIATION
Linking consonants and vowels 2

4 **a** **2.24** Listen and notice how the consonant and vowel sounds link in this sentence.

Go out‿of here‿and turn left.

b Mark the consonants and vowels that link in these directions.

    1 Turn right and go past the palace. (x1)
    2 You'll go past a big building on your left, the Beurs. (x2)
    3 You'll see the National Monument on your left and the Royal Palace on your right. (x3)

c **2.25** Listen to check. **P** Practise saying the directions.

SPEAKING

5 **a** Work alone. Choose two places on the map. Think about how to give directions from the tourist office.

b Listen to each other's directions and guess the places.

Tourist information centre
" " officer

Get tourist information

7.3 goals
⊙ make recommendations ♻
⊙ give directions ♻
⊙ get information in a tourist office

Sergei is in Amsterdam on business, but has some free time to see the city.

TASK LISTENING

1 a What can you remember about:

the Van Gogh Museum?   the Keukenhof Gardens?   Anne Frank's house?

b ◦◦ **2.26** Listen to Sergei's conversation in the tourist office. Which places does he decide to visit?

TASK VOCABULARY

Getting tourist information

2 a Can you remember what Sergei says? Tick (✓) the highlighted expressions he uses.

  1   I'm looking for somewhere to stay.
✓2   Do you organise tours of the city?
✓3   Have you got a map?
✓4   Can you recommend some things to see?
  5   Do you have any information about art galleries?
✓6   Do you sell tickets?

b ◦◦ **2.26** Listen again to check.

3 Can you think of more ways to continue the highlighted expressions in 2a? Use these and your own ideas.

- day trips
- guidebooks
- a leaflet
- a restaurant
- the railway station
- travel passes
- a hotel

I'm looking for a good hotel.

TASK

4 a You're going to do a role play in a tourist office. Work in A/B pairs.

Student B, tell Student A the name of a neighbourhood, town or city you know well.
A, you're visiting this place. Think of five questions to ask.
B, you work in the tourist office. Decide where the tourist office is, then think of five things to recommend and how to get there.

b Have a conversation in a tourist office.

A, start the conversation with one of your questions.
B, listen, make recommendations and give directions.

> Hello, I'm looking for …

c Change roles and have another conversation.

EXPLORE

Keyword *will*

will for predictions

1 a Put the lines of each conversation in the correct order, 1–3. *2.27* Then listen to check. **P**

- [ ] It'll be Leona. I invited her for a coffee.
- [ ] Rob! Can you answer the door? I'm doing the washing up.
- [ ] Yeah, OK. Who is it?

- [ ] Ah, yes. How old is he?
- [ ] Don't forget, it's Deiter's birthday on Monday.
- [ ] He'll be twenty-five, I think.

b In which conversation is *will* ('ll):
   a about the future?   b about now?

c Write a list of five important people in your life. Then look at each other's lists and find out about the people. Use these questions and your own ideas.

1 Who are they? How do you know them?
2 Where do you think they are at the moment?
3 When will you see them again?
4 How do you think their lives will change in the next five years?

will for offers, promises, requests

2 a You can also use *will* to make:

offers

```
A   Can I put my case in the back?
B   I'll do that for you. Unit 4
```

promises

```
OK, I'll give her the message and ask her to
contact you. Unit 2
```

requests / orders

```
I'll take these postcards, please. And do you
have any maps? Unit 5
```

Can you remember who said these sentences and where?

b *2.28* Listen to three short conversations. Which is:
   a a phone call?   b in a car?   c in a café?

c *2.28* Listen again. Think of a sentence with *will* to continue each conversation and then compare your ideas.

> Yes, I'll have some water, please.

Across cultures Tourism

1 a Read statements 1–6. Find a highlighted expression which means:

a a place where a lot of people go for holidays.
b the people who live in a place, not tourists.
c important places in a country's history.
d people's habits and ways of behaving.

1 Tourism helps people from different places to understand each other.
2 When you visit another country, you should try to speak the local language.
3 In a tourist resort, restaurants should sell food from tourists' countries *and* local food.
4 Tourism is bad for a country's areas of natural beauty and historical sites.
5 Visiting a place during a festival is a great way to learn about the customs and traditions there.
6 Tourism is good for the local people and local businesses.

b Tick (✓) the statements you agree with.

2 a *2.29* Listen to Natalie and Paula talking about statement 2. Do they generally agree or disagree with the statement?

b *2.29* What do they say are the good points about the statement? What are the problems? Listen again, then read the script on p150 to check.

3 Tell each other what you think about statements 1–6. Explain your ideas.

63

7 EXPLORE Writing

1 a Choose a city, or a place you know well, to write about. Make a list of things you could write about.

buildings, parks, the weather ...

b Compare your ideas and add more things to your list.

2 a Read the web postings about home towns. Who writes about these things, Kelly, Madu or both of them?

K 1	people	M 3	flowers	M K 5	the weather
KM K 2	homes	K 4	popular activities	M 6	the city's atmosphere

---

File Edit View Favorites Tools Help

Address www.myhometown.com/welcome ⬇ ➡ Go Links »

WELCOME TO MY HOME TOWN!

KELLY – SHERIDAN, WYOMING (USA)

¹ Ten years ago, Sheridan had 15,500 people. Now it has 16,000. The growth has all been outside the city. They're building a lot of homes four or five miles out of town.
² Sheridan's about 1,200 metres above sea level. We get lots of snow and there are good ski slopes near here. Drive an hour west and you'll be in the best camping and fishing areas.
³ Sheridan has some of the best schools in the country. Great football and soccer teams. We also have street dances and kids' groups. There's always something going on around here.

MADU – ABUJA (NIGERIA)

¹ In Nigeria, people often talk about the beauty of Abuja. It was a nice surprise when I stepped into this city for the first time. The city gate has many flowers planted around it. Nearby is the very modern National Stadium and the Games Village, which was used for the All African Games.
² Abuja is the federal capital city of Nigeria and a lot of the country's oil money has been spent on it. The streets and buildings look new, clean and beautiful.
³ There are modern houses and lots of trees and flowers. A nice wind blows in from the Sahara Desert. It's quiet and peaceful. After my first visit, I decided to make Abuja my home.

---

b Would you like to visit these places? Why? / Why not?

3 a Add words and expressions from the postings to these groups.

1. places and buildings *ski slopes, ...*
2. groups of people *football teams, ...*
3. events *street dances, ...*
4. the weather, nature *snow, ...*

b What words or expressions could you use to talk about your city? Add more things to each group.

4 a What adjectives do Kelly and Madu use? Try to complete the list, then check in the postings.

g*ood*   gr_____   ni_____   mo_____   ne_____
cl_____   be_____   qu_____   pe_____

b What adjectives could you use to talk about your city? Add them to the list.

5 a Plan a posting describing a place you know well.

1. Decide what things you want to talk about.
2. Organise the things into three or four paragraphs.
3. Think of words and expressions to use in each paragraph.

Look at the language in 3–4 and use your own ideas.

b Explain your ideas to each other.

6 Write your posting.

7 Read each other's postings. Ask questions to find out more information.

Review

GRAMMAR Real conditionals

1 a Paul is talking about his life in the next five years. Put the words in order to make sentences.

1 be happy have I I'll if job same the .
I'll be happy if I have the same job.
2 a annoyed be better can't car get I I'll if .
3 be don't exams I I'll if my pass sad .
4 be get I I'll if married surprised .
5 be children have I I'll if shocked .

b Write sentences like 1–5 about your life in the next five years.

c Listen to each other's sentences. Ask questions to find out more.

VOCABULARY Giving directions

2 a ◆ 2.30 Look at the map of a language school and listen to the receptionist's directions to a student. Where does the student go?

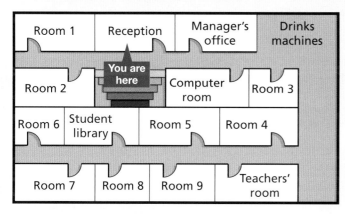

b Read the script on p150 to check. Then look at the map and try to remember the directions.

c Take turns to ask for and give directions to other rooms from the reception. Listen and check the directions are correct.

CAN YOU REMEMBER? Unit 6 – Chores, habits

3 a Look at the sentence about chores. In groups, think of words or expressions which could replace each part of the sentence 1–4.

I usually clean the windows once a month.
   1   2   3   4
tend to do the ironing every day

b Work alone. Think about how to describe a normal day in your life:

• during the week. • at the weekend.

c Tell each other about your days. Who spends the most time:

at work? doing chores? studying? relaxing?

Extension

SPELLING AND SOUNDS *ui, uy*

4 a ◆ 2.31 You can say ui and uy in three ways. Listen and repeat.

/ɪ/	/aɪ/	/uː/
build	buy	fruit

b Add these words to the correct group. Practise saying the words.

guide suit guy juice guitar biscuit

c (Circle) the correct answer. Which letters do we use:

1 in the middle of words? ui / uy
2 at the end of words? ui / uy

d ◆ 2.32 Spellcheck. Close your books. Listen to nine words and write them down. Then look at the script on p150 to check your spelling.

NOTICE Noun + infinitive

5 a Complete the sentences from this unit with these nouns.

place queue something
somewhere things time

1 The _____ to get in can be quite long.
2 I'm looking for _____ to stay.
3 One of the most popular _____ to see is Anne Frank's house.
4 The best _____ to go is early evening.
5 It's definitely a good _____ to visit.
6 Would you like _____ to drink?

b Think about these questions. Then ask and answer in groups.

1 Can you recommend a city to visit? When's the best time to go?
2 In the city, can you recommend:
  a somewhere to stay?
  b some things to see? Are there long queues to get in?
  c somewhere to have a meal?

Self-assessment

Can you do these things in English? (Circle) a number on each line. 1 = I can't do this, 5 = I can do this well.

◎ make guesses and predictions	1 2 3 4 5
◎ make recommendations	1 2 3 4 5
◎ give directions	1 2 3 4 5
◎ get information in a tourist office	1 2 3 4 5
◎ write a description of a place	1 2 3 4 5

• For Wordcards, reference and saving your work ›› e-Portfolio
• For more practice ›› Self-study Pack, Unit 7

Things

Portobello Market

LISTENING

Carolina lives in London.

1 Look at the photos of stalls in Portobello Market, London. Ask and answer the questions together.

1 Do you like shopping in markets? Why? / Why not?
2 Do you usually just pay the full price at market stalls, or do you bargain?
3 What do markets in your town sell? (food, antiques, second-hand clothes ...)
4 Are there any famous markets in your country? Have you ever visited them?

2 ◆ 2.33 Carolina is from Spain but lives and works in London. Listen to her shopping in Portobello Market. What thing in each photo does she ask about?

3 ◆ 2.33 Listen again. What does Carolina buy? How much does she pay?

VOCABULARY
Buying things

4 a Complete the highlighted expressions from Carolina's conversations with the stallholders with verbs from the box.

| give | have (x2) | is | leave | ~~looking~~ | see | take (x2) | try | want |

Looking

1 s Do you need any help?
   c No, thanks, I'm just _looking_.

2 c Can I _____ a look at those ones there?
   s These big ones?
   c No, the smaller ones.

3 c Can I _____ the big rug at the top?
   s The orange one?
   c No, the white one.

Bargaining

4 c I could _____ you eighty.
   s I'll do it for eighty-five.
   c Well ... OK, I'll _____ it.

5 c Would you _____ twenty?
   s I can take thirty.
   c Thanks, but I'll _____ them.

6 c How much do you _____ for them?
   s These ones are thirty-five.

Buying clothes

7 c What size _____ it?
   s It's a medium.

8 c Can I _____ it on?
   s Yes, of course.

9 c Do you _____ any other colours?
   s I'm afraid not, no.

b Look at the script on p150 to check.

PRONUNCIATION

Contrastive stress

Can I see that jacket, please?

The blue one?

No, the black one.

5 a ● **2.34** Listen to 2 and 4 from 4a. Notice that two of the words have strong stress.

c Can I have a look at those ones there? c I could give you eighty.

s These big ones? s I'll do it for eighty-five.

c No, the smaller ones. c Well ... OK, I'll take it.

b Now look at 3 in 4a. Which two words have strong stress? What about in 5?

c ● **2.35** Listen to check. ❷ Practise saying 2–5 in 4a.

6 In pairs, take turns to start the conversations from 4a. Answer with your own ideas.

Do you have any ... ?

GRAMMAR

some, any

1 Look at the examples in the table. Then complete 1–4 with some and any.

➕	❓
There are some second-hand stalls just over there. I might have some other sizes.	c Excuse me? s Yeah, do you need some help? Do you have any silver candlesticks? Do you have any other colours?
➖	
We don't have any second-hand clothes.	s Do you need any help? c No thanks, I'm just looking.

1 In positive sentences, we usually use _____.

2 In negative sentences, we usually use _____.

3 In questions, we use _____ when we don't know the answer.

4 In questions, we use _____ when we expect the answer 'yes' (offers, requests, etc.).

2 a Add some or any to sentences 1–5 in the conversation.

some

1 STALLHOLDER Hello. Do you need ⁄ help?

2 CAROLINA Yes. Do you have bookcases?

3 s Yes, we do. We've got nice bookcases over here.
   c Oh, right. How much is the big one?

4 s It's 110, but we've got cheaper ones. This black one's just 80.

5 c Hm. Do you think you'll get more?
   s Yes, I get them in quite often, so you could try again in a few weeks.

Grammar reference and practice, p138

b ● **2.36** Listen to a conversation with possible answers. Are your answers the same?

c In pairs, change the underlined expressions and have more conversations.

SPEAKING

3 a Work in A/B pairs. Choose the rug, antique or jacket stall in the photos on p66.

A, you're the stallholder. Decide on prices for things in the photo.
B, you want to buy something for a good price. Choose something.

b Role play together.

4 Change roles and choose another stall. Role play again.

5 Tell the class what you bought and how much you paid.

Portobello Market, London

Mystery objects

A

B

C

READING

1 a Look at the three objects. What do you think they are?

b Read the webpage and check your ideas.

Mysteries.com

The Voynich Manuscript This strange book was discovered in 1912 in Frascati, near Rome, by Wilfred Voynich, an antique book collector. It's small, 25 by 18 cm, but thick, with 235 pages. The pages are illustrated with strange coloured pictures of different things, including unknown plants and herbs. The book uses a kind of writing which no one can understand. Some people think it's written in an unknown, secret language. Others think the whole manuscript must be a very complicated (and expensive) joke. No one knows for sure where it came from, but many experts believe it was made in Europe, sometime between the fifteenth and seventeenth centuries.

The Baghdad Battery This small pot, about 15 cm tall, was probably discovered in a village near Baghdad in the 1930s. It's about 2000 years old and is made of light yellow clay but also has two pieces of metal inside. In 1940, an article was written suggesting that the pot was in fact a very old electric battery. In the 1970s, a copy of the 'Baghdad battery' was made and filled with grape juice. It produced a small amount of electricity – 0.87 volts – so it seems possible that electric batteries were used in the ancient world, nearly 2000 years before their 'invention' by Alessandro Volta in 1800.

The Saqqara Bird This object, made of wood, was found in 1898 in Saqqara, Egypt. It's about 18 cm across and weighs about 40 g. At first it was thought to be a model of a bird, made in about 200 BC, and it was put in a box in the basement of the Egyptian Museum in Cairo. Then, in 1969, it was rediscovered by Dr Khalil Messiha. He believed that the object looked very similar to a modern aeroplane – for example, it has wings like an aeroplane, not a bird. The ancient Egyptians often made small models of things they planned to build, so could this be a model of a simple aeroplane that was built over 2000 years ago?

2 Read again and complete the table.

	Voynich Manuscript	Baghdad Battery	Saqqara Bird
place found	*Frascati, near Rome*		
when found			
size			
age			

3 Which ideas about each object do you think are correct or incorrect? Talk together.

VOCABULARY

Describing
objects

4 **a** Match the descriptions, 1–6, with pictures A–C.

1 It's light yellow.
2 It's small but thick, with 235 pages.
3 It's 25 by 18 cm.
4 It's made of clay.
5 It has wings like an aeroplane.
6 It weighs about 40 g.

b Answer the questions in groups, then compare your ideas.

1 What's the opposite of *light* in sentence 1?
2 How many more colours can you think of?
3 Find things in your classroom which are made of these materials.

| cotton | glass | leather | metal | paper | plastic | stone | wood |

c Choose some things in your classroom and write two or three sentences about each one.

SPEAKING

5   Listen to each other's sentences. Can you guess the objects?

> It's blue with white letters.
> It's about 20 by 12 cm.

> A dictionary?

It was made in …

GRAMMAR

Passives

D

1 **a** Which sentence, 1 or 2, is used in the paragraph about the Voynich Manuscript?

1 Wilfred Voynich discovered this strange book. (active)
2 This strange book was discovered by Wilfred Voynich. (passive)

b Why does the writer use the passive? Is the writer more interested in the book or Wilfred Voynich?

2 **a** Complete the sentences in the table with the correct form of be.

present simple passive am / is / are + past participle	past simple passive was / were + past participle
Some people think it _____ written in an unknown, secret language. The pages _____ illustrated with strange coloured pictures.	Many experts believe it _____ made in Europe. It seems possible that electric batteries _____ used in the ancient world.

b Find and <u>underline</u> nine more examples of the passive in the text.

3   Work in two groups, Group A and Group B.

A, turn to p125 and complete the information about the object in picture D.
B, turn to p129 and complete the information about the objects in picture E.

Use the active or passive. You can look up irregular past participles on p160, *Irregular verbs*.

Grammar reference
and practice, p138

SPEAKING

E

4 **a** Prepare to tell someone from the other group about your object. Use these expressions to help you remember.

> **Group A**
> Istanbul, 1929   animal skin
> Piri Reis, 1513   Africa   America
> Antarctica?   1820?   a bad drawing?

> **Group B**
> 300   Costa Rica, 1930s
> people in Central America   why?
> 2 cm   2 m   how old?   *Las Bolas*

b Work in A/B pairs. Tell each other about your objects.

5   Which of the five objects, A–E, do you think is the most interesting? Why?

Talk about a favourite possession

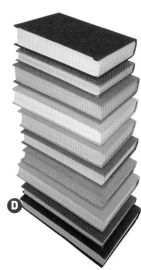

Anna from the USA

Alba from Venezuela

Claudia from Austria

Eren from Turkey

TASK LISTENING

1 **2.37** Listen to four people talking about their favourite possessions. Match the people and possessions.

TASK VOCABULARY

Talking about a possession

2 **a** Can you remember who uses these sentences?

1 I think my favourite thing is my TV.
2 I need it for work.
3 It helps me relax after a long day at work.
4 I've had some of them since I was five.
5 They were given to me by my mother.
6 It just reminds me of those days, the sunny summer days.
7 I just like it because it means I can do a lot of different things.
8 I absolutely love it because it is like a mosaic.

b **2.37** Listen again to check.

TASK

3 **a** Think of one of your favourite possessions. Think about how to describe:

1 what it looks like. *It's made of ...*
2 how long you've had it. *I've had it ...*
3 how you got it. *It was given to me by ...*
4 how you feel about it. *I like it because ...*
5 any other details.

b Tell each other about your favourite possessions. Ask questions to find out more.

4 As a class, make a list of everyone's favourite possession. Which are the oldest? Which are the smallest? Which are the most unusual?

Keyword *by*

1 Add the <u>underlined</u> expressions from previous units to the correct groups in the table.

```
1  This strange book was discovered in 1912 by Wilfred Voynich. Unit 8
2  It was drawn in 1513 by an admiral in the Turkish navy, Piri Reis. Unit 8
3  The house is by the canal, just here. Unit 7
4  Can I pay by card? Unit 5
5  I'll be at home by the time you arrive. Unit 5
6  No one really talks. Everyone's a bit tired by Friday. Unit 3
7  Supermarkets bring a lot of their stuff here by plane and that's bad for the environment. Unit 3
8  You have to stop the luge by putting your feet on the ice. Unit 1
```

A who? *by a person*	B how? *by (noun / -ing)*	C no later than *by a time*	D next to *by a place*
by Alessandro Volta	by taxi	by two o'clock	by the park

2 a Add **by** to these questions.

1 Do you have to do anything important the end of this week?
2 What things do you keep your cooker at home?
3 How often do you contact people letter?
4 Were any of the things in your home made your family or friends?
5 When you're on holiday, do you prefer to travel car or use public transport?
6 Would you prefer to live the sea or in the mountains?
7 Do you think you'll still live in the same place the end of next year?
8 What do you hope to have done 2020?

b Ask and answer the questions together.

Independent learning Ways of reading

1 Which of these do you usually read on a computer?
Which do you usually read on paper? Why?

bank statements   dictionaries   essays
newspaper and magazine articles   recipes
stories and poems   transport timetables
TV and film listings   work documents

2 a Think about how you read the things in 1. Which do you:

a   read quickly to get a general idea of what it's about?
b   read quickly to find information (e.g. a price)?
c   read slowly and carefully so you can understand everything?
d   read slowly and carefully because you enjoy it?

b Compare your ideas in groups. Do you read things in the
same way?

3 Talk about your reading in English.

1 What kinds of English texts do you read?
2 What ways of reading in 2a do you use for each one?
3 What ways of reading do you use the most often and the
least often?

4 Look again at the article Mysteries.com on p68. Which ways
of reading do you think tasks 1b and 2 practise?

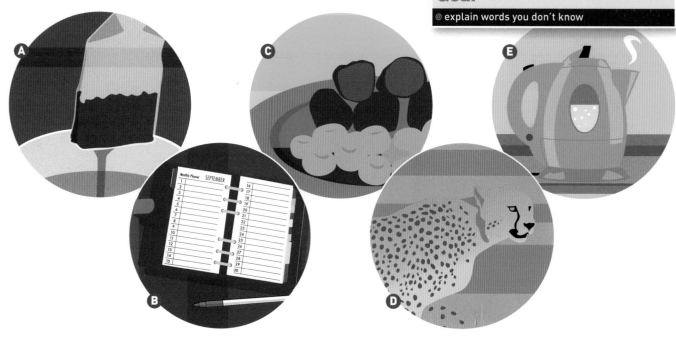

1 **a** ◆ 2.38 Listen to three conversations. In each conversation:

1 Where are the people?
 a classroom   an office   a restaurant
2 Which thing in pictures A–E do they talk about?

b Read the scripts to check. In which conversation does someone:

a describe something in other words because they can't remember an English word?
b help someone by explaining an English word?
c explain a word in their language that doesn't have an English translation?

2 Look at the highlighted expressions 1–9 in the scripts. Which are for:

1 saying you don't know a word? ☐☐
2 describing size, shape, material, similar things? ☐☐☐☐
3 describing use, location? ☐☐☐

3 **a** In pairs, think about how to describe the things in pictures A and D. Use expressions from 2.

b Compare your descriptions with another pair.

4 **a** Work alone. In your first language, write down the names of four things in your home or workplace. Choose things you don't know the English words for.

b Work in groups. Don't show your words but take turns to describe your things to your group. Can anyone tell you the English word?

> I don't know what you call it in English. It's a kind of …

c Check each word in a bilingual dictionary.

---

①

AGNIESZKA	So, what are we having to eat?
BRENDA	I don't know. Is there a menu in English?
AGNIESZKA	I don't think so. Can I help?
BRENDA	Yeah … *barszcz* I know, *placek* I know … what's '*kluski*'?
AGNIESZKA	*Kluski*. ¹They're made of potato.
BRENDA	Potato?
AGNIESZKA	Yeah, ²they're like little balls. Sometimes ³they have meat inside them.
BRENDA	OK. What about this?

②

NAZIF	Hi, Helen.
HELEN	Afternoon. Have you lost something?
NAZIF	Yes, I'm looking for my blue … erm … ⁴What's it called?
HELEN	Your pen?
NAZIF	No. ⁵I don't remember the word in English. ⁶It's a kind of book. ⁷You write in it, you know, times, things to do …
HELEN	You mean your diary?
NAZIF	That's it, a diary.
HELEN	Is that it over there?

③

HAE-WON	Manuel, what's a 'kettle'?
MANUEL	A what?
HAE-WON	A 'kettle'.
MANUEL	Where's that?
HAE-WON	Em … it's in paragraph two.
MANUEL	Hang on. Oh, it's a … ⁸you usually find it in the kitchen.
HAE-WON	OK …
MANUEL	⁹You use it to make water hot.
HAE-WON	Right …
MANUEL	When you make tea or coffee, for example.
HAE-WON	Oh, I see. Thanks.

Review

VOCABULARY Describing objects

1 a 🔊2.39 Listen to Sandra describing an object that's important to her. Guess what it is.

b Think of an important object you have at home. Plan how to describe it without saying what it is.

It's made of plastic and ...

c Listen to each other's descriptions. Can you guess the objects?

GRAMMAR The passive

2 a Complete the quiz questions with the correct form of the passive, present or past.

> **1** Farsi _____ (speak) in
> **a** Turkey **b** Iran **c** Iraq.
>
> **2** The first colour photographs _____ (take) in the
> **a** 1860s **b** 1890s **c** 1920s.
>
> **3** The Yellow River _____ (locate) in
> **a** Cambodia **b** China **c** Korea.
>
> **4** In 1867, Alaska _____ (sell) to the USA by
> **a** Russia **b** Britain **c** Canada.
>
> **5** *Ulysses*, by James Joyce, _____ (write) in the
> **a** 18th century **b** 19th century **c** 20th century.
>
> **6** The 2005 Nobel Prize for Literature _____ (give) to
> **a** V S Naipaul **b** Kenzaburo Oe
> **c** Harold Pinter.
>
> **7** In English, baby elephants _____ (call)
> **a** 'kids' **b** 'calves' **c** 'cubs'.
>
> **8** The first football World Cup _____ (win) in 1930 by
> **a** Argentina **b** Brazil **c** Uruguay.

b 🔊2.40 Do the quiz and then listen to check.

c In groups, write four more quiz questions.

d Exchange quizzes with another group. Do the quiz and then check your answers together.

CAN YOU REMEMBER? Unit 7 – *will, might*

3 a What do you think will happen in your life in the next five years? Complete the sentences. Think about these topics:

- family • work • studies • travel
- free time • possessions

1 I'll ...   4 I hope I'll ...
2 I'll probably ... 5 I think I'll ...
3 I might ...   6 I don't think I'll ...

I might get married.

b Listen to each other's sentences. Ask questions to find out more.

Extension

SPELLING AND SOUNDS *ow*

4 a 🔊2.41 You say *ow* in two ways. Listen and repeat.

/aʊ/	/əʊ/
now down shower	show yellow known

b Add these words to the correct group.

borrow brown crowded flower flown follow
how snow tomorrow town vowel window

c 🔊2.42 Spellcheck. Close your book. Listen to ten words with *ow* and write them down.

d Look at the script on p151 to check your spelling.

NOTICE Describing opinions and beliefs

5 a Which of these sentences are about the Voynich Manuscript? Which are about the Piri Reis map?

1 No one knows for sure where it came from.
2 Many experts believe it was made in Europe.
3 Some people think it shows the coast of Antarctica.
4 Other people say it's really just a bad drawing of part of South America.

b What else can you remember about these mystery objects?

- the Baghdad Battery • the Saqqara Bird
- the Stone Balls of Costa Rica

Use the expressions in 5a.

> Some people say it's a model aeroplane.

Self-assessment

Can you do these things in English? Circle a number on each line. 1 = I can't do this, 5 = I can do this well.

ask about and buy things	1	2	3	4	5
describe objects	1	2	3	4	5
talk about possessions	1	2	3	4	5
explain words you don't know	1	2	3	4	5

- For Wordcards, reference and saving your work » e-Portfolio
- For more practice » Self-study Pack, Unit 8

Why do we do it?

 **A**  **B**  **C**  **D**  **E**

VOCABULARY

yawn, laugh ...

1 Match the highlighted words with the pictures.

Did you know:
1 babies start to yawn _____6_____ months before they're born?
2 adults laugh, on average, _____17_____ times a day?
3 the average baby cries for _____2-3_____ hours a day?
4 you use _____12_____ muscles in your face to smile; you use about _____70_____ muscles to speak?
5 when you sneeze, air leaves your nose at _____150_____ kilometres per hour?

2 a Can you guess how to complete the sentences 1–5 with these numbers?

2 or 3   6   12   17   70   150

b 🔊 **2.43** Listen to check. ℗

READING

breathe – to take air into and out of your body
deaf – not able to hear
blind – not able to see
hormones – chemicals that make the body grow and change
oxygen – a gas in the air, O_2
tears – drops of water from the eyes

3 a Read the sentences, using the glossary to help you. Which do you think are true? Which are false?

F 1 People who are deaf and blind don't laugh.
F 2 People usually laugh because they see or hear something funny.
F 3 People yawn when their brains need more oxygen.
T 4 If you breathe through your nose, this will stop you from yawning.
T 5 The human eye makes three different kinds of tears.
F 6 When people cry, their bodies make a lot of hormones.

b Work in groups of three, A, B and C.

A, read the article about laughing on this page and check sentences 1–2 in 3a.
B, read the article about yawning on p125 and check sentences 3–4 in 3a.
C, read the article about crying on p130 and check sentences 5–6 in 3a.

Why do people laugh?

Babies start laughing very soon after they're born. Deaf and blind people can laugh even though they've never seen or heard anyone laughing. Laughing seems to be a part of human nature, but what's it for?

Many people think that we laugh because we see or hear something funny, but most of the time this isn't true. In one study, a professor of psychology and his students listened in and made notes on hundreds of conversations in public places. They heard about 1,200 laughs, but only 10–20 percent came after a joke or something funny. The other 80–90 percent followed normal, everyday expressions like, "I'll see you later" or, "It was nice to meet you".

No one really knows why we laugh, but one idea is that the most important reason for laughing is to make other people feel good. When you laugh, the people around you often start laughing too. Soon, the whole group is cheerful and relaxed. Laughter can stop negative feelings and help people to feel closer to each other. It may be that thousands of years ago, before people could speak, laughter helped them to form groups and work together.

It also seems that laughter can be good for your health. Laughing a hundred times uses the same energy as riding on an exercise bike for fifteen minutes. The writer Norman Cousins, who suffers from back pain, wrote that watching comedy programmes on TV helped him to feel better. He said that ten minutes of laughter gave him two hours of pain-free sleep.

c Talk together. Are sentences 1–6 in 3a true or false?

4 Read your article again. Choose two or three more facts, then tell your group about them.

5 Which ideas from the articles do you find most interesting? Do you have any different ideas?

How do you feel?

VOCABULARY

Extreme adjectives

1 a Choose words from the table to complete the conversations.

ordinary adjectives	extreme adjectives
angry cold pleased hot hungry frightened sure surprised tired	amazed boiling delighted exhausted freezing furious positive starving terrified

1 **A** I'm very hungry. Shall we make some dinner?
  B Good idea. I'm absolutely _____ .
2 **A** Are you sure the shops will be open tomorrow?
  B Yes, I'm _____ . Don't worry.
3 **A** You look really _____ . Have you had a long day?
  B Yeah, I'm exhausted. I'm going to bed.
4 **A** It's very hot in here, isn't it?
  B Hot? It's _____ ! Can we open a window?
5 **A** How could you do that parachute jump? Weren't you _____ ?
  B Yeah, I was absolutely terrified, but it was fun!
6 **A** I heard Kirsten found a job. She must be really _____ .
  B Oh, yes, she's delighted.
7 **A** Will Ron be _____ if we don't go to the meeting?
  B I think he'll be absolutely furious!
8 **A** Is it cold there at the moment? Should I bring a winter coat?
  B Yes. It's _____ .
9 **A** Were you surprised you passed the exam?
  B I was really _____ . I don't know how I did it.

Handwritten notes:
1 : starving
2 : positive
3 : tired
4 : boiling
5 : frightened
6 : pleased
7 : angry
8 : freezing
9 : amazed

b **2.44** Listen to check. **P**

c Work in pairs. Take turns to start the conversations 1–9 and remember the responses.

2 Which of these words in the box can we use:

1 only with ordinary adjectives?
2 only with extreme adjectives?
3 with both kinds of adjective?

absolutely really very

SPEAKING

3 a Try to think of a time when you were:

• delighted • exhausted • amazed • freezing • furious • boiling

When was it? What happened?

b Tell each other about your experiences.

I was delighted when I passed my driving test.

Oh yes. When was that?

Just good friends

9.2 goals
- give and respond to different kinds of news
- thank people and apologise

 **A**
 **B**
 **C**
 **D**

LISTENING

1 a These pictures tell a story. Can you guess:

1 what's happening in each picture?
2 how Jean-Paul and Rachel feel about each other?

b 🔊 **2.45** Listen to Rachel and Jean-Paul's conversation in each picture. Check your ideas.

2 a Can you complete these sentences?

Conversation 1
1 Jean-Paul bought Rachel a cactus because she needed some plants in her _____ .
2 In the evening Rachel's going out with _____ .
Conversation 2
3 She didn't get the job with NBS because she doesn't have enough _____ .
4 She's worked for the company for almost _____ years.
Conversation 3
5 She didn't come to the cinema because she had a call from her _____ .
6 Jean-Paul and Rachel planned to meet at _____ .
Conversation 4
7 Rachel's new job is _____ miles away.
8 She thinks she should start looking for a _____ .

Handwritten notes: 1 - flat; 2 - some friends; 3 - experience; 4 - J; 5 - sister; 6 - outside the cinema; 7 - 200; 8 - new place to

b 🔊 **2.45** Listen again to check.

3 What do you think Jean-Paul should do?

VOCABULARY
Reacting to news, thanking, apologising

Handwritten: Congratulations / Good Job / Well done / Awesome! / Cool man? / Sorry for your loss / Please accept my condolences

4 a Add these expressions from the conversations to the correct group.

Cheers. Congratulations. I'm really sorry. (x2) Sorry. That's not good. That's very kind of you. Well done.

Good news	Bad news	Thanking	Apologising
That's great! You did well.	I'm sorry to hear that.	Thanks very much.	I'd like to apologise.
	I'm really sorry	Cheers.	I'm really sorry
	That's not good	That's very kind of you	Please accept
	Sorry	It's much appreciated	my apologies

b 🔊 **2.46** Listen to check. 🅟

5 Look at conversations 1 and 3 on p151. Find two expressions Jean-Paul uses to respond to an apology and two expressions he uses to respond to thanks.

PRONUNCIATION

Intonation –
speaking with
emotion

6 a **2.47** Listen to the expressions in A and B. Notice how the speakers use intonation to express different emotions.

A Thanks very much.
That's great!

B I'd like to apologise.
I'm sorry to hear that.

b Practise saying all the expressions from 4a.

SPEAKING

7 a In pairs, choose one of the pictures A–D, and role play Jean-Paul and Rachel's conversation.

b Change roles and role play another conversation.

What's happened?

GRAMMAR

Present perfect
3 – giving news

1 Look at the examples in the table, then circle the correct words in 1 and 2.

You use the present perfect to talk about an action which:
1 is finished / not finished.
2 has a result in the past / present.

have / has + past participle	Result
I've **bought** you a present. They've **given** the job to someone else. She's just **had** her second baby. I've **found** a new job!	(Here is your present.) (Someone else has the job now.) (My sister has two children now.) (I have a new job now.)

2 a Complete the sentences with these verbs in the present perfect.

build   buy   decide   finish   forget   lose   move   pass

1 I'm really sorry. I _____ your name.
2 I _____ my keys. Can you help me find them?
3 Have you heard? Jean-Paul _____ his driving test.
4 We don't have a lot of money at the moment because we _____ just _____ a new car.
5 The town's changing really fast. They _____ two new hotels in the last six months.
6 Rachel and Jean-Paul don't work here any more. They _____ to another company.
7 That was the boss on the phone. He _____ to cancel tomorrow's meeting.
8 I _____ my work for today. Let's go for a coffee.

You can look up irregular past participles on p160, *Irregular verbs*.

Handwritten notes:
1 – I've forgotten
2 – 've lost
3 – has passed
4 – have bought
5 – have built
6 – have moved
7 – has decided
8 – 've finished

b Change the underlined words in the sentences in 2a with your own ideas. Write five sentences.

I'm really sorry. I've forgotten your email address.

Grammar reference
and practice, p139

c Compare your sentences.

SPEAKING

3 a Talk about pictures 1–5 in pairs. How do you think each person feels? Why?

She looks happy.

Yeah, maybe she's passed an exam. Or she's just got a new job.

b Compare your ideas. How many do you have for each person?

Catch up with friends

9.3 goals
◎ say how you feel ♻
◎ give and respond to different kinds of news ♻
◎ ask for news

Jenny from Dublin, Ireland and Sharmila from Mumbai, India are old friends.

TASK LISTENING

1 Talk together. Which of your family and friends do you see:

every day?　about once a week?　two or three times a year?　less than once a year?

2 ◖2.48 Listen to Sharmila and Jenny. Tick (✓) the things they talk about.

a movie　Sharmila's new home　Sharmila's new job　Mani's new job　a concert

3 a What do they say about the things? ◖2.48 Listen again to check.

b How often do you think they see each other?

TASK VOCABULARY

Asking for news

4 a Match the expressions from the conversation.

A		B		C	
1	What have you been up to?	a	He's really happy.	v	I'm still teaching maths.
2	I've just started a new job.	b	Not much.	w	No? How are things at work?
3	How is it?	c	Oh, great. So what are you doing?	x	Oh, that's good.
4	How's Mani?	d	Some of the kids are difficult!	y	Really?
5	Anyway, what's new with you?	e	Erm, things are very busy right now.	z	Hm, that's not good.

b Read the script on p152 to check.

c Take turns to say 1–5 and remember the responses.

TASK

5 a You're going to a café to meet a group of friends you haven't seen for six months. Think of five pieces of news to tell them about. For example:

• work　• family　• trips and holidays　• home studies　• free time

b Think about how to:

1　give news about the things in 5a. *I've started ...*
2　say how you feel. *I'm a bit ...*
3　ask your friends about their news. *How are things at ... ?*
4　react to your friends' news. *That's great!*

6 In groups, tell each other your news. Ask questions to find out more.

Keyword *just*

1 **a** In which of these sentences from previous units does just mean: a short time ago? only, simply?

```
1   I've just started a new job. Unit 9
2   My sister called, the one from New Zealand. She's just had a baby. Unit 9
3   I've just bought you a present. Unit 9
4   Some of the balls are very small – just two centimetres. Unit 8
5   In 1900, just 13 percent of the world's population lived in cities. Unit 7
6   Cities won't have just one centre where everyone goes to work and shop. Unit 7
```

b In the sentences where just means a short time ago, which verb form is used?

2 **a** Add just once to each line, 1–6, of the phone call.

BEN Hi, Rosy, it's Ben. Look, would you like to come out to dinner tonight?

1 **ROSY** Maybe. I've got back from a hard day at work. Who's going?

2 **BEN** Well, me actually.

3 **ROSY** Oh, right. You know, I think I'm going to stay in.

BEN That's OK, don't worry. By the way, do you think Jen'll be at home?

4 **ROSY** Actually, I've seen her at the bus stop.

5 **BEN** Really? What's her mobile number? I have her home number.

6 **ROSY** Oh, a second. Here you are. It's 077 145 96 70.

BEN Thanks, Rosy. You're a star. Well, have a nice evening.

b ◆ **2.49** Listen to check. ℗ Then practise the conversation in pairs.

3 **a** Match the sentences. Where do you think the conversations take place?

1 Can I have the bill, please?
2 Can I get you a coffee?
3 Do you need any help?
4 Hello, we have a reservation.
5 Where are you going?
6 I'm sorry but Lisa's not in at the moment.

a Could you just tell me your names, please?
b Oh. Could I just leave a message?
c I'm just looking, thank you.
d No thanks, I've just had one.
e I just have to go to the bank. I'll be back soon.
f Yes, of course. Just a moment.

b Take turns to say 1–6 and remember a–f.

Across cultures Gestures

1 Where you live, do people use gestures to communicate these things? What are they? Talk in groups.

1 Hello.
2 Goodbye.
3 Yes and no.
4 I don't know.
5 I'm not sure.
6 Come here.
7 I'd like the menu.
8 I'd like the bill.
9 OK, I understand.
10 Please wait.
11 Stop!
12 Be quiet.
13 What's the time?
14 It's good.
15 It's bad.
16 It's a secret.
17 He's crazy.
18 He's rich.
19 Thank you.
20 Sorry.

2 **a** ◆ **2.50** Listen to Pete talk about a gesture he saw when he lived in Egypt.

1 Did he understand the gesture?
2 What does it mean?

b Read the script on p152 to check.

3 Ask and answer the questions together.

1 Have you ever had an experience like Pete's?
2 Do you know any different gestures from other countries or places you've visited?
3 Do you think people where you live use a lot of gestures when they speak?

EXPLORE Writing

1 Sometimes we get invitations to parties but can't go. What reasons can you think of?

2 Read the two emails from Adam.

1 Why didn't he go to Kim's party?
2 Why can't he go to the lunch on the 14th?

3 Read the emails again and put these events in order from 1 (first) to 7 (last).

Kim's party 1   go to Porto 4   meet Sean 7
phone Kim 2   return from Porto 6
retirement lunch for Marina 5   see Kim 3

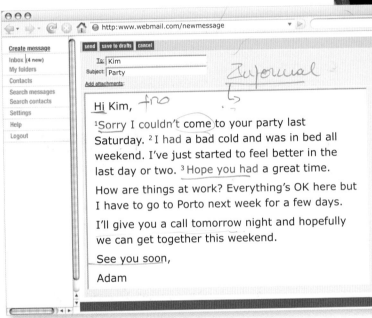

Informal

Hi Kim, two

¹Sorry I couldn't come to your party last Saturday. ²I had a bad cold and was in bed all weekend. I've just started to feel better in the last day or two. ³Hope you had a great time.

How are things at work? Everything's OK here but I have to go to Porto next week for a few days.

I'll give you a call tomorrow night and hopefully we can get together this weekend.

See you soon,

Adam

Formal

Dear Sean,

Thank you very much for the invitation to the retirement lunch for Marina Lopez on the 14th.

⁴Unfortunately I won't be able to come because ⁵I'll be in Porto. ⁶I have to make a couple of presentations to our sales team there but I'll be back on Friday. Is it possible to see you on the 19th (Monday)? I've just received a copy of Yulia's report and would like to discuss it with you.

⁷I'm sorry I'll miss the lunch. ⁸I hope you have a good time. Please give Marina my best wishes.

Yours, Adam

Adam Clarke
Technical Manager

---

4 a Match the highlighted expressions 1–8 with possible endings a–f.

a ☐ away on business. / on holiday.
b ☐☐ a great party. / a wonderful evening.
c ☐ take my children to the doctor's. / work late.
d ☐☐ come to your party. / attend the meeting.
e ☐ a bad cold. / a dentist's appointment.
f ☐ I'll miss the lunch. / I won't see you.

b Which expressions 1–8 are for:

1 apologies
2 excuses
3 good wishes

5 a You're going to write an email of apology. Choose one of the situations.

1 You've been invited to an event by a friend or relative. You can't go because you have other things to do on that day.
2 You were invited to an event by someone from another company. You didn't go because you had to do something important, or something you didn't expect.

Then think about:

Who invited you?
What is / was the event? When is / was it?
Why can't / didn't you go?

b Write your email.

6 Read some other students' emails. Do you think they give good reasons for not going?

Review

Handwritten annotations:
2 - fridge   6 - delighted
3 - terrified 7 - positive
4 - boiling   8 - amazing
5 - starving 9 - exhausted

Extension

VOCABULARY Extreme adjectives

1 a Can you remember the extreme adjectives?

1 angry – f *urious*
2 cold – f_____
3 frightened – t_____
4 hot – b_____
5 hungry – s_____
6 pleased – d_____
7 sure – p_____
8 surprised – a_____
9 tired – e_____

b Ask and answer the questions in groups.

How do you feel:
1 on Monday morning?
2 at the end of a working week?
3 when you meet an old friend?
4 after you've just finished some housework?
5 when you've been too busy to eat lunch?

GRAMMAR Present perfect

2 a Complete the questions with *Have you ever*, *recently*, *How long*.

Handwritten: Have you ever
1 _____ ridden a camel or an elephant? (present perfect 1, Unit 2)

Handwritten: How long
2 _____ have you known your closest friend? (present perfect 2, Unit 2)

Handwritten: Recently
3 Have you bought anything nice _____? (present perfect 3, Unit 9)

b Which questions in 2a are about:

Handwritten: 1
a an unfinished action or situation?

Handwritten: 3 –
b a finished action with a present result?

Handwritten: 2 –
c your whole life up to now?

c Write three more questions for a partner, with *Have you ever*, *recently*, *How long*.

d Ask and answer all the questions. Find out more details.

CAN YOU REMEMBER? Unit 8 – Buying things

3 a Match sentences 1–7 with responses a–g.

1 Can I try it on?   *1 - e*
2 Do you need any help?   *2 - c*
3 Can I see the big rug at the top? *3 - f*
4 I could give you seventy. *4 - b*
5 What size is it?   *5 - a*
6 Can I have a look at those shoes there? *6 - g*
7 Do you have any other colours? *7 - d*

a It's a medium.
b I'll do it for seventy-five.
c No, thanks, I'm just looking.
d I'm afraid not. Only red.
e Yes, of course.
f The blue one?
g The black ones?

b In pairs, cover a–g and take turns to answer 1–7 with your own ideas.

SPELLING AND SOUNDS -ge, -dge, -age

4 a ▶ 2.51 You say -ge and -dge as /dʒ/. When it's not stressed, you say -age as /ɪdʒ/. Listen and repeat.

/dʒ/		/ɪdʒ/
age	bridge	average
huge	judge	language

b Add the correct endings for these words, -ge, -dge or -age.

vill...   chan...   lugg...   fri...   mess...   oran...
pa...   lar...   arran...

Handwritten (right margin):
village
change
luggage
fridge
message
orange
page
large
arrange

c ▶ 2.52 Spellcheck. Close your book. Listen to ten words and write them down.

d Look at the script on p152 to check your spelling.

NOTICE Describing ideas

5 a Can you complete the sentences about laughing? Look at the article on p74 again to check.

Handwritten: health
1 It seems that laughter can be good for your ...

Handwritten: good
2 One idea is that the most important reason for laughing is to make *other people* feel ...

Handwritten: form groups or work together
3 It may be that, before people could speak, laughter helped them to ...

b Why do people yawn? Why do they cry? Read one of the texts on p125 and p130 that you haven't read before. Then tell each other what you remember using the highlighted expressions.

Self-assessment

Can you do these things in English? Circle a number on each line. 1 = I can't do this, 5 = I can do this well.

⊚ say how you feel	1	2	3	4	5
⊚ give and respond to different kinds of news	1	2	3	4	5
⊚ thank people and apologise	1	2	3	4	5
⊚ ask for news	1	2	3	4	5
⊚ write an email or note of apology	1	2	3	4	5

• For Wordcards, reference and saving your work » e-Portfolio
• For more practice » Self-study Pack, Unit 9

Getting organised

A place to stay

Kuala Lumpur, Malaysia

VOCABULARY
Hotel facilities

1 Answer the questions.

1 Have you ever stayed in any hotels? Which were the best? Which were the worst? Why?
2 Are there any hotels near where you live? Which one would you recommend to a visitor? Why?

2 Read the introduction to the Sun Hotel's website. Where's the hotel located? What's it close to?

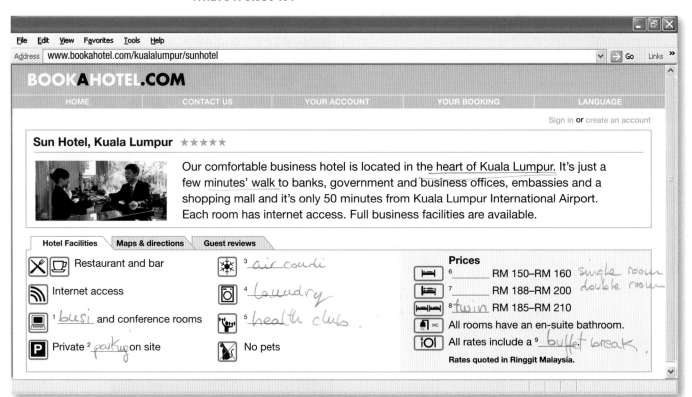

3 a Complete the web page with these words.

| double room | parking | air conditioning | buffet breakfast | health club |
| twin room | laundry | single room | business centre | |

b ◄ **3.1** Listen to check. **℗**

4 Which things do you think are important when choosing a hotel?

Booking a room, checking in

LISTENING

Leonardo Barreiros works for Brazilian company Rio Amazonia. He's preparing for a business trip to Kuala Lumpur.

1 ⚫ **3.2** Listen to Leonardo calling the Sun Hotel to ask some questions.

1 Tick (✔) the things he asks about.
parking internet access breakfast laundry
late arrival swimming pool air conditioning

2 Does he decide to reserve a room?

2 ⚫ **3.2** Listen again. Answer the questions.

1 How much does internet access cost?
2 What time is Leonardo arriving at the hotel?
3 What kind of room does he want?
4 What day is he arriving?
5 How many nights is he staying?

3 ⚫ **3.3** Listen to Leonardo checking in a week later. Which of these things does he want?

1 ✗ a map 2 some sandwiches 3 help with his suitcase

4 ⚫ **3.3** Listen again and circle the correct words.

1 Leonardo's leaving on the 3rd / 13th.
2 The receptionist asks for his credit card / passport.
3 Leonardo / The receptionist fills in the registration card.
4 His room number is 1406 / 1416.
5 The check-out time is 10.00 / 11.00.

VOCABULARY

Staying in a hotel

5 a Complete the sentences from Leonardo's conversations with these words.

check-out have reservation book says included is charge

Checking and booking

1 Your website _says_ you have internet access. Is it wireless?
2 And is internet access _incl_ ? Or is there an extra _char_ for that?
3 Does the hotel _have_ a swimming pool?
4 I'd like to _book_ a single room for three nights, from the tenth of November.

Checking in

5 I have a _reserv_. My name's Leonardo Barreiros.
6 What time _is_ breakfast?
7 What's the _check_ time?
        out

b ⚫ **3.4** Listen to check. ⓟ

Examen
Vocabulario
1 - says
2 - included /charge
3 - have
4 - book
5 - reservation
6 13
7 - check out

6 a Match Leonardo's sentences in 5a with answers a–g.

3 a Yes, and we also have a fitness room.
1 b Yes, it is.
6 c It's from 6.30 to 10 am, in the dining room.
4 d Certainly, and what's your name, please?
7 e It's 11 am.
5 f Sorry, could you spell your surname, please?
2 g No. It's included in the room rate.

b In pairs, cover 6a and take turns to remember the answers to 5a. Then cover 5a and try to remember what Leonardo said.

SPEAKING

7 a Work alone. Look at the Sun Hotel's webpage. Prepare to:

1 book a room on the phone. Decide what kind of room you want, when and for how long.
2 check in. Decide what questions you want to ask, for example, about the health club, a map, breakfast time …

b In pairs, practise booking a room and checking in. Take turns to be the guest and the receptionist.

Remember me?

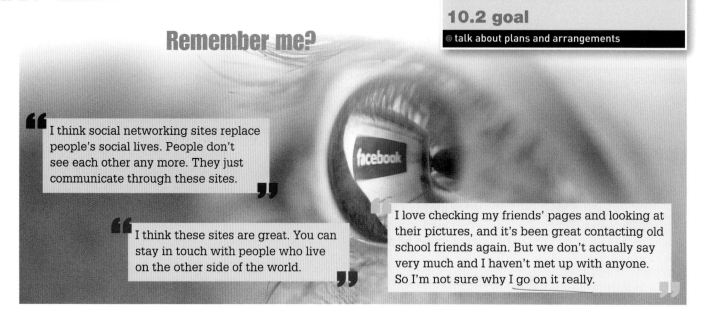

"I think social networking sites replace people's social lives. People don't see each other any more. They just communicate through these sites."

"I think these sites are great. You can stay in touch with people who live on the other side of the world."

"I love checking my friends' pages and looking at their pictures, and it's been great contacting old school friends again. But we don't actually say very much and I haven't met up with anyone. So I'm not sure why I go on it really."

READING

1 Read the opinions about social networking sites. Then ask and answer the questions together.

1 Which opinions do you agree with? Why?
2 Have you ever used a social networking site? Why? / Why not?
3 Have you ever found an old friend online? Did you contact or meet the friend? Are you still in touch?

2 Read the message from Min to Leonardo Barreiros on a social networking site.

1 How do they know each other? 3 Where does Min live now?
2 When did they last see each other?

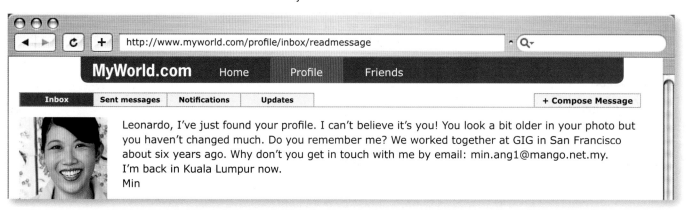

http://www.myworld.com/profile/inbox/readmessage

MyWorld.com   Home   Profile   Friends

Inbox | Sent messages | Notifications | Updates | + Compose Message

Leonardo, I've just found your profile. I can't believe it's you! You look a bit older in your photo but you haven't changed much. Do you remember me? We worked together at GIG in San Francisco about six years ago. Why don't you get in touch with me by email: min.ang1@mango.net.my. I'm back in Kuala Lumpur now.
Min

3 Read the emails between Leonardo and Min. What are their jobs now?

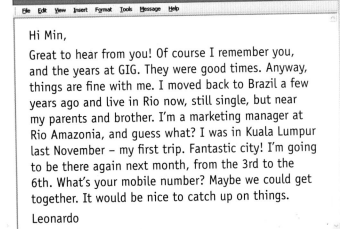

File Edit View Insert Format Tools Message Help

Hi Min,

Great to hear from you! Of course I remember you, and the years at GIG. They were good times. Anyway, things are fine with me. I moved back to Brazil a few years ago and live in Rio now, still single, but near my parents and brother. I'm a marketing manager at Rio Amazonia, and guess what? I was in Kuala Lumpur last November – my first trip. Fantastic city! I'm going to be there again next month, from the 3rd to the 6th. What's your mobile number? Maybe we could get together. It would be nice to catch up on things.

Leonardo

Hi Leonardo,

It's great to know you're coming here soon. I'd love to meet you. Give me a call when you arrive and we can arrange something. My mobile's 012-3242349, office phone 03-3241-3456.

Maybe you're wondering why I left the States. After GIG, I went to work for CIS Management in LA but it wasn't very challenging – I'll tell you about that later – so anyway, I returned to Malaysia and got a good job with MalayTech as Advertising Manager. I'm single, too, but have lots of family and friends here in KL.

Min

4 Read the emails again. What do Leonardo and Min have in common?

Well, they both moved back to their home countries ...

Plans and arrangements

LISTENING

1 🔊 **3.5** Listen to a phone call between Leonardo and Min. Why does Leonardo call Min?

   a to make a business appointment   c to change an arrangement
   b to make a social arrangement

2 🔊 **3.5** Listen again. When and where do they arrange to meet?

3 🔊 **3.6** Listen to their second phone call. What new arrangement do they make?

4 **a** After Leonardo returns to Brazil, Min writes him an email. What do you think she says?

   b Read her email on p129 to check.

GRAMMAR
Future plans and arrangements

Petronas Towers,
Kuala Lumpur

**Grammar reference
and practice, p140**

5 You can use different forms to talk about future plans and arrangements. Match a–d with examples 1–4.

> a   present progressive for arrangements with people, organisations, etc.
> b   be going to + infinitive for personal plans
>   The difference between a and b is very small. Often, you can use either.
> c   present simple for things with fixed times (train timetables, flight schedules, etc.)
> d   am / is / are (with adjectives, prepositions, etc.)
>
> _b_ 1 I'm going to be there again next month from the 3rd to the 6th.
> _c_ 2 My flight leaves on Saturday morning at 11.15.
> _a_ 3 What are you doing on Friday evening?
> _d_ 4 Friday's difficult … I'm free on Wednesday evening.
>
> We usually use time expressions with forms a–d to say when something is happening. For example, _next month, on Friday evening, at 11.15_.

6 **a** Choose the best form (or forms) to complete the questions.

   1 What _____ (you do) after class? _are you doing_
      What are you doing after class? or _What are you going to do after class?_
   2 What time _____ (this class finish)? ~~finish this class~~ _does this class finish?_
   3 _____ (you go) anywhere on your next holiday? _Are you going_
   4 What _____ (you have) for dinner tonight? _are you having_ (PP)
   5 _____ (you be) busy tomorrow evening? _Are you_ (ADJ)
   6 What time _____ (the shops close tonight)? _does the shops_
   7 _____ (you meet) any friends this weekend? _Are you meeting_
   8 _____ (you work) tomorrow afternoon? _Are you working_

   b 🔊 **3.7** Listen to check. 🅟

PRONUNCIATION
Intonation in questions

7 **a** 🔊 **3.7** Listen to the questions in 6a again. Circle the correct underlined word in rules a and b.

   a In yes / no questions (starting _Are_, _Do_, etc.), the intonation often goes up / down at the end.
   b In information questions (starting _What_, _Who_, etc.), the intonation often goes up / down at the end.

   b Practise saying the questions with the right intonation. 🅟

SPEAKING

8 Ask and answer the questions in 6a. Find out more information.

9 Tell the class about your partner's most interesting plans and arrangements.

> This weekend, Alba's driving to the sea with her family and they're going to …

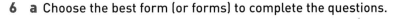

Arrange to meet up

10.3 goal
◎ talk about plans and arrangements ♻
◎ make and change arrangements

TASK LISTENING

1 Ask and answer the questions together.

1 What do you think is the best way to spend time with friends?
2 Does anyone you know cancel arrangements a lot? What reasons do they give?

2 🔘 **3.8** Listen to Jason and Akio arranging to meet in their free time. What do they arrange to do?

3 🔘 **3.9** Listen to their next conversation. Who's going to the performance on Saturday? Who's going on Sunday?

TASK VOCABULARY

Arranging to meet up

informal

fancy + ing

4 🔘 **3.8** 🔘 **3.9** Listen to both conversations again. (Circle) the underlined expressions that they say.

Checking
1 Are you doing anything this week? / tonight?
2 Do you fancy having lunch? / going too?   *Would you like to*
Arranging a date and time
3 Can you make Saturday? / the 12th?   *available for/at*
4 Can you do tomorrow? / 3.30?
Cancelling and rearranging
5 I'm sorry but I can't make it tomorrow. / on Saturday.
6 Can we postpone? / Can we do it another time?

TASK

5 a Work alone.

1 Think of three things you'd like to do with friends. For example:
   • have a meal at your home   • watch a sports event
   • go to a concert   • have a party   • go for a picnic
2 Write down four times when you're free.

> 1 tomorrow, 12 am
> 2 Monday, 7 pm
> 3 Tuesday, 1 pm
> 4 Saturday evening

b Make arrangements with three different people. Find someone to do each thing with.

> Hi, Ahmed. Are you doing anything tomorrow?

6 a Work alone. You have to cancel two of your arrangements. Decide which two and why.

1 tomorrow, 12 am – go for lunch with Ahmed cancel because: meeting at work

b Talk to the two people you made the arrangements with. Cancel and agree on a different date and time.

> Hi, Ahmed. Sorry but I can't make it tomorrow. I've got a meeting at work. Can we postpone?

EXPLORE

Keyword *make*

make + noun

1 a Add the expressions with make to the table.

(handwritten: lunch.)

> make an appointment   make friends
> make a profit   make a snack   make mistakes
> make some salad   make repayments

(handwritten circled numbers: 3, 1, 2, 3)

A money	B food, drink	C other things
make money *(handwritten: make a loss, a fortune, a living)*	make dinner *(handwritten: lunch, juice)*	make arrangements *(handwritten: suggestion, a fuss, up your mind)*

b Can you think of more expressions for A–C?

2 a Complete the questions with the correct form of make and these words.

a list   a meal   a phone call   presentations

(handwritten left margin: make a/to the call)

1 When was the last time you _____ to another country?

(handwritten left margin: make a list)

2 Do you usually _____ before you go shopping?

3 Have you ever _____ for more than six people?

4 Do you ever have to _____ *(handwritten: make presentation)* to a lot of people?

b Write two more questions with make for a partner. Then answer all the questions.

(handwritten: make a meal)

Patterns with *make*

3 a Look at the highlighted expressions with make. Does make mean:

a cause something to happen or cause a state?
b create something?

> 1 The most important reason for laughing is to make other people feel good. Unit 9
> 2 Why do some illnesses make people yawn more? Unit 9
> 3 You can use it to make water hot. Unit 8
> 4 Not many people would say that shopping in their local supermarket makes them happy. Unit 3

b Which highlighted expressions are:

a *make* + object + verb?
b *make* + object + adjective?

4 Talk together about what makes you:

furious   happy   feel exhausted
feel energetic   cry   laugh

> Well, this sounds strange but weddings always make me cry.

Independent learning Improve your listening

1 Ask and answer the questions in groups.

1 What would you like to be able to understand better in English? (songs, the news, conversations in shops ...)
2 Is there anything that makes listening difficult for you?

2 **3.10** Listen to three people talking about how they improve their listening. Who:

1 needs English for travel?
2 studies English at home?
3 needs English for work?

3 a Can you remember who does these things?

1 Listen to other people's conversations.
2 Listen to things on the Internet and learn new words.
3 Ask people to repeat or explain words.
4 Imagine what other people might say and prepare the answers.

b **3.10** Listen again to check.

c What do you think about their ideas? Give reasons.

4 a In groups, make a list of ideas about how to improve your listening:

1 if you live in or visit an English-speaking country.
2 in your own country.

b Compare your list with the one on p126. Which ideas would you like to try?

Martin from France

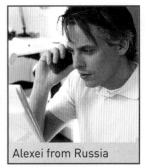

Alexei from Russia

Ae-Young from South Korea

1 Read the information. Why is it a good idea to use questions: before invitations? before requests?

> Before invitations, a question makes it easier for the other person to say 'no'.
> *Are you free?* → *Erm, I'm a bit busy.* → *Do you want to go for a quick coffee?* → *No, sorry, I've got too much to do.*
> Before requests, a question prepares the other person for the request.
> *Do you have a pen?* → *Yes, I think so.* → *Can I use it for a moment?*

2 🔊 **3.11** Listen to three conversations. Match them with pictures A–C.

3 In conversation 1, Anna asks a <u>question</u> (1) and then gives an <u>invitation</u> (2).
In conversations 2 and 3, underline:

1 a question to preface an invitation or request.
2 an invitation or a request.

❶

ANNA	Did I tell you? I'm going to the cinema next week with some friends.
ROSE	Oh, yeah? What are you going to see?
ANNA	'Metropolis'. It's on at the Roxy.
ROSE	Oh, right. That's a good film.
ANNA	¹<u>Are you free on Thursday evening</u>?
ROSE	Erm, yes, I am, actually.
ANNA	²<u>Well, would you like to come with us</u>?
ROSE	That would be really nice, Anna. <u>What time</u>?

❷

LEO	Hello.
JO	Hi, Leo. It's Jo. How are you?
LEO	Not bad. Is everything OK with you?
JO	Yeah, fine. <u>Erm, what are you doing tomorrow</u>?
LEO	I'm working all day … from twelve to eleven. Why, Jo?
JO	<u>Do you want to meet up for a coffee in the morning</u>?
LEO	Sorry, I'll be too tired. I never get up in the morning.
JO	Oh, OK. Well, maybe next time …

❸

ANNA	Sorry to bother you, Rose. <u>Have you got a moment</u>?
ROSE	Yes. Go ahead.
ANNA	Sorry, but <u>could you help me with my computer</u>?
ROSE	I can try. What's the problem?
ANNA	I need to print something but it's not working.
ROSE	Again? OK. Let's have a look.

4 a Read the beginnings of six conversations. In pairs, decide what speakers A and B could say next.

1 A Do you like Chinese food?
  B Yes, I do.
  A Well, would you like to …?
2 A What are you doing tomorrow?
  B Nothing, really.
  A …
3 A Are you interested in art exhibitions?
  B …
  A …
4 A Have you got your mobile here?
  B …
  A …
5 A Are you going to the party tonight?
  B …
  A …
6 A Do you have any plans for the weekend?
  B …
  A …

b Practise your conversations.

5 a Choose one activity. Think about the language you'll need for requests and invitations.

1 You want to go to a football match tomorrow. You have four free tickets.
2 You want to buy some new clothes. You'd like some friends to come with you.
3 You're moving flat or house this weekend. You need a few people to help.
4 You want to go to a concert or show with some friends.

b Talk together. Find people to do the activity with you.

c Which activity did you choose? Who's going to do it with you? Tell the class.

Review

VOCABULARY Hotel collocations

1 a Match words from A and B to make hotel collocations.

A	B
air en-suite	breakfast parking
internet business	bathroom club
buffet double	room conditioning
private health	access centre

b Can you think of more hotel collocations?

c In groups, imagine the perfect hotel for you. What facilities would it have? Why?

GRAMMAR Future plans and arrangements

2 a Complete the telephone conversation with the correct form of these words.

have get (x2) is can't go
can (x2) leave take

KIM   Hi, John. How are you? I haven't heard from you for ages.

JOHN I know, sorry. Where are you? [1]_____ you talk now?

KIM   I'm at the airport, actually.

JOHN Really? Where [2]_____ you [3]_____?

KIM   To Italy. I [4]_____ a meeting there tomorrow.

JOHN Oh, right. Look, Julie and I [5]_____ married in June.

KIM   Congratulations!

JOHN Can you come? The wedding [6]_____ on the 16th.

KIM   The 16th? Oh, sorry, I [7]_____. I [8]_____ a holiday in June.

JOHN That's too bad. Well, maybe we [9]_____ meet another time.

KIM   Sure. Listen, I have to run. My plane [10]_____ in 20 minutes.

JOHN OK. Give me a call when you [11]_____ back, OK?

KIM   I will. Bye, and speak to you soon.

b In pairs, change five or six details in the conversation. Then practise your conversation.

CAN YOU REMEMBER? Unit 9– Reacting to news, thanking, apologising

3 a Circle the best response to these statements.

1 **A** I passed my driving test yesterday.
    B Cheers. / Well done!

2 **A** My mum's not very well.
    B I'd like to apologise. / I'm sorry to hear that.

3 **A** Can I get you a drink?
    B That's very kind of you. / That's great!

4 **A** I've had a headache for three days now.
    B That's not good. / Sorry!

b In pairs, take turns to say 1–4 and remember the responses.

Extension

SPELLING AND SOUNDS *au*, *aw* /ɔː/

4 a ●3.12 You usually say au and aw as /ɔː/. Listen and repeat these words.

laundry sauna saw awful

b Complete these words with au or aw.

__tumn d__ghter dr__ exh__sted
l__yer s__ce str__berry y__n

c ●3.13 A few words have a different pronunciation. Listen and repeat.

laugh aunt Australia sausage

d ●3.14 Spellcheck. Close your book. Listen to ten words and write them down.

e Look at the script on p153 to check your spelling.

NOTICE *Work*

5 a Look at the sentences with work from this unit. Match the words with the definitions a–d.

I need to print something but it's not working[1]. (Anna, script p153)

I chat with the people I work[2] with, usually after work[3], and when they say something I can't understand, I say, 'Wait!' (Martin, script p153)

I plan everything and then when I get there, I can understand things better. It usually works[4] quite well. (Alexei, script p153)

3 a the thing you do to earn money (noun)
2 b do a job (verb)
1 c is broken (verb)
4 d is successful (verb)

b Ask and answer the questions in groups.

1 Is there anything that doesn't work in your home or place of work or study at the moment?

2 What do you do when something you need to use doesn't work?

3 What's the best way to learn a language? What works best for you?

4 Do you chat to people at work during the day? When?

Self-assessment

Can you do these things in English? Circle a number on each line. 1 = I can't do this, 5 = I can do this well.

◎ book a room and check into a hotel	1	2	3	4	5
◎ talk about plans and arrangements	1	2	3	4	5
◎ make and change arrangements	1	2	3	4	5
◎ use questions to preface invitations and requests	1	2	3	4	5

• For Wordcards, reference and saving your work » e-Portfolio
• For more practice » Self-study Pack, Unit 10

11

11.1 goals
- ⊚ talk about homes and housing
- ⊚ describe imaginary situations

Spaces

[handwritten: verbs = move / moving / moved]
[handwritten: noun = move -s]

Moving

[handwritten: Duda: An Average / On Average]

www.homechange.org/forum/australia/general

⌂⟷⌂ homechange.org

☐ homechange forum > australia > general

☐ **An average Australian will move eleven times in their life.** Originally posted by Craig84

When I read this statistic, I was SHOCKED! I'm from a small town and I now live 2 km from where I grew up. *LaurenF*

I'm moving at the end of this month and that makes 21 moves since I was 18. I'm 42 this month. *TR*

I hate moving. I want to stay in one place for my kids but we're always having to move because of my job. *Domo2000*

VOCABULARY

Describing homes

1 Read the postings from a website about moving home. Then ask and answer the questions.

1 What do you think about the information in the postings?
2 How many times have you moved in your life?
3 What are the reasons you or people you know have moved?
4 How do you feel about moving home?

2 Read the advertisements from an estate agent's in Sydney, Australia. Match the pictures and descriptions.

[handwritten: in the]
[handwritten: sin prep]

❶ *[handwritten: C]*
A comfortable house in the countryside with two bedrooms, a spacious modern kitchen, a fireplace and air conditioning. Barbecue area next to swimming pool and beautiful garden with trees. Perfect for people who love peace and quiet.

[handwritten: far from the city center]

A

$200 per week
**Longbeach Road,
Long Beach**

B

$350 per week
**Century Tower,
Sydney**

[handwritten: B] ❷
This modern one-bedroom apartment on the 31st floor is close to the city centre. It faces east and has great views of the city. Comfortable living room, wooden floors and balcony. Modern bathroom. No parking.

❸
Just around the corner from the beach, this two-storey home has two bedrooms, a traditional kitchen and a large bathroom. The living room faces north, so it's warm in winter and cool in summer. The balcony at the back is perfect for relaxing. 3.5 hours from Sydney.

C

$380 per week
**Wallacia, Far North
Coast**

[handwritten left margin: swimming pool / garden / balcony parking / air conditioning / wooden floors]

3 **a** Read the advertisements again and find words for:

outdoor features 1 barbecue 2 s... p... 3 g... 4 b... 5 p...
indoor features 6 fireplace 7 a... c... 8 w... f...
describing rooms 9 comfortable 10 s... 11 m... 12 t... 13 l... 14 w... 15 c...

b ◀ 3.15 Listen to check. ℗

[handwritten bottom: spacious / modern / traditional / large / warm / ~~cool~~ cosy / small]

4 Match 1–6 with a–f to make sentences about homes.

1 I live in a
2 It's on
3 There's a large living room with
4 It's close to
5 It has a wonderful view of
6 It's perfect for

a the city centre.
b the mountains.
c people who love peace and quiet.
d two-storey apartment.
e the 10th floor.
f a balcony.

SPEAKING **5** Talk about your home or a home you know well. Ask questions to find out more.

> I live in a three-storey building.

> Which floor do you live on?

A dream home

LISTENING **1** ● **3.16** Listen to Donna and José outside the estate agent's.

1 Who likes the idea of moving? Who doesn't like the idea?
2 Which places A–C on p90 do they talk about?

2 ● **3.16** Listen again.

1 Why does José think they can't move? (two reasons)
2 What solution does Donna suggest?

GRAMMAR
would

3 Read part of the conversation. Circle the correct answer in 1 and 2.

DONNA Imagine it, we'd come home from work, go for a swim …
JOSÉ That would be nice, yeah.

1 They're talking about the past / the present or future.
2 They're talking about a situation that is real / is not real.

4 a Complete the grammar table with 'd, would (x3) and wouldn't (x2).

❓ What _____ I do in the middle of nowhere?	_____ you change your job?
➕ I bet you _____ find a nice little school nearby.	Yes, I think I _____, actually.
➖ I _____ want to move schools.	No, I _____.
'd = would	

b ● **3.17** Listen to check. ℗

5 a Complete these descriptions of ideal homes with would or 'd and verbs from the box.

be (x3)   have (x2)   like (x2)

> My ideal home ¹_____ pretty much like the place I live in now but I ²_____ it to be fifteen degrees warmer, so instead of growing lettuce and spinach I could grow things like mangoes and oranges and tomatoes. That ³_____ really perfect.

Natalie from Trinidad and Tobago (now lives in England)

> Right now I live in a very small apartment, so I think my ideal home ⁴_____ a lot more space. It ⁵_____ a big living room, a big kitchen, big everything. I ⁶_____ to have maybe two bedrooms, one for me and one for guests. Also there ⁷_____ really big windows with views of the mountains, like my old home in Brazil.

Eduardo from Brazil

Grammar reference
and practice, p140

b ● **3.18** Listen to check. What do you think of Natalie's and Eduardo's ideas?

SPEAKING **6 a** What would your ideal home be like? Think about:

- location • size • rooms • indoor features • outdoor features • climate

b Talk in groups. What do you think of each other's ideas?

Le Corbusier

11.2 goals
- ◎ talk about homes and housing ♻
- ◎ discuss pros and cons

Le Corbusier (1887–1965) was a Swiss-French architect. He built this tower block called *Unité d'habitation*.

READING

1 Look at the photos and answer the questions together.

1 What can you see in the pictures?
2 Would you like to live in a place like this?
3 Do many people live in <u>tower blocks</u> where you live?
4 What do you think are the good and bad points about living in a tower block?

2 Read the article about Le Corbusier. Which paragraphs A–F are about:

D 1 a city he designed? ___
E 2 why some people dislike his ideas? ___
F 3 why his ideas might be important for the future? ___
  4 people's different opinions about his work? _A_
B 5 his ideas for tower blocks? ___
C 6 his tower block in France? ___

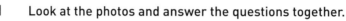

¿siluardo?

Le Corbusier – architect of the future?

^A To some people, he is the father of a million ugly tower blocks, shopping centres and multi-storey car parks. To others, he was a genius, a man who dreamed of safe and comfortable cities for everyone, rich or poor. His name was Le Corbusier and his buildings can be seen in Europe, North and South America and Asia.

^B Le Corbusier saw concrete and tower blocks as a way of providing inexpensive, quiet and spacious homes for everyone. He thought tower blocks should have their own indoor 'streets' with shops, cafés, schools and sports centres, and be close to historic city centres.

^C Le Corbusier used these ideas in one of his most famous designs, the twelve-storey *Unité d'habitation* in Marseille, built in 1952. Today, the tower block is home to 1,600 people. It's a popular address and neighbours get on well. It has an indoor shopping street, social clubs, a kindergarten, a gym and a hotel. There is even a swimming pool and a rooftop garden.

^D However, perhaps the best example of Le Corbusier's vision for modern urban living is in India, 250 km north of Delhi. There, he built one of the world's most unusual cities, Chandigarh. It is set around a large man-made lake and is full of parks, trees and flowers. It has 46 areas, each with its own apartment blocks, shops and services. One resident, Ranjit Sehgal, says, "Chandigarh was for many a dream in the desert, a new beginning. People are terribly proud of being from Chandigarh."

^E However, there is another side to the story. Other architects tried to use Le Corbusier's ideas, but their tower blocks were sometimes very different. They were cheaply built with small, dark apartments and paper-thin walls. They were built far from city centres, with no indoor shops or streets. Some writers on urbanisation believe tower blocks like these create social problems, like crime and violence, and they blame Le Corbusier for the problems of modern city life.

^F Laurent Bouvier, an expert on the architect, disagrees. "With more than half the world's population now living in cities," he says, "it's time to look at Le Corbusier's work again. His ideas were misunderstood in the 20th century, but they may be the answer to the problems of the 21st."

3 Read the article again. According to the writer, who has or had these opinions?

1 Tower blocks should have their own facilities. LC
2 People from Chandigarh are proud to live there. One Resident
3 Le Corbusier is responsible for some of the problems in cities today. Some writer
4 People should think about Le Corbusier's ideas again. Laurent
5 Le Corbusier's ideas could help create better cities in the future. Laurent

SPEAKING

4 Talk together. Which opinions in 3 do you agree and disagree with? Why?

The thing is …

VOCABULARY

Talk about pros and cons

1 Read what some people say about Chandigarh. Which highlighted expressions show positive, negative or neutral opinions?

see do

"The worst thing about Chandigarh is, it's too quiet. My parents live there and it's perfect for them – a city for retired people. But it's not for me. I like the noise, the sounds, the smells of Delhi!

Randeep Gupta, who lives in Delhi

"The best thing about the college is, it's so green, with lots of light inside.

Sehar Mohan, student at the College of Art in Chandigarh ↳ bright

Le Corbusier was the artist of concrete. The trouble is, concrete is not beautiful to look at. It can look dirty and depressing if it's not cleaned regularly.

Devi Rameesh, resident of Chandigarh

The thing is, Chandigarh is too popular. Designed for a population of up to 500,000, it's now home to double that or more. — neutral

Neena Ramesh, resident of Chandigarh

2 Choose one of these topics and complete 1–4 with your opinions:

• tower blocks • living in the country • modern architecture • living in the city

1 The bad / worst thing about … is, …
2 The good / best thing about … is, …
3 The thing is, …
4 The trouble / problem is, …

The best thing about tower blocks is, you get a great view.

PRONUNCIATION

Groups of words 1

3 a 🔊 **3.19** People speak in groups of words. Listen and put // between the two groups in each sentence:

1 The worst thing about Chandigarh is // it's too quiet.
2 The best thing about the college is, it's so green.
3 The thing is, Chandigarh is too popular.
4 The trouble is, concrete is not beautiful to look at.

b Practise saying the sentences.

4 Listen to each other's ideas from 2. Do you agree?

SPEAKING

5 a Work alone. Think about the area where you live, and areas near where you live. What are the pros and cons of each place?

• location • travel services and shops • things to do
• the environment • other

b Listen to each other's opinions and ask questions to find out more. If you're from the same place, do you agree?

Talk about a problem

11.3 goals
- describe imaginary situations ♻
- discuss pros and cons ♻
- talk about ways to solve problems

Donna and Marisa are talking about Marisa's daughter, Eva.
Eva rents a room in Canberra with a family, the Pierces.

TASK LISTENING

1 🔊 **3.20** Listen to Donna and Marisa's conversation. What problem do they talk about?

2 🔊 **3.20** Listen again. Which suggestion for Eva does Marisa think is a good idea?

1 Organise her day so she doesn't see the Pierces' daughter.
2 Talk to the daughter.
3 Talk to Mr and Mrs Pierce.
4 Write to Mr and Mrs Pierce.
5 Move to a different flat.

TASK VOCABULARY

Solving problems

3 a Match 1–5 with a–e to make sentences from the conversation.

e 1 Could she organise   a talk to the parents, actually.
c 2 Maybe she should   b write to them?
a 3 I'd probably   c talk to her.
b 4 Would it be possible to   d if that doesn't work!
d 5 I'd tell her to move   e her day so she doesn't see the daughter?

b Read the script on p154 to check.

c Cover 1–5 and look at a–e. In pairs, try to complete the suggestions.

4 What do you think Eva should do? Why?

TASK

5 🔊 **3.21** Listen to Paula and Leonardo talking about problems they have with people. What problem does each person have?

6 a Think about each situation.

1 How you would feel? *I think I'd feel ...*
2 What would you do? Think of two or three ideas. *I'd say ...*

b Talk about your ideas in groups. Who has the best ideas?

> My brother lives in a block of flats, and the person in the flat above him often has parties.

7 a Think about similar problems you, or someone you know, has had with people at home or at work.

b In groups, discuss the problems and ways to solve them.

Keyword *there*

1 Put the words in order to make sentences from previous units with there + be.

> 1 There / with / a large living room / 's / a balcony. Unit 11
> 2 There / second-hand stalls / some / just over there / are. Unit 8
> 3 There / less traffic / 'll / be / in 2050 / on the roads. Unit 7

2 **a** Notice the difference between there and it / they. Which highlighted words:

1 introduce new ideas?
2 refer back to earlier ideas?

There's a café round the corner. It opens at ten. There are lots of lovely parks to go to. They're usually free.

b Complete Ela's description of her flat with there (x2), it (x2) and they (x1).

> " Well, in our flat _____ are five rooms. _____ 's a living room, and a bedroom – _____ 're quite big – and we also have a study, a kitchen and a bathroom. I suppose my favourite room is the study. _____ 's also the smallest room but _____ 's the room that I really feel is mine. I don't just work in the study; I also like to lie on the sofa and read a good book. "

c **3.22** Listen to check. **P**

d Write a description of your home and favourite room, like Ela's.

e Listen to each other's descriptions. What are other people's favourite rooms? Why?

3 **a** You can also use there to avoid repeating places. Replace a group of words in 1–5 with there.

there
1 I love the Golden Lion cafe. I go ⋀ to the Golden Lion quite often on my way home.
2 My favourite room at home is the kitchen. We do everything in the kitchen, cooking, talking, everything.
3 I usually arrive at work at the same time every day. I usually get to work at eight thirty.
4 When I need to relax, I go to the river near my house. I probably go to the river once or twice a week.
5 I spend a lot of time at my parents' house. I stay at my parents' house two or three times a week.

b Change the sentences in 3a so they're true for you. Then compare your sentences.

I spend a lot of time at my friend's house. I go there almost every day.

Across cultures Neighbours

1 Look at the expressions in the box. Tick (✓) the places you have lived in. Compare in groups.

> a house   a suburb   a village   a city centre   a town centre
> a student hall ᵁᴷ / a dormitory ᵁˢ   a block of flats ᵁᴷ / an apartment block ᵁˢ

2 **a** Who are your neighbours? Do you know them? Are they friendly?

b **3.23** Listen to Megan talking about her experience of neighbours in different countries.

1 Where does she live now?
2 Where did she live in the past?

3 **3.23** Listen again. What does she say about her neighbours in each place?

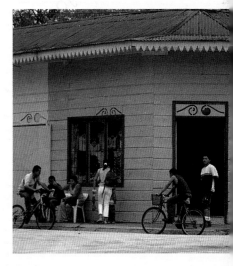

4 Tell each other about the places where you live now.

1 Do neighbours usually say hello when they see each other? Do they stop and chat?
2 Do they ever help each other with things like shopping or taking care of children?
3 Is it normal for people to visit new neighbours and introduce themselves?
4 Do neighbours spend free time together, or organise things together? What do they do?
5 Do their children play or go to school together?
6 Do people generally live near other members of their family?

5 What are your experiences of neighbours in other places you've lived?

1 a Have you ever rented an apartment? What problems can people have? Make a list.

Can't open a window, a broken light …

b Read José's letter. Are his problems on your list?

2 a Cover the letter. Can you remember the missing information in this summary of the problems?

1 The … is broken.
2 José and Donna can't find …
3 The … doesn't work properly. *some but*
4 They've asked for someone to … but …
5 They are very unhappy about the …

b Read the letter again to check.

3 Which words or expressions in the letter are used to:

1 explain the reasons for writing? (x2)
2 make a list of complaints? (x4)
3 make requests? (x1)

4 a You're going to write a letter or email of complaint. With a partner, read the situation and decide on details together.

1 You're renting a home. When did you move in?
2 You have two or three problems with the home. What are they?
3 What do you want the owner or agency to do about the problems?

b Think about:

1 how many paragraphs to write.
2 what should go in each paragraph.
3 which expressions from 2 and 3 you'd like to use.

5 Work alone and write an email or letter of complaint about your situation.

6 a With a new partner, read each other's letters or emails. Can you answer these questions?

1 What's the reason for writing?
2 What are the problems?
3 What does the writer want to happen?

b Talk about your emails or letters together and improve them if necessary.

3105 Century Tower
Sydney
December 20, 2010

Dear Mr Scott,

I am writing to complain about the service provided by your agency. My wife and I moved into 3105 Century Tower on September 12. We are generally happy with the apartment, but unfortunately there are a number of problems.

First, the air conditioning is broken, which is making the apartment very uncomfortable. Another problem is, we can't find the key for the balcony door. Also, the intercom doesn't work properly, so visitors sometimes can't hear what we're saying.

We've telephoned your agency three times and asked for someone to come round and fix these things, but no one has come. In addition, I emailed your office on December 12 but again, I haven't had a reply. I am very unhappy about this level of service.

Would you please contact me as soon as possible to let me know what you are going to do about this?

Yours sincerely,

José De Souza

Review

VOCABULARY Discuss pros and cons

1 a Which expression, 1 or 2, do these words go with?

bad	problem	thing	best
good	trouble	worst	

1 The _____ is, I don't like hot weather.
2 The _____ thing about summer here is, it's absolutely boiling.
3 The _____ thing about my flat is, it's got air-conditioning.

b Talk together. What do you think are the pros and cons of these things?

• summer • winter • Internet • football
• flying • driving • pets • fast food

GRAMMAR would

2 a What would you do in these situations?

1 Your friend is trying to give up smoking. However, when you go out together, he always asks people for cigarettes.
2 It's early in the morning and your neighbour is playing really loud music. You want to sleep.
3 You're looking after your sister's flat and you break one of her plates. She has lots and probably won't notice.
4 You're driving to a party but you're lost. You don't have a map and your mobile phone doesn't work.
5 It's Monday morning and you're not feeling well. You have an important meeting at work in the afternoon.

b Talk about situations 1–5 in groups.

CAN YOU REMEMBER? Unit 10 – Hotel collocations

3 a Work in A/B pairs.

A, look at five hotel expressions on p128.
B, look at five hotel expressions on p127.

Think of definitions for your expressions.

A big room for business meetings (conference room)

b Test each other. Listen to each other's definitions and say the expressions.

c Put the words in order to make sentences.

1 a I'd four like book double room to for nights .
2 breakfast included buffet Is the ?
3 a have I reservation .
4 time breakfast is What ?
5 the time check-out is What ?
6 have access you internet Do wireless ?

d Role play a conversation in pairs. Make a hotel reservation by telephone, then check in. Take turns to be the guest and receptionist.

Extension

SPELLING AND SOUNDS ck, k, ch, qu

4 a ● 3.24 Listen and repeat the words. How do you say ck, k and ch? How do you say qu?

1 ck /k/ block back
2 k /k/ fork broken
3 ch /k/ school architect
4 qu /kw/ quiet question

b ● 3.25 Spellcheck. Close your books. Listen to twelve words and write them down.

c Look at the script on p154 to check your spelling.

NOTICE Expressions with prepositions

5 a Complete the highlighted expressions in the estate agent's advertisements with the correct prepositions.

around	at	from	in	of	to

1 A comfortable house _____ the countryside. *in*
2 It has wonderful views _____ the city. *of*
3 Just _____ the corner from the beach. *around*
4 The balcony _____ the back is perfect for relaxing. *at*
5 3.5 hours _____ Sydney. *from*
6 This apartment is close _____ the city centre. *to*

b Check in the adverts on p90.

c Write an estate agent's advert for your home or a home you know well. Use the prepositions from 5a. You can use the adverts on p90 to help you.

Self-assessment

Can you do these things in English? Circle a number on each line. 1 = I can't do this, 5 = I can do this well.

⊚ talk about homes and housing	1	2	3	4	5
⊚ describe imaginary situations	1	2	3	4	5
⊚ discuss pros and cons	1	2	3	4	5
⊚ talk about ways to solve problems	1	2	3	4	5
⊚ write a letter or email of complaint	1	2	3	4	5

• For Wordcards, reference and saving your work » e-Portfolio
• For more practice » Self-study Pack, Unit 11

People and places

Where is it?

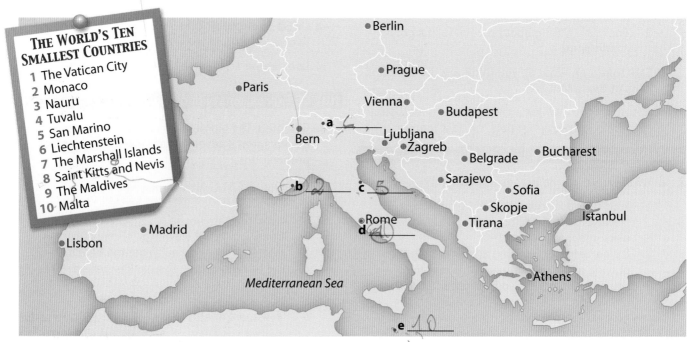

THE WORLD'S TEN SMALLEST COUNTRIES
1 The Vatican City
2 Monaco
3 Nauru
4 Tuvalu
5 San Marino
6 Liechtenstein
7 The Marshall Islands
8 Saint Kitts and Nevis
9 The Maldives
10 Malta

VOCABULARY

Location

1 Look at the list of the world's ten smallest countries.

  1 What do you know about them?
  2 Which ones can you put on the map in a–e?
  3 Do you know where the other countries are?

2 a Work in groups. Can you match the countries with these descriptions?

  a It's in Rome in Italy.
  b It's in the east of Italy.
  c It's an island in the South Pacific.
  d It's a group of islands in the Pacific Ocean. (x2)
  e It's an island nation in the Caribbean Sea.
  f They're in the Indian Ocean, south-west of Sri Lanka.
  g It's in the Mediterranean Sea, to the south of Sicily.
  h It's between Austria and Switzerland.
  i It's in the south of Europe, on the Mediterranean coast, and it borders France.

b 3.26 Listen to check. **P**

c Add words from 2a to these lists. Can you think of any more words?

  a *the Atlantic Ocean, ...*
  b *Africa, Asia, ...*
  c *the north, the south, ...*

SPEAKING

3 a Think about how to describe the location of:

  1 another city on the map.
  2 a town or country you've visited or would like to visit.

b Listen to each other's descriptions. Can you guess the places?

Two small countries

The Vatican City

Tuvalu

ROME

1 Work in A/B pairs. A, read about the Vatican on this page. B, read about Tuvalu on p127. Find the answers to these questions.

1 Where is it? How big is it?
2 How many people live there?
3 What jobs do people do?

4 Does it get many visitors?
5 What languages do people use?
6 How does it make money?

The Vatican City

VATICAN CITY

ROME

The smallest independent country in the world, the Vatican City covers an area the size of a golf course in Rome, the capital of Italy. It was founded in 1929 and is ruled by just one man, the Pope, who is also the head of the Catholic Church. Its buildings – such as St Peter's Basilica and the Sistine Chapel – are home to some of the world's most famous art, including works by Botticelli, Raphael and Michelangelo.

The Vatican has its own bank, army, police force, fire brigade, post office, satellite TV channel, radio station and internet domain (.va). The Vatican army, called the Swiss Guard, is the smallest in the world. It has about 100 soldiers, all unmarried, and all from Switzerland. The Vatican postal service has an excellent reputation: an international letter posted in the Vatican will arrive faster than one dropped just a few hundred metres away in Italy.

Millions of people visit the Vatican every year, but the Vatican has a population of only about 800 people. The Vatican has no official language. The Swiss Guard use German, but most people use Italian and Latin. In fact, the Vatican's bank machines are the only ones in the world that give instructions in Latin.

The country's economy is unique. It receives most of its money from Catholics around the world and from tourism. It also makes money from a petrol station where Italians can buy fuel 30 percent more cheaply than in Italy – because the Vatican has no taxes!

2 Read the descriptions again. Choose two more interesting facts to tell your partner.

3 Tell each other about the Vatican and Tuvalu.

Describing a country

4 What can you remember about the Vatican and Tuvalu? Complete the sentences together.

1978   800   art collection   Britain   four years   Funafuti
tourism   Tuvaluan and English   the UN

1 The capital is … Funafuti
2 The population is about …800
3 The official languages are …Tuvaluan English
4 It's a member of … U N
5 It has elections every …four years

6 It makes its money from …tourism
7 It's famous for its … art collection
8 In the past it was governed by …Britain
9 It became independent in … 1978

5 a Write six sentences about your country, five true and one false.

The capital of Slovenia is Ljubljana.

b In groups, listen to each other's sentences. Which sentence is false?

6 a Work in groups of three, A, B and C.

Student A, look at the profile of San Marino on p127.
Student B, look at the profile of the Maldives on p123.
Student C, look at the profile of Saint Kitts and Nevis on p125.

Prepare to talk about your country.

b Tell each other about your countries in 6a. Would you like to visit any of these countries? Why?

Big in Japan

LISTENING

1 a Look at the picture of Akebono Taro. Guess the answers to these questions.

1 Where is Akebono from?
2 Where did he become famous?
3 What was unusual about him?
4 What is a *yokozuna*?

b ⏺ 3.27 Listen to a radio interview with the author of a book, *Yokozuna*, about sumo wrestling. Check your ideas in 1a.

Akebono Taro, sumo wrestler and *yokozuna*

2 a Read the summary. Can you correct the <u>underlined</u> information?

> " Akebono was born in ¹<s>Japan</s> *Hawaii*. At first he was interested in ²<u>football</u>. He flew to ³<u>Hawaii</u> in 1988 and started practising sumo seriously. His first professional match was in ⁴<u>1989</u>. He became a *yokozuna* in ⁵<u>1994</u>. He was the first foreigner to achieve this in ⁶<u>1800</u> years. During his thirteen years of sumo wrestling, he won the Emperor's Cup a total of ⁷<u>12</u> times. His last fight was in ⁸<u>2000</u>. "

(handwritten notes in margin:)
— basketball
— Japan
— 1988
— 1993
— 1500
— 11
— 2001

b ⏺ 3.27 Listen again to check.

3 Who are the best-known sportspeople where you live? What sports do they play or do?

Achievements

VOCABULARY

Life and achievements

1 a What can you remember about Akebono? Match 1–8 with a–h to make sentences.

g 1	He was born	a	study hotel management.
e 2	He won	b	sumo from watching it on TV.
a 3	He wanted to	c	in 2001.
b 4	He became interested in	d	become a *yokozuna* in 1500 years.
h 5	He flew to Japan to join	e	a basketball scholarship.
f 6	Akebono defeated	f	Konishiki.
d 7	He was the first foreigner to	g	in Hawaii.
c 8	He retired	h	Azumazeki's stable.

b ⏺ 3.28 Listen to check. ℗

2 In pairs, cover 1–8 and look at a–h. Can you remember the complete sentences?

SPEAKING

3 a Prepare a short talk about your life or the life of someone you know. Use the expressions in 1a and your own ideas.

b Listen to each other's talks. Ask questions to find out more.

> My dad was born in 1955. He was the first person in my family to go to university ...

GRAMMAR

Infinitives and gerunds

4 a Circle the correct expressions in these sentences from the interview.

1 For foreigners, it was very difficult to become / becoming a *yokozuna*.
2 As a young man, he enjoyed to play / playing basketball.
3 He also wanted to study / studying hotel management.
4 He became interested in sumo from to watch / watching it on television.

b Look at the script on p155 to check.

c Match the sentences 1–4 in 4a with these rules.

You can use infinitives with *to* (*to go*, *to have*, etc.):	You can use gerunds (*going*, *having*, etc.):
a after adjectives ☑	c after prepositions ☑
b after some verbs ☑	d after some verbs ☑
Some common verbs + the infinitive with *to* are: *agree, decide, hope, learn, need, plan, want, would like.*	Some common verbs + the gerund are: *enjoy, finish, practise, suggest, can't stand.*

5 a Choose verbs from the box to complete questions 1–6. Use the infinitive or the gerund.

> learn   move   retire   speak   start

Do you know anyone who ...

1 decided _____ a new career after they were 30?
2 practises _____ English outside class?
3 finds it easy _____ new languages?
4 is planning _____ before they're 60?
5 is thinking about _____ to another country?
6 would like to become ...
7 is interested in studying ...
8 enjoys ...
9 is hoping ...

Grammar reference and practice, p141

b Complete 6–9 with your own ideas.

PRONUNCIATION

Stress in verbs

6 a 🔊 3.29 Listen to the verbs with two syllables. Which syllable is usually stressed, the first or the second?

agree   become   decide   defeat   enjoy   finish   practise   retire   study   suggest

b 🔊 3.30 Listen to the verbs. Does the stress move or stay the same when you add an ending?

decide – decided   practise – practises   buy – buying   speak – spoken

c Find the verbs in the sentences in 5a and mark the stress. Practise saying them.

SPEAKING

7 In groups, ask and answer the questions in 5a. Find out more.

Talk about people and places in your country

12.3 goals
- say where places are ♺
- describe countries ♺
- talk about people's lives and achievements ♺

Kraków

Lech Wałęsa

TASK LISTENING

Renata from Poland

1   Look at the pictures. What do you know about Lech Wałęsa and Kraków?

2   ♦ **3.31** Listen to Renata talking about Lech Wałęsa. Tick (✓) the things she mentions.

Solidarity   Gdańsk   communism   education   election   1995

3   a ♦ **3.31** Listen again. What does she say about the things you ticked?

b Check your ideas in groups. Then check in the script on p155.

4   ♦ **3.32** Now listen to Renata talking about Kraków. Tick (✓) the things she mentions.

the capital   atmosphere   industry   jazz   Warsaw   south   population

5   a ♦ **3.32** Listen again. What does she say about the things you ticked?

b Check your ideas in groups, then check in the script on p155.

TASK VOCABULARY

Expressions with *know*

> Do you know anything about Kraków?
>
> Well, I know that it's in Poland and it's ...

6   a Match 1–7 with a–g to complete the sentences.

b	1	You probably know it was	a an ordinary worker.
g	2	I know that he worked	b the capital of Poland.
	3	I don't know much about its	c he did before that.
c	4	I don't know what	d the population is less than a million.
e	5	Do you know anything about	e his life?
d	6	I don't really know for sure, but I think	f history.
a	7	As far as I know, he was	g in Gdańsk.

b Look at the pictures at the top of the page again. In pairs, talk about them, using the highlighted expressions.

TASK

7   a Choose a person and a place in your country that you think are important or interesting, and prepare to talk about them. Think about these questions.

The person
1   Why do you think they're important or interesting?
2   When and where were they born?
3   What do you know about their life?
4   Are they well known in your country nowadays?

The place
1   Why do you think it's important or interesting?
2   Where is it exactly?
3   What do you know about its history?
4   Have you been there? What's it like?

b Talk in groups and ask each other questions to find out more. If you chose the same people or places, do you have the same information and opinions?

8   Which people and places did you find interesting? Tell your group.

Keyword *to*

INFINITIVES WITH *to*

1 a Match the <u>underlined</u> expressions with the correct groups, A–C, in the table.

> 1 He <u>wanted to change</u> the country. Unit 12
> 2 Is it <u>possible to see</u> you on the 19th? Unit 9
> 3 Can you recommend some <u>things to see</u>? Unit 7
> 4 There are often long queues, so <u>the best time to go</u> is early evening. Unit 7
> 5 We're <u>planning to have</u> a sauna. Are you interested in using a sauna? Unit 6
> 6 Having a great time here in Scotland. <u>Hope to see</u> you soon. Unit 5

A verb + infinitive	B adjective + infinitive	C noun + infinitive
plan to go need to buy	difficult to do ready to order	a good place to visit the best way to learn

b Write five or six questions. Then ask and answer the questions in groups.

Do you want / need … ?   Are you planning / hoping … ?   Is it possible … ?
Do you think it's difficult / easy … ?   What's the best time / way / place … ?

PREPOSITION *to*

2 a Write *to* in the correct place in the questions.

1 Do you like listening music when you're working or studying?
2 Do you ever read stories friends or people in your family?
3 Have you ever sent a text message the wrong person?
4 Do you always reply emails on the same day?
5 When was the last time you wrote a letter someone?
6 How often do you give presents people?

b Ask and answer the questions.

Independent learning Guessing what words mean

1 What do you do when you see a word you don't know? Do you:

1 look the word up in a dictionary?
2 ask your teacher?
3 ask someone else in class?
4 try to guess what the word means?

2 Read the web page, then close your books. How much can you remember about Christopher's story?

3 a Look at the highlighted words 1–4.

1 Can you say which word is a noun, verb or adjective?
2 Can you guess what the words mean?

b Match the words with these explanations.

a brothers and sisters
b got together in a group
c the top part of your legs when you sit down
d very clear and strong

4 Look at the highlighted words 1–4 in two more stories on p130. Try to guess what they mean and then check your ideas in a dictionary.

File   Edit   View   Favorites   Tools   Help

Address

1969 – 'One small step for man'

On 21 July 1969, millions of people around the world watched on television as man walked on the moon for the first time. Some of you sent your memories:

I was only five years old but I have a ¹vivid memory of that day. We all ²gathered in front of the TV – my mum, dad and all my ³siblings. I was the smallest boy, so I sat on my dad's ⁴lap. I remember he was very quiet. Then when Neil Armstrong stood on the moon, I felt something wet on the top of my head. My father was crying.
Christopher

<u>Click to read similar stories.</u>

1 a **3.33** Listen to three conversations.

1 What's the relationship between Helen and Pat, and between Helen and Luis?
2 What's each conversation about?

b Read scripts 1–3 to check your ideas.

2 Look at the highlighted expressions in the script. Which ones do you use:

1 to describe things when you can't be exact?
   _____ , _____
2 to mean 'and similar things'
   _____ , _____
3 to mean 'or similar things'
   _____ , _____

3 a Which expressions from 2 can you use in 1–6 in this conversation? Two expressions are always possible.

PAT   It's so quiet here, isn't it?
HELEN Yes, sometimes there are kids on motorbikes racing around and shouting ¹_____ , but it's usually fine.
PAT   So, what are we going to do today?
HELEN Well, maybe see some sights. There are a few museums, art galleries, the aquarium ²_____ .
PAT   Yes, or we could have a ³_____ quiet day, maybe walk around a bit, then go out for lunch ⁴_____?
HELEN Definitely. There's a great restaurant up the road. It does a ⁵_____ local fish dish which I'm sure you'd love.
PAT   Great. And then maybe we could visit a museum or gallery ⁶_____ tomorrow.
HELEN Sure, good idea.

b Practise the conversation twice. Try to use different expressions each time.

4 Talk in groups. Tell each other:

1 where you were born and grew up and what you remember about it.
2 about the ingredients of a nice meal you ate recently.
3 what someone visiting your country in this season should bring with them.
4 what you'd like to do with a close friend or relative visiting you for the first time in a new place.

①

Pat is planning to visit her daughter in Mendoza, Argentina.

PAT   I'm so looking forward to seeing you, Helen, and meeting your new boyfriend … Luis, right? But what clothes should I bring? Is it warm?
HELEN Yes, it's warm in the day but bring some jumpers or a jacket or something for the evenings.
PAT   Jumpers? Thick ones, woolly ones, you mean?
HELEN Er, yes, maybe.
PAT   Like my blue one? You know the one?
HELEN Yes, the blue one or your red one or whatever. It doesn't matter.

②

A week later, in Mendoza. It's lunchtime.

PAT   So, what are we having for lunch, darling?
HELEN Er, I'm not sure yet. Maybe some soup?
       (later)
PAT   Mmmm, this soup's absolutely delicious. Your cooking has got much better, Helen. What's in it?
HELEN Oh, er, vegetables mainly. Onions, peppers, potatoes and stuff like that.
PAT   Right. So, you, er, chop the veg, and then what?
HELEN Well, I think you add water and some herbs and things … Sorry, I didn't actually make it. Luis did.
PAT   Ah, OK. Well, tell him it was lovely, and I'd like the recipe! When are we seeing him again?
HELEN This afternoon, at three.

③

Later that afternoon, Pat is chatting to Helen's boyfriend, Luis.

PAT   So, Luis, you were born in Spain, right?
LUIS   Yes, that's right. In Galicia.
PAT   Oh, yes. Where exactly?
LUIS   Well, actually, in a farmhouse in the middle of nowhere! It was sort of surrounded by mountains. The nearest town was Ortigueira, which is on the, er, the north-west coast.
PAT   Oh, right. And did you stay there throughout your childhood?
LUIS   No. We moved to Argentina, to Buenos Aires, when I was three, so I don't really remember it at all. But I've always had a, a kind of special feeling about the mountains. It's difficult to explain, but I love being able to see the mountains. It gives me a sense of space, I guess.

Review

VOCABULARY Location, describing a country

1 a In groups, design your ideal country. You can use some of these ideas:

location   size   population   languages   work
free time   government   the economy   transport

Prepare to talk about your country. You can use the expressions on p98 and p99.

Our ideal country is a group of three islands. It has ...

b Change groups. Tell each other about your ideal countries. Decide which you'd most like to visit.

GRAMMAR Infinitives and gerunds

2 a Put the verbs in the correct groups.

promise   agree   can't stand   would like
offer   dislike   enjoy   want   finish   miss

_____ / _____ / _____ / _____ / _____ + to do
_____ / _____ / _____ / _____ / _____ + doing

b Do these verbs go with an infinitive or a gerund? In groups, use dictionaries to check.

> **enjoy** /ɪnˈdʒɔɪ/ *verb* **1** If you enjoy something, it gives you pleasure. *I hope you enjoy your meal.* [+ doing something] *I really enjoyed being with him.*

hope   learn   plan   don't mind

c Use the verbs to write six sentences about yourself, four true and two false.

When I was six, I wanted to be a policeman.

d Listen to each other's sentences. Can you guess which are false?

CAN YOU REMEMBER? Unit 11 – *would*

3 a Add the missing words to Theo's description of his dream home. would (x7) wouldn't (x1)

" My dream home? Well, I live in a house in the mountains but it be close to a village so we could go shopping and things like that. It be too big – it have maybe four rooms – but the living room have a big balcony with wonderful views. I live there with my wife and son of course, and every day we get up, make coffee and just look out over the mountains. That be perfect. "

b Think about your dream home. Where would it be, what would it be like and what would you do there?

c Talk in groups. Listen to each other's ideas. What do you think about them?

Extension

SPELLING AND SOUNDS -ent, -ant

4 a ● 3.34 You say the endings –ent and –ant in the same way, /ənt/. Listen and repeat.

student   president   parliament   government
important   elephant

b Read the information and then complete the words.

1   -ent (including -ment) is much more common that -ant.
2   After the sounds /f/, /g/, /k/ and /t/, we usually use -ant.

account____   apartm____   assist____   differ____
excell____   independ____   mom____
monum____   inst____   pres____

c ● 3.35 Spellcheck. Close your books. Listen to ten words and write them down.

d Look at the script on p156 to check your spelling.

NOTICE Expressions with *of*

5 a Complete the expressions with *of* using the words from the box.

member   head   group   south

1   The Vatican's ruled by the Pope, who is also the _____ of the Catholic Church.
2   Monaco is in the _____ of Europe.
3   Tuvalu is a _____ of nine islands.
4   Nowadays it's a _____ of the United Nations.

b Think about your answers to these questions.

1   What are you a member of? What groups do you belong to?
2   Who's the head of state in your country? Who's the head of your company, school or club?
3   Which part of your town do you live in? For example, the centre or the east? What about your friends and family?

c Ask and answer the questions. Find out more.

> I'm a member of a cycling club.

> Oh yeah? How often do you meet?

Self-assessment

Can you do these things in English? Circle a number on each line. 1 = I can't do this, 5 = I can do this well.

◉ say where places are	1	2	3	4	5
◉ describe countries	1	2	3	4	5
◉ talk about people's lives and achievements	1	2	3	4	5
◉ use vague language	1	2	3	4	5

• For Wordcards, reference and saving your work » e-Portfolio
• For more practice » Self-study Pack, Unit 12

13

13.1 goals
◎ talk about electronic gadgets you use
◎ use the phone in different situations

Now and then

I couldn't live without it!

a webcam

a printer and scanner

a laptop

a mobile phone

a digital camera

a music player

LISTENING

1 a Look at the picture. Which of these electronic gadgets do you have?

b What other gadgets do you use? Make a list.

c Compare your lists. Which are the most common gadgets? Which are the most unusual?

2 ◆ 3.36 Listen to two conversations. Tick (✓) the gadgets that the people mention.

		mobile phone	music player	computer
1	Natalie and Paula			
2	Metin and Fabio			

Natalie and Paula

3 a What can you remember about 1–3? Talk together.

1 How do Natalie and Paula feel about their mobile phones? Do they feel the same?
2 How often does Metin use his music player? Why is it important to him?
3 How does Fabio feel about gadgets in general? Which ones does he have?

b ◆ 3.36 Listen again to check.

Metin and Fabio

4 Do you know anyone like Natalie, Paula, Fabio or Metin? Who are you most similar to?

VOCABULARY

How I feel about gadgets

5 a Can you remember what each of these sentences is about?

1 I need to have it with me. *mobile phone*
2 I use it all the time.
3 I use it for my job.
4 I don't know how to use them.
5 It makes life easier.
6 I have one but I hardly ever use it.
7 I don't even have one at home.
8 I don't bother with it.
9 I think I would die without it.
10 I couldn't live without mine.

b Read the scripts on p156 to check.

SPEAKING

6 a Think about the different gadgets you use.

1 How often do you use them?
2 Do you use them for work, for studies or for your personal life?
3 How do you feel about them?
4 Are there any gadgets you're not interested in having? Why not?

b Ask and answer the questions.

Four phone calls

LISTENING

1 Ask and answer the questions.

   1 Do you ever use the phone to manage your bank account or book holidays? Why? / Why not?

   2 Do you or people you know get a bonus at work? How often? What's it usually for?

2 **3.37** Listen to three phone calls with Christine. Answer the questions after each one.

Call 1
1 Christine calls her bank. Why is she surprised?
2 Where does she think the money has come from?

Call 2
1 Christine calls a company. Who does she want to talk to?
2 What message does she give the receptionist?

Call 3
1 Christine talks to her husband John. What does she tell him?
2 What do they decide to do?

3 **a** The bank manager phones Christine. What do you think he says?

   b **3.38** Listen to check your ideas.

4 Has something like this ever happened to you or someone you know?

VOCABULARY

Telephone expressions

5 **a** Who said sentences 1–12?

Christine (C)   receptionist (R)   John (J)   bank manager (B)

   1 Can I speak to John Andrews, please? *C*
   2 It's Christine, his wife.
   3 I'm sorry, but John isn't here.
   4 Listen, the reception's really bad here.
   5 Just a moment, please.
   6 Is that Christine Andrews?
   7 Do you want me to take a message?
   8 Could you ask him to call me?
   9 I'll call you back later.
  10 This is Paul Jennings.
  11 Is this a good time to talk?
  12 Can you hear me now?

   b Read the scripts on p156 to check.

PRONUNCIATION

Groups of words 2

6 **a** **3.39** Listen to sentences 1–5 in 5a again. Mark // between the two groups of words.

   1 Can I speak to John Andrews // please?

   b Practise saying the sentences.

7 **a** Look at the sentences in 5a again. In pairs, change the names. Then decide what the next line could be.

   1 Can I speak to Anna, please? *Yes, just a moment.*

   b Take turns to say 1–12 and respond with your ideas.

SPEAKING

8 **a** Work alone. Think about the language you'll need for these conversations.

   1 **Caller,** you want to speak to a relative (brother, mother …). Phone the place where they work and ask to speak to the person. You have important news to tell them. **Receptionist,** the person's not in. Take a message.

   2 **Caller,** call a friend. The reception is bad. Call back, then ask about recent news and arrange to do something. **Friend,** talk about recent news. Agree on a day to meet, a time and a place to go.

   b Role play the conversations. Take turns to be the caller.

ABC International. How can I help you?

I'd like to speak to …

When I was a child

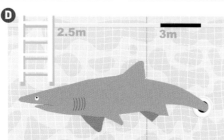

READING

1 The pictures show what five people believed when they were children. Can you guess what they thought?

2 Read the people's web postings. Match them with pictures A–E.

Cam ☐   Leonardo ☐   Natalie ☐   Raquel ☐   Dave ☐

---

  www.childhoodbeliefs.com ▼ ▷ 🔍

childhoodbeliefs.com is a collection of strange and funny ideas we had when we were children. Add your own to our site.

I used to think my grandmother was inside the telephone. I'd hear her voice and say, 'Come out, Gran!' but she never did. **Cam from New Zealand**

When I was little, I used to believe there were little men inside the television and I used to get close to the TV and turn it on and off to see if I could hear the little men working inside it … And I still don't understand how it works. **Leonardo from Costa Rica**

When I was a little girl, I lived in a very big neighbourhood and we shared a garden and a pool between forty-eight houses. There were a lot of children around my age and we all used to play together, and we'd often swim in the pool. But there was one boy about five years older than us and he told me once, when I was swimming in the pool, "I hope you know that if you're alone in the pool, there's a shark that will come out of the light bulb and get you." I was terrified, and up until today – I'm twenty-five now – I still get nervous if I'm in a pool alone and I always check the light to make sure there's no shark. **Natalie from Trinidad and Tobago**

When I was little, I used to believe the moon followed me and my family everywhere we went. When we went to my uncle's, the moon would come with us. When we went on holiday, the moon would be there. I was so surprised when I told my friend and she said it followed her, too. How could the moon follow me and her at the same time when we weren't together? It couldn't be true! **Raquel from Mexico**

When I was about six years old, I used to believe that monsters lived under my bed. I'd jump out of bed so they couldn't get me. Later I decided they just wanted to be friends and felt bored under the bed. After that, I'd always leave a book under my bed so they could read it while I slept. **Dave from England**

3 Read the postings again. Who:

    1   was afraid of something as a child? (x2)
    2   is still a bit afraid now?
    3   didn't understand something as a child? (x3)
    4   still doesn't really understand it as an adult?

4 Which story do you like the best? Why?

I used to …

1 Read the sentences. Answer questions 1 and 2.

I **used to** get close to the TV and turn it on and off. (Leonardo)
We all **used to** play together, and we**'d** often swim in the pool. (Natalie)

    1   Are they about the present or the past?
    2   Did they do these things once or many times?

2 **a** <u>Underline</u> more examples of used to and would ('d) in the web postings on p108.

  b Complete the rules 1 and 2 with used to or would.

I used to believe that monsters lived under my bed. I used to jump out of bed so they couldn't get me. I'd jump out of bed so they couldn't get me. 'd = would	1 We can use both _____ and _____ to talk about actions: go, come, look, jump … 2 We can only use _____ to talk about states: believe, be, have, live, think, like, hate …

  c ◀ **3.40** Listen and say the sentences. ℗

3 **a** Which sentences can you complete with: **a** used to or would?   **b** only used to?

When I was a child …
    1   I *used to / would* play in the woods near my house after school.
    2   I *used to* like swimming in the sea. Now I find it too cold.
    3   I _____ have a wonderful red bicycle.
    4   I _____ live in a small village in the countryside.
    5   I _____ walk to school with my best friend every day.
    6   I _____ read one or two comic books every week. I loved reading.
    7   I _____ believe the moon was a light bulb in the sky.
    8   I _____ talk to my toys all the time.
    9   I _____ go to dance and exercise classes after school.
    10 I _____ buy sweets at a wonderful little shop near my home.

Grammar reference and practice, p140

  b Use the highlighted verbs in 3a to write five sentences about your childhood.

I used to play baseball with my friends after school every day.

4 Think about things you used to do in your childhood, and things you used to believe.

  • things you did: games you played   school friends   places you went on holiday …
  • beliefs about: food   nature   machines   animals   toys   science   transport
                          people   money …

5 In groups, talk about your childhood memories.

> When I was a child we used to go camping nearly every summer.
>> Really? Where did you go?

6 How many of you believed or did the same things?

Talk about technology and change

TASK READING

1 Have you done all these things? When was the first time you did them?

- used the Internet • opened an email account • bought something online
- watched TV online • talked online

2 Read Mark Glaser's web page about how the Internet has changed people's lives. Does he think the changes are good, bad or both?

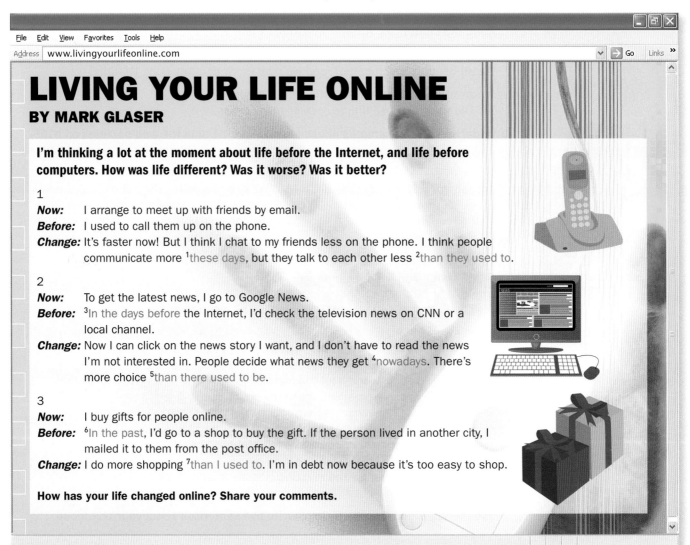

File   Edit   View   Favorites   Tools   Help

Address www.livingyourlifeonline.com   Go   Links »

LIVING YOUR LIFE ONLINE
BY MARK GLASER

I'm thinking a lot at the moment about life before the Internet, and life before computers. How was life different? Was it worse? Was it better?

1
Now: I arrange to meet up with friends by email.
Before: I used to call them up on the phone.
Change: It's faster now! But I think I chat to my friends less on the phone. I think people communicate more [1]these days, but they talk to each other less [2]than they used to.

2
Now: To get the latest news, I go to Google News.
Before: [3]In the days before the Internet, I'd check the television news on CNN or a local channel.
Change: Now I can click on the news story I want, and I don't have to read the news I'm not interested in. People decide what news they get [4]nowadays. There's more choice [5]than there used to be.

3
Now: I buy gifts for people online.
Before: [6]In the past, I'd go to a shop to buy the gift. If the person lived in another city, I mailed it to them from the post office.
Change: I do more shopping [7]than I used to. I'm in debt now because it's too easy to shop.

How has your life changed online? Share your comments.

TASK VOCABULARY

Comparing past and present

TASK

> People are always in contact with each other nowadays. It's more difficult to get away from everyone than it used to be.

3 Read the web page again. Which highlighted expressions:

1 are about now? (x2)
2 are about the past? (x2)
3 compare the present and the past? (x3)

4 **a** You're going to talk about how technology has changed lives. Think about these questions.

1 What technology do you use at home and at work? What about other people you know?
2 How have these things changed your life?
3 How have they changed life in your country, or around the world?

Think of the language you need. Make notes.

b Talk together. Do you have the same ideas?

5 Do you think these changes have made life better or worse? Why?

Keyword *time*

1 a Use expressions with time from the box to complete the sentences from previous units.

> all the time   another time   Any time
> too much time   for the first time
> have a good time   your first time

1 I need my mobile phone with me _____ . Unit 13
2 In 1969, man walked on the moon _____ .
   Unit 12
3 If you're busy tomorrow, we can meet _____ .
   Unit 11
4 I'm sorry I'll miss the lunch. I hope you
   _____ . Unit 9
5 Is this _____ in Canada? Unit 4
6 We probably spend a bit _____ surfing the
   Internet. Unit 2
7 Would you mind changing our appointment?
   _____ is fine. Unit 1

b Write four sentences about when you were a child or teenager with expressions from 1. Then compare your sentences.

I flew for the first time when I was fourteen.

2 a Complete the sentences from previous units with words from the box.

> to go   to think   to talk

1 Is this a good time _____ ? Unit 13
2 There are often long queues, so the best
   time _____ is early evening. Unit 7
3 At that speed, you don't have time _____ .
   Unit 1

> you arrive   I hear that expression   I go on holiday

4 And then next time _____ , I know it. Unit 10
5 I need my passport every time _____ . Unit 8
6 I'll be at home by the time _____ . Unit 5

b Make questions for the people in your class. Then ask and answer the questions.

When's the best time ... ?
Do you have time ... ?
What will you do the next time ... ?

> When's the best time to call you?

Across cultures Time

1 ◆ 3.41 Listen to Leonardo and Megan talking about attitudes to time in Costa Rica. Answer the questions.

1 Which does Leonardo say is faster, Costa Rican time or regular time?
2 What do they say about how people in Costa Rica feel about:
   a having meals?   b getting to meetings?
3 How does Megan feel about time?

2 a ◆ 3.41 Listen to Leonardo and Megan again. Tick the sentences you hear.

1 I'm usually right on time.
2 I always try to be on time but I'm sometimes late.
3 I'm in a hurry to get where I'm going.
4 People are always rushing to get somewhere.
5 People take their time having their breakfast.

b Which expressions are about:

1 doing things at the agreed time?
2 doing things quickly, often with stress?
3 doing things slowly without stress?

3 a Write three sentences about yourself with the expressions in 2a.

I'm always in a hurry to get to my classes.

b Compare your sentences and ask questions to find out more. Are your attitudes to time the same or different?

4 Think about other places you've been to or know about. Do you think people's attitudes to time there are similar to yours?

Leonardo is from Costa Rica, Megan is from Canada. They talk about time in Costa Rica.

1 Look at the pictures in the web page. Can you remember your first calculator, music player or camera?

1 How old were you?
2 How did you feel about them?
3 What were they like?

2 Read three people's web postings about their 'firsts'. What are their answers to the questions in 1?

TECHNOMEMORIES > MY FIRST >

http://www.technomemories.com

> MY FIRST CALCULATOR

I got my first calculator when I was about eleven, when I went to junior high school. It was really big and heavy but it could do lots of complicated things. I loved it so much that I used to carry it in my jacket pocket all the time. It nearly pulled my jacket off my shoulder! Then a few years later, I began to dislike it. I was doing a maths exam, which I found really boring, and I had to study all the time, and the calculator just represented the exam. I still have it – see pic. Very old-fashioned! Whenever I see it, I still think of that exam. *Koji H., Japan*

> MY FIRST WALKMAN

I remember getting my first Sony Walkman. My older brother had one and I didn't, so I used to use his Walkman a lot, usually without asking. We had so many arguments that my parents eventually gave me my own Walkman for Christmas. I think I was twelve or thirteen. I remember that my brother was really jealous because it was smaller and more modern than his old one. I loved my Walkman. I used to use it all the time, especially when I was delivering papers early in the morning before school. It made the experience almost enjoyable. *Cam, New Zealand*

> MY FIRST DIGITAL CAMERA

I remember when I got my first digital camera, a little silver one. My husband gave it to me for my twenty-eighth birthday. I was a bit disappointed – another boring gadget. I love taking pictures and I used to take good ones with my old camera, before it broke. But as soon as I started using the digital camera, my pictures were terrible! The quality wasn't good, the battery always died just when I had the perfect shot ... it was all too complicated. I have a much better digital camera now but I still miss my old camera. *Elmira E., Turkey*

---

3 a Cover the postings. Match 1–5 with a–e to complete the sentences.

1 I got my first calculator when
2 But as soon as I started using the digital camera,
3 I remember getting my first
4 I remember that my brother
5 I remember when I got my first digital camera,

a Sony Walkman.
b was really jealous.
c a little silver one.
d my pictures were terrible!
e I was about eleven.

b Read the web postings again to check.

4 Choose a 'first' gadget to write about. In pairs, talk about your ideas for your web postings.

1 When did you get it?
2 What was it like? How often did you use it?
3 How did you feel about it then? What do you think about it now?
4 Which highlighted expressions from 3a can you use? Can you use used to or would?

5 Work alone and write your web posting.

6 Read your partner's posting. Ask questions to find out more.

Review

VOCABULARY Telephone expressions, expressions with *time*

1 a Play in groups of three, A, B and C.

A and B, take turns to choose a number in the box. Listen to C read a sentence with a gap. Say the missing word and win a square. You win the game by getting three squares in a line.
C, read the sentences for Game 1 on p128.

1	4	9
7	6	2
3	8	5

b Draw another grid with numbers 1–9. Change roles and play again.

C, read the sentences for Game 2 on p122.

GRAMMAR *used to*, *would*

2 a Which verbs usually go with:

1 used to and would?
2 used to, but not would?

think 2	buy ☐	go ☐	enjoy ☐
walk ☐	believe ☐	take ☐	dislike ☐
have ☐	listen to ☐	play ☐	live ☐

b Choose six verbs from 2a and write sentences about your past. You can write about your life:

1 as a teenager.   3 at college.
2 at school.   4 in your last job.

c Listen to each other's sentences. Ask questions to find out more.

CAN YOU REMEMBER? Unit 12 – Life and achievements

3 a Complete the sentences about Akebono, the sumo wrestler, with words and expressions from the box.

join   retired   became interested in
was the first   study   won

1 He wanted to _____ hotel management.
2 He _____ sumo from watching it on television.
3 He flew to Japan to _____ Azumazeki's stable.
4 Akebono _____ foreigner to become a *yokozuna*.
5 He _____ a basketball scholarship.
6 He _____ in 2001.

b Write sentences about a famous person in your country. Use the expressions in 3a.

c Read your sentences to a partner. Ask questions to find out more.

Extension

SPELLING AND SOUNDS *ei, ey*

4 a 🔊 **3.42** You can say ei and ey in two ways. Listen and repeat.

A /iː/	B /eɪ/
receive money	eight they

b Do you usually use ei or ey:

1 at the start of a word?
2 in the middle of a word?
3 at the end of a word?

Note that ei often goes:
1 after *c*   2 before silent *gh*

c Complete these words with ei or ey. Then put them in the correct groups above, A or B.

c___ling   gr___   journ___   k___
n___ghbour   rec___pt   Turk___   w___gh

d 🔊 **3.43** Listen to check. 🅟 Repeat the words.

e 🔊 **3.44** Spellcheck. Close your book. Listen to ten words and write them down. Then look at the script on p157 to check your spelling.

NOTICE *without*

5 a Match 1–3 with a–c to make sentences from this unit.

1 I used to use his Walkman a lot, usually without
2 I think I would die without
3 How do you live without

a the Internet?
b my mobile phone.
c asking.

b Ask and answer the questions.

1 What three gadgets can you live without?
2 What three gadgets can't you live without?
3 When you were a child, what could you do without asking?

> I could play in the street without asking. But when I wanted to go to the park, I had to ask my parents.

Self-assessment

Can you do these things in English? Circle a number on each line. 1 = I can't do this, 5 = I can do this well.

◎ talk about electronic gadgets you use	1 2 3 4 5
◎ use the phone in different situations	1 2 3 4 5
◎ talk about past habits and states	1 2 3 4 5
◎ write about a memory	1 2 3 4 5

• For Wordcards, reference and saving your work » e-Portfolio
• For more practice » Self-study Pack, Unit 13

14.1 goals
- express and respond to opinions
- have a discussion

A matter of opinion

Boxing

LISTENING

1 **a** Find these things in the picture.

boxers   gloves   the referee   the ring

b What other sports similar to boxing can you think of? *wrestling, karate ...*

c Are these kinds of sports popular in your country?

2 🔊 **3.45** Listen to the first part of Lewis and Amelia's conversation. Who likes boxing? Who doesn't?

3 **a** Which of these opinions do you think are Lewis's (L)? Which do you think are Amelia's (A)?

Lewis and Amelia from the USA are watching a boxing match at home.

1   Boxing is dangerous.
2   Other sports are more dangerous.
3   In boxing, the goal is to hurt other people.
4   People are naturally aggressive.
5   Boxers are great athletes.
6   People can choose to box or not.
7   Children under sixteen shouldn't box.
8   If you ban boxing, it will become more dangerous.
9   Boxers could do other sports because they're good athletes.

b 🔊 **3.46** Listen to the rest of the conversation and check your ideas.

4 Do you agree with the opinions? Talk in groups.

What do you think?

1 a Complete Lewis's and Amelia's opinions with words from the box.

feel   course   ~~think~~   know   find   thing (x2)   anyway

1 I _think_ it's awful.
2 I _____ it quite exciting.
3 We all _____ that people are aggressive.
4 And _____, nobody has to box.
5 I really _____ that if people want to box, we shouldn't stop them.
6 Of _____ that's not the same.
7 The _____ is, they have rules and there's a referee.
8 Another _____ is, being a boxer is a job, you know.

b 🔊 **3.47** Listen to check. ℗

2 a Think about your opinions on some of these things.

- the environment • supermarkets • banks
- health and fitness • the Internet

> I think we should buy fresh food in markets, not supermarkets.

b Listen to each other's opinions. Do you agree?

3 Read six extracts from Lewis and Amelia's conversation. Which highlighted expressions can we use if we want to:

1 agree?   2 disagree?   3 finish what we're saying?

1 L I mean, a lot of boxers get injured. Some even die.
   A Sorry, but more people die in football matches, you know.
2 A Lots of sports can be dangerous.
   L Yes, but in football, you're not trying to hurt someone, are you?
3 A People are aggressive. Naturally.
   L Well, not really. I think it depends on their environment.
4 L Yeah, but …
   A Just a second. The thing is, they have rules and there's a referee.
5 A … and that'll be a lot more dangerous.
   L OK, that's a good point.
6 L But you said boxers are great athletes, right?
   A Yes, exactly.

4 🔊 **3.48** Listen to the responses in 3. Which words are stressed in the highlighted expressions? ℗

5 Work in A/B pairs. A, say the first lines in 1–6 above. B, cover 1–6 and give responses. Then change roles.

6 a Think about these statements. Do you agree or disagree? Why?

1 People's writing and spelling are getting worse because of texting and email.
2 Tower blocks are the best places to live.
3 You don't really need to worry about your health until your 30.
4 It's best to work for one company all your life.
5 Everyone should learn at least two other languages.
6 University education should be free for everyone.

b In groups, talk about 1–6.

c Which topics did your group agree and disagree about? Tell the class.

Carbon footprint

14.2 goals
◉ have a discussion ♻
◉ discuss imaginary situations

READING

1 A carbon footprint is the amount of carbon dioxide (CO_2) we produce from our daily activities. What activities do you think create a carbon footprint?

Nandita is a writer and lives in Mumbai, India. She's also a doctor and has her own blog about cooking, called *Saffron Trail*.

2 a You're going to read an article by Nandita, 'Ways to reduce your kitchen's carbon footprint'. What do you think she'll say about these things?

microwave   dishwasher   light bulb   oven   pressure cooker

cars   herbs   bottled water   solar power

b Read the article. Were your ideas correct?

Address http://saffrontrail.blogspot.com/ways-to-reduce-your-kitchens-carbon.html

Ways to reduce your kitchen's carbon footprint

June 5 is World Environment Day. I thought it would be a perfect opportunity to see how I could improve the environment in my own small way. These ideas helped me reduce my carbon footprint in the kitchen and helped me save money, too.

• Do you keep the microwave and other kitchen machines on standby? Does your refrigerator need to be so cold? Is your dishwasher only half full? It all wastes energy.

• If you use light bulbs in your kitchen, change to low-energy bulbs. They waste less energy, heat up the place less and last longer. If everyone changed to low-energy bulbs, the world would use 4% less electricity.

• When I'm using the oven, I bake two or three dishes together. For those with a small oven, if you prepare everything ahead of time and bake the dishes one after the other, you won't have to pre-heat the oven again.

• Please learn to use a pressure cooker if you don't already. It takes 90% less time to cook rice, vegetables and lentils than by boiling.

• If your tap water is drinkable, don't drink bottled water. It just increases the amount of plastic in the environment.

• Plan your shopping for food and kitchen supplies so you can get everything in one trip. If you share a car with friends, you'll have fun and save fuel.

• Grow as many green herbs as possible. They'll make your kitchen look nice, you can use them in cooking and they'll also increase the oxygen supply.

• Solar heaters are very popular in the South of India and many new buildings have them. If we get a lot of sunlight, we shouldn't waste it.

The biggest problem we have today in India is the feeling '*Ek mere se kya hoga?*' (Hindi for 'What difference will one person make?') But if everyone thought like that, we wouldn't change anything. If we all managed our homes better, our cities would soon be cleaner and greener.

SPEAKING

3 Talk about each of Nandita's points. Which do you think is:

- a good idea?
- a good idea but a lot of people do it already?
- a good idea but difficult to do?
- a waste of time?

> I think it's a good idea not to keep machines on standby, but I often forget to turn them off.

Imagine

GRAMMAR

Real and unreal conditionals

1 a Read the two sentences. Then answer the questions.

A If you share a car with friends, you'll have fun and save fuel.
B If everyone changed to low-energy bulbs, the world would use 4% less electricity.

1 Are they about: a the past? b the present or future?
2 Which sentence means:
  a the situation is possible (real conditional)
  b the situation is imaginary and probably won't happen (unreal conditional)

b Complete the sentences in the table with thought, prepare, won't have and wouldn't change.

A If + present simple, *will* + infinitive
If you share a car with friends, you'll have fun and save fuel.   If you _____ everything ahead of time, you _____ to pre-heat the oven again.
B If + past simple, *would* + infinitive
If everyone changed to low-energy bulbs, the world would use 4% less electricity.   If everyone _____ like that, we _____ anything.
You can change the order: The world would use 4% less electricity if everyone changed to low-energy bulbs.

2 a Read the situations, then circle the correct underlined words in the sentences.

situation	what the person says
1 I might see Susan this afternoon.	'If I see / saw Susan, I'll / I'd give her your message.'
2 I don't have a bike.	'If I have / had a bike, I'll / I'd use it to get to work.'
3 He hates exercise.	'He'll / He'd be a lot healthier if he does / did some exercise.'
4 We might go to Spain in July.	'If we go / went to Spain, we'll /we'd visit Andalusia first.'
5 You don't have a computer.	'If you have / had a computer, your life will / would be a lot easier.'
6 She'll probably work late tonight.	'If she works / worked late, she'll / she'd get a taxi home.'

b 🔊 **3.49** Listen to check. ℗

3 Complete these sentences. Think about your situation, then choose the correct form.

1 If I have / had time this weekend …
   If I have time this weekend, I'll go and see that exhibition. (You probably have time.)
   If I had time this weekend, I'd go and see that exhibition. (You don't have time.)
2 If I need / needed some new clothes …
3 If my friend calls / called later …
4 If I change / changed jobs …
5 If I can / could change one thing in my country …

Grammar reference and practice, p142

PRONUNCIATION

Groups of words 3

4 a Think about how to say your sentences from 3. Mark // between groups of words.

1 If I have time this weekend // I'll go and see that exhibition.

b Say your sentences to each other. Are your situations the same or different? Compare your ideas.

SPEAKING

If everyone turned down their heating or air conditioning, we'd use less energy.

5 a Nandita says, 'If we all managed our homes better, our cities would soon be cleaner and greener.' Think about more things people could do to reduce their carbon footprint:

• at home (heating, air conditioning, waste …)
• travelling (long-distance, fuel, public or private transport …)
• shopping (local products, packaging, second-hand …)
• free-time activities (cycling, walking …)
• at work (machines, recycling, working from home …)

b Talk in groups. What do you think about each other's ideas? Why?

Have a debate

14.3 goals

- ◉ express opinions
- ◉ have a discussion
- ◉ discuss imaginary situations
- ◉ take part in a meeting

TASK READING

1 Ask and answer the questions.

1 What are the most important airports in your country?
2 Are there any plans to make them bigger or to build new ones?
3 What do you think are the advantages of living near an airport? What are the disadvantages?

2 a Read the information. Match the photos 1–3 with the places A–C on the map.

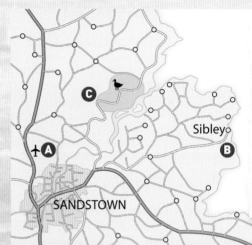

It's clear that this area of the country needs a bigger airport. The present airport, very near Sandstown, is extremely important for business and for local tourism, but everyone agrees that it's too small. It gets thousands of passengers every day, both from other cities in the country and from abroad, and this number will probably increase by at least fifty percent in the next five years. Some people think the best solution to this problem would be to make the airport bigger by adding a new terminal. Others believe that Sandstown Airport should be closed, and a new airport built further away from the town. There are two possible locations for a new airport: near the village of Sibley on the coast, or on the road going through the Nature Reserve. Department of Transport officials are coming to meet local people and to hear their opinions ...

b Read the information again and then answer the questions together.

1 What's the problem with the airport now?
2 There are three possible solutions to the problem. What are they?
3 What are the good and bad points of each solution?

TASK

3 You're going to have a meeting to talk about the airport. Work in four groups.

Group A, you live in Sandstown, near the airport. Look at the role card on p122.
Group B, you live in Sibley. Look at the role card on p124.
Group C, you work at the Nature Reserve. Look at the role card on p128.
Group D, you work for the government, at the Department of Transport. Look at the role card on p130.

Follow the instructions on your card.

4 Get into groups of four, with one person from each of the groups A–D.
Student D, start the meeting.

5 a When you finish your meeting, go back to your original group.

Groups A, B, C, how was your meeting? What do you think the government will decide?
Group D, what did you think about the arguments you heard? Decide where the airport should be and why.

b Listen to group D's decision. Do you think it's the right decision? Why? / Why not?

Keyword *would*

Two uses of *would*

Expressions with *would*

1 We use *would* to talk about:

A imaginary things in the present / future:

> It'd be really nice to get out of the city. Unit 11

B habits in the past:

> When I was a little girl, we'd often swim in the pool. Unit 13

Which sentences, 1–5, are like A? Which are like B?

1 <u>It would be a good idea to</u> ban music in supermarkets and other public places.
2 <u>The world would be a lot</u> happier <u>if</u> people didn't have to work so much.
3 <u>When I was</u> a student, <u>I'd always</u> get a job in the summer.
4 <u>I think it would be</u> interesting <u>to</u> learn another language.
5 <u>I'd often</u> sleep late on Saturday mornings, <u>when I was</u> a teenager.

2 Write four sentences which are true for you, using the underlined words. In pairs, talk about your sentences.

It would be a good idea to have more free parking in this city.

3 Match sentences 1–8 with the responses a–h.
3.50 Then listen to check. **P**

1 Can I take you out for dinner?
2 Would you close the window, please?
3 Let's eat and then go to the cinema.
4 Brandon Hotel. Can I help you?
5 We're going for a drink. Can you come too?
6 Would it be possible to meet up tomorrow?
7 Would you mind lending me your dictionary?
8 How about coffee at three o'clock?

a Yes. I'd like to book a room, please.
b I'd love to. I'll just get my jacket.
c I'd rather meet today if we can.
d Four would be better for me.
e Yes, it is rather cold.
f That would be lovely!
g I'd prefer to go to the cinema first.
h Sorry, but I'd rather not. I'm using it now.

4 In pairs, take turns to say 1–8 and remember the responses in a–h.

Independent learning Improve your speaking

1 How can you use these things outside the classroom to improve your speaking? Talk in groups.

2 **3.51** Listen and answer the questions.

1 Which picture, A or B, does each person talk about?
2 Were their ideas successful?

3 a In pairs, put Miguela's and Aslan's instructions in the correct order.

Miguela's idea
☐ Then try to say everything at the same time as the recording.
☐ Read the scripts and repeat each line after the recording.
☐ Listen to the conversations on your coursebook CD.

Aslan's idea
☐ Plan what you want to say.
☐ Check your grammar, look up new words and check pronunciation.
☐ Listen and write down what you said.
☐ Listen and do steps 3–5 again if necessary.
☐ Practise again and then record yourself again.
☐ Record yourself speaking.

b Read the scripts on p157 to check.

4 What do you think about their ideas? What other ways have you tried to improve your speaking?

Aslan from Turkey and Miguela from Spain talk about how they tried to improve their speaking.

1 Can you remember the answers to these questions? If you need help, look back at the text on p118.

1 What was the problem with the airport in Sandstown?
2 What were the three possible solutions to the problem?
3 What were some of the good and bad points of each solution?

2 🔊 **3.52** Listen to interviews with three people living in Sandstown. Who thinks the airport should stay in Sandstown? Who thinks it should move?

3 a 🔊 **3.52** Listen again. What reasons do the people give?

b Read the conversations below to check.

4 a Which of the highlighted expressions 1–8 make an opinion softer? (x3) Which make a disagreement softer? (x5)

b 🔊 **3.53** Listen to 1–8. Which words are stressed in the highlighted expressions?

c Listen again and repeat. 🅿

Goal
⊚ use expressions to soften opinions and disagreements

Leona is a local radio journalist. She's asking people in Sandstown what they think should be done about the airport.

5 a Work alone. Choose two or three topics and make notes about your opinions and reasons.

- a good place to live
- interesting TV programmes or films
- a nice place to visit
- a good time of year to have a holiday
- good places to shop

a good place to live – the countryside, quiet and clean.

b In pairs, take turns to give your opinions and say whether you agree or disagree. Use the highlighted expressions in the script. Ask questions to find out more.

> I think the best place to live is in the countryside because it's quiet and clean.

> Well, I'm not so sure because ...

❶

LEONA Excuse me, I'm Leona Cook from UPC news. Can you tell us, what do you think about Sandstown airport?

KARL Well, ¹I haven't thought about it a lot, but I suppose it should be moved. It's very old. I remember when it was built ... 35, 40 years ago?

LEONA Forty-two years. What do you think about the idea of simply extending the airport by building another terminal? Wouldn't that be better?

KARL Well, ²I'm not sure about that. There isn't room, unless they build over the North Park, and I wouldn't want that. I don't think there are enough green spaces in the town as it is.

❷

LEONA Excuse me. Can I ask you what's your opinion about the airport? Where do you think it should be?

CAROLE I know some people think we should move it, but ³I don't really agree. I use the airport quite a lot and it's good to have the airport near the town. ⁴It's true we need a bigger airport, but the location isn't a problem.

LEONA But if they made the airport bigger, they'd have to build over the North Park, wouldn't they? Surely that wouldn't be a good thing?

CAROLE Actually, ⁵I'm not so sure. I grew up near that park and I don't think it's anything special, and it's already very noisy because of all the planes. But there's lots of lovely countryside outside the town, and we don't want to lose that.

❸

LEONA Excuse me, Leona Cook, UPC news. There's a lot of discussion at the moment about the airport here and where it should be. Do you have any thoughts on that?

ABBAS Well, ⁶I might be wrong, but I think they should build the airport near Sibley. But not in the Nature Reserve.

LEONA But Sandstown already has an airport. Wouldn't it be cheaper just to make that airport bigger?

ABBAS ⁷That's a good point, but I think they could sell the land in Sandstown. ⁸I guess it's worth a lot of money. Then they could use that money to pay for the new airport. Yeah.

Review

VOCABULARY Expressing opinions, responding to opinions

1 a Complete the expressions for:

giving opinions
I t_ _ _ _ _ _ ...   We all k_ _ _ _ _ that ...
I really f_ _ _ _ _ that ...   The t_ _ _ _ _ is ...
I f_ _ _ it ...

disagreeing
S_ _ _ _ _ _ but ...   Y_ _ but ...
Well, not r_ _ _ _ _ _ _ .

agreeing
OK, that's a good p_ _ _ _ _ _ .
Yes, e_ _ _ _ _ _ _ .

b In groups, take turns to start conversations with these sentences and reply to them.

1   Let's go out tomorrow night. Do you know any good shows or films?
2   Let's go to a fast-food place after class.
3   Let's open the window. It's too hot in here.
4   Let's start running for fitness. We can go every morning.
5   Let's go for a picnic this weekend.

c Did you agree in the end? Tell the class.

GRAMMAR Unreal conditionals

2 a What would you do? Complete the sentences with your own ideas.

1   If I had the time, I'd ...
2   If I had the money, I'd ...
3   If I had the chance, I'd ...
4   If I had more energy, I'd ...
5   If I had a larger home, I'd ...
6   If I had a time machine, I'd ...

b Compare your ideas in groups. Ask questions to find out more.

CAN YOU REMEMBER? Unit 13 – Gadgets

3 a Match 1–6 with a–f to make sentences.

1	I use it	a	easier.
2	I don't know	b	have one at home.
3	It makes life	c	without it.
4	I have one but I	d	all the time.
5	I don't even	e	hardly ever use it.
6	I couldn't live	f	how to use them.

b Think of different gadgets you own such as:

• kitchen gadgets   • cleaning gadgets
• electronic dictionary or other study aids
• hairdryer, electric shaver, etc.

c Talk about them, using sentences 1–6.

> I have a hairdryer but I hardly ever use it.

Extension

SPELLING AND SOUNDS -le, -el, -al, -ul /əl/

4 a ● 3.54 These four endings have the same sound, /əl/. Listen and repeat.

people   channel   usual   awful

-ul is nearly always in the ending -ful.

b In pairs, complete the words with the correct endings.

nation___   skilf___   trav___   simp___
vow___   troub___   anim___   chann___
possib___   beautif___   capit___   wonderf___
usef___   vegetab___   hospit___

c ● 3.55 Spellcheck. Close your book. Listen to twelve words and write them down.

d Look at the script on p158 to check your spelling.

NOTICE waste, save

5 a Complete these sentences from Nandita's article with waste or save in the correct form.

1   These ideas helped me _____ money, too.
2   Does your refrigerator need to be so cold? Is your dishwasher only half full? It all _____ energy.
3   Change to low-energy bulbs. They _____ less energy, heat up the place less and last longer.
4   If you share a car with friends, you'll have fun and _____ fuel.
5   If we get a lot of sunlight, we shouldn't _____ it.

b Read the article on p116 to check.

c Think of ways you could waste less or save:
a   energy   b   money   c   time

d Compare your ideas. Are they the same or different?

Self-assessment

Can you do these things in English? Circle a number on each line. 1 = I can't do this, 5 = I can do this well.

⊚ express opinions	1	2	3	4	5
⊚ have a discussion	1	2	3	4	5
⊚ talk about imaginary situations	1	2	3	4	5
⊚ take part in a meeting	1	2	3	4	5
⊚ use expressions to soften opinions and disagreements	1	2	3	4	5

• For Wordcards, reference and saving your work » e-Portfolio
• For more practice » Self-study Pack, Unit 14

Activities

Unit 1, p12, An unusual athlete 8b (Student A)

Michelle Sung Wie
- (be) Korean-American professional golfer
- (be) born in Honolulu, Hawaii in 1989
- (begin) playing golf at the age of four
- (win) two major golf tournaments in Hawaii at the age of 11
- (become) a professional player at 15
- (be) 185cm tall and very strong
- (train) hard every day
- (want) to play in the Masters one day
- (prepare) for a tournament at the moment

Read the information about Michelle. Think about these questions.

1 What does she do?
2 How did she get into golf?
3 What's she doing at the moment?

Unit 14, p118, Target activity 3 (Group A)

You live in Sandstown, near the airport. You're going to have a meeting with someone from the government who wants to hear different people's opinions.

You don't want them to make the airport bigger because:
- the roads to and from the airport are too small and there's already too much traffic.
- the only possible space for a new terminal is a beautiful park near your home.

You think they should build a new airport further away from the town.

Discuss these questions.
1 What will you say? Can you think of more arguments?
2 Where do you think the new airport should be (near Sibley, or in the Nature Reserve)? Why?

Unit 13, p113, Look again 1a and b

Game 2 – Expressions with *time*

C, read the sentences. Say 'gap!' for the missing word.

Answers	
1 I need my mobile phone with me _____ the time	(all)
2 'Piensa en mi' is my favourite song of _____ time.	(all)
3 If you're busy tomorrow, we can meet _____ time.	(another)
4 In 1969, man walked on the moon for the _____ time.	(first)
5 I'm sorry I'll miss the lunch. I hope you _____ a good time.	(have)
6 Is this your _____ time in Canada?	(first)
7 We probably _____ a bit too much time surfing the Internet.	(spend)
8 Would you mind changing our appointment? _____ time is fine.	(Any)
9 I need my passport _____ time I go on holiday.	(every)

Unit 12, p99, Two small countries 6a (Student B)

The Maldives

Geography:	More than 1000 small islands (though only 250 populated) in Indian Ocean. Smallest country in Asia. Smallest Muslim country.
Population:	380,000
Language(s):	Dhivehi (official), English
Capital:	Malé
Government:	Elections every five years. Parliament (Majlis) elects a president.
Economy:	Tourism (about 0.5 million visitors a year), fishing
History:	Buddhist for over 2,000 years. Islam introduced 1153. Independence 1965.

Unit 4, p37, Telling a story 6a

beggar

sacar dinero → with deposit

Unit 4, p39, Independent learning 2b

1   Change the language on your computer to English.
2   Change the language on your mobile phone to English.
3   Listen to English radio programmes and podcasts.
4   Listen to English songs. Find the words on the Internet.
5   Make cards with English words on one side and a definition / picture on the other. Test yourself.
6   Make recordings of new English words and expressions. Listen to them on your way to work / school.
7   Meet your classmates half an hour before class begins. Chat in English.
8   Practise reading aloud a short text with the correct sounds and stress.
9   Read books in English. These can be special books for students, or children's books.
10   Visit Internet chatrooms for students of English.
11   Watch English-language films with subtitles in your own language.
12   Watch English-language TV programmes with a story – for example, soap operas.
13   Watch films with subtitles in English.
14   Write a diary in English. Write every day or every few days.
15   Write down new English words and expressions in a notebook. Read through them every few days.

chandal →

Unit 5, p43, How would you like to pay? 6a (Student A)

CONVERSATION 1	CONVERSATION 2
You're a customer in a small shop.	You're a receptionist in a museum.
Tick (✓) three things you'd like to buy.	You sell:
postcards of Glasgow	tickets £10 (adults) £6 (children) £4.50 (students, over-65s)
stamps	guided tours £2.50 extra
a drink	museum guidebooks £1.99 each
a local newspaper	postcards £1.50 each
a sandwich	books about Glasgow's history £10 each
a phone card	
	You don't have:
You'd like to pay by card.	maps of Glasgow
You have cash, but only a £50 note.	stamps
	You take cash or cards.
	You don't have any bags.

Unit 14, p118, Target activity 3 (Group B)

You live in the village of Sibley. You're going to have a meeting with someone from the government who wants to hear different people's opinions.

You don't want them to build the airport near the village because:
○ too many people will want to move there, it will get too crowded and there will be too much traffic.
○ tourists come to Sibley for the peace and quiet.

Discuss these questions.
1 Do you think they should make Sandstown Airport bigger, or build a new airport in the Nature Reserve? Why?
2 What will you say? Can you think of more arguments?

Unit 5, p45, Microcredit 6b (Student B)

http://www.microcreditsummit.org/stories/rukmani.htm

BORROWER SUCCESS STORIES
MICROCREDIT SUMMIT CAMPAIGN

"I had eleven children. Life wasn't easy," says Rukmani from Bidar in India. "There were days when we didn't have any food.

"When my children got married and left home, I got a loan of 200 rupees, and bought some pieces of metal from the shop where my husband worked. We used the metal to make useful things like knives. Then we sold them and made a profit.

"With a second loan, I started a small shop. Now my husband and I work together in the shop and make up to 100 rupees a day."

Unit 6, p50, Burning calories 4b

The cycle washer

Have you ever felt that there aren't enough hours in the day? These days we have to do our jobs, look after our homes, save energy to help the environment, and do exercise to stay healthy! Like many of us, Alex Gadsden never had enough time. He ran a business and a home and needed to lose weight. So he decided to do something about it. He invented the cycle washer.

The 29-year-old now starts each day with a 45-minute cycle ride. He not only feels healthier but he saves on his energy bills and does the washing too.

He said, "It gives the user a good workout. I've only used it for two weeks but I've already noticed a difference."

"I tend to get up at around six-thirty now and get straight on the cycle washer. I keep it in the garden, so it's nice to get out in the fresh air. Afterwards, I feel full of energy. Then I generally have breakfast and a shower and I really feel ready to start the day."

The green washing machine uses 25 litres of water a wash, and takes enough clothes to fill a carrier bag. He normally cycles for 25 minutes to wash the clothes, and then for another 20 minutes to dry them. And it doesn't use any electricity, of course.

Mr Gadsden, the boss of a cleaning company, believes his machine could become very popular. With an invention which cleans your clothes, keeps you fit and reduces your electricity bill, he may well be right.

[handwritten note: Bien puede/podría estar en lo cierto / tener razón]

5 a Read your article again and answer the questions about Alex.

1 Who had the idea?
2 How much time does he spend doing exercise at the moment?
3 What's his morning routine now?
4 How has it changed his life?

Unit 8, p69, It was made in ... 3 (Group A)

Mysteries.com

http://www.mysteries.com/sar.htm

The Piri Reis Map

This map _____ (find) in 1929 in Istanbul. It _____ (make) of animal skin. It _____ (draw) in 1513 by an admiral in the Turkish navy, Piri Reis. It _____ (show) the west coast of Africa and the east coast of South America.

It's famous because some people _____ (think) it also shows the coast of Antarctica. If true, this would be amazing, because the history books say the Antarctic _____ (discovered) in 1820. But other people _____ (say) that the map's 'Antarctica' is really just a bad drawing of part of South America.

Unit 9, p74, Why do we do it? 3b (Student B)

Why do people yawn?

Everyone yawns – babies, children, teenagers, adults – but the truth is that we don't completely understand why.

Many people think that we yawn when we're tired or bored because our bodies are trying to get more oxygen to the brain. In 1987, Robert Provine from the University of Maryland decided to test this idea. He asked groups of students to breathe different levels of oxygen for 30 minutes, and counted how many times they yawned. The result? All the students yawned about the same number of times.

So the traditional theory probably isn't true. It also fails to answer a lot of other questions. Why do some illnesses make people yawn more? Why do Olympic athletes sometimes yawn before a race? And what about 'group yawning', when people start yawning because they see other people yawning?

One study suggests we yawn when our brains are too hot. Yawning is simply a way of cooling the brain and helping it to work better. In the study, students were asked to watch videos of other people yawning, and the number of times they yawned in response was counted. It was found that the students yawned less often if they had something cold on their heads. People who breathed through their noses – another way of cooling the brain – did not yawn at all.

So it seems that we yawn not when we're bored, but as a way of cooling our brains when we're tired or ill. 'Group yawning' probably started many thousands of years ago, when it helped small groups of people to concentrate and notice dangers.

Unit 12, p99, Two small countries 6a (Student C)

Saint Kitts and Nevis

Geography:	Two islands in the Caribbean Sea: St Kitts (bigger) and Nevis (smaller, 3 km to the south-east of St Kitts). Smallest country in the Americas.
Population:	45,000. High emigration: population is 25% less than in 1960.
Language(s):	English
Capital:	Basseterre
Government:	Elections every four years. Parliament of 14 members.
Economy:	Banking, tourism, sugar
History:	Governed by Britain / France from 17th century. Independence 1983. Newest independent country in the Americas.

Unit 10, p87, Independent learning 4b

If you're in an English-speaking country:

Everyday situations

1 Restaurants, airports, stations, post offices, ticket offices, etc.
   - Plan what to say ahead of time. Look up useful words or expressions. Imagine what the other person might say and prepare answers.
2 Phone calls: making appointments, buying tickets, ordering food, etc.
   - Do the same as 1. Think of useful telephone expressions, then think of other useful language to use.
3 Announcements: airports, stations, etc.
   - Practise listening to announcements. Try to pick out key information: times, numbers, names, places.

The media

News on the television, radio or Internet: the weather, sports, etc.
- Think about or look up words or expressions for topics that are in the news. Then watch or listen to the news.

Other people

- Ask people to explain the meanings of interesting new words or expressions they use. Try to use them as soon as possible.

If you're in your own country:

The media

1 News on the Internet or radio: the weather, sports, etc.
   - Listen to or read the news in your own language first. Then listen to the news in English. It will be easier to understand.
   - Listen to the news on the Internet. Write down new words for one news item. Look them up, then listen to the news item again.

2 Films, TV shows
   - Watch English-speaking films or TV shows with subtitles or dubbed into your language. Then watch them in English. Repeat. Each time the film or TV show will be easier to understand.
   - Copy the English subtitles for a short scene from the screen. Translate them into your own language. Then listen to check.
3 Songs
   - Listen to songs to understand the main topic (love, etc.). Listen again and write down as many words as possible. Try to guess the story or the singer's ideas. Then read the lyrics to check.

Unit 2, p24, Explore speaking 5a (Student A)

Role card 1

You work for CSP.

Answer the phone and:

- explain that the person is not there
- take the caller's contact details and a message.

Unit 2, p24, Explore speaking 5b (Student A)

Role card 3

You work for Findajob. You want to find out about an ex-employee of CSP, Andy Koch.

Your name: Mukami Lelei

Your phone number: 0481 301 991

Your email address: m.lelei@findajob.com.au

Call CSP and:

- say you want to talk to Mrs McLachlan. You want to find out about an ex-employee, Andy Koch.
- leave your contact details and a message.

Unit 12, p99, Two small countries 1 (Student B)

SOUTH PACIFIC

Tuvalu

no ✏️

Tuvalu is a group of nine small islands in the South Pacific, between Australia and Hawaii. Polynesian people first came to the islands about 3000 years ago and, because they only lived on eight of the nine islands, they called them 'Tuvalu', which means 'eight standing together'. Tuvalu was governed by Britain from the late nineteenth century until 1 October 1978, when it became an independent country.

live in city
live on an island

Nowadays Tuvalu is a member of the United Nations and its official languages are Tuvaluan and English. Most of its 12,000 people live in Funafuti, the capital. It has a prime minister and a parliament (*Fale i Fono*) of just fifteen members. Although Tuvalu has elections every four years, there are no political parties. People generally vote for friends, family members and well-known people.

The government's largest source of income is renting out its internet domain name, which is '.tv'. It also rents out its international phone code (900) and makes money by selling stamps and coins to collectors. Traditionally, each family on Tuvalu has its own work to do (*salanga*), for example fishing, farming, defence, or house-building. There are very few tourists in Tuvalu simply because it's so difficult to get to. There is one small airport with flights to and from Fiji, no railway, and just eight kilometres of roads.

La mayor fuente de ingre-
sos del gobierno es alquilar
su dominio de internet

The highest point in the islands is only five metres above the sea, so climate change is a big worry for the people of Tuvalu. If the water rises by a few centimetres, it will be impossible to live there.

Answer the questions.

1 Where is it? How big is it?
2 How many people live there?
3 What jobs do people do?

4 Does it get many visitors?
5 What languages do people use?
6 How does it make money?

Unit 12, p99, Two small countries 6a (Student A)

San Marino

Geography:	In the Apennine Mountains in Italy. 61 km². 33% the size of Washington DC.
Population:	30,000
Language(s):	Italian (official), Emiliano-Romagnolo
Capital:	City of San Marino
Government:	Elections every five years. Parliament (*Consiglio*) with 60 members chooses two 'captains' from different parties every 6 months.
Economy:	More than 2 million tourists a year. Also banking, electronics, wine, stamps. Now one of the world's richest countries.
History:	Founded over 2,300 years ago by Marinus of Rab (Croatia). The world's oldest republic.

Unit 11, p97 Look again 3a (Student B)

Hotel expressions
- private parking
- air conditioning
- a single room
- an en-suite bathroom
- a business centre

Activities

Unit 13, p113, Look again 1a and b

Game 1 – Telephone expressions

C, read the sentences with telephone expressions. Say 'gap!' for the missing word.

> Can I *gap!* to John Andrews, please?

Answers
1	Can I _____ to John Andrews, please?	(speak)
2	Is _____ Christine Andrews?	(that)
3	_____ Christine, his wife.	(It's)
4	Just a _____, please.	(moment)
5	I'm sorry but John isn't _____ at the moment.	(here)
6	Do you want me to take a _____?	(message)
7	Could you ask him to _____ me?	(call)
8	Is this a good _____ to talk?	(time)
9	I'll call you _____ later.	(back)

Unit 14, p118, Target activity 3 (Group C)

You're an environmentalist working in the Nature Reserve. You're going to have a meeting with someone from the government who wants to hear different people's opinions.

You don't want them to build the airport in the reserve because:
- the reserve has a lot of unusual birds and animals, which you can't find anywhere else in the country.
- local people need somewhere quiet and beautiful where they can spend time.

Discuss these questions.
1   Do you think they should make Sandstown Airport bigger, or build a new airport in Sibley? Why?
2   What will you say? Can you think of more arguments?

Unit 1, p12, An unusual athlete 8b (Student B)

Vincent Mantsoe
– (be) a dancer, choreographer and teacher
– (be) born in Soweto, South Africa
– as a boy (dance) with youth clubs, practising street dances
– (copy) dance moves from videos
– (train) with the Johannesburg Moving into Dance company
– (create) own style of dance, called Afro-fusion
– now (have) his own international company of dancers
– the company (include) dancers from France, South Africa, the USA and Japan
– (prepare) a big new show at the moment

Read the information about Vincent. Think about these questions.

1   What does he do?
2   How did he get into dancing?
3   What's he doing at the moment?

Unit 11, p97, Look again 3a (Student A)

Hotel expressions
- a business hotel
- a double room
- a twin room
- a health club
- a buffet breakfast

Unit 10, p85, Plans and arrangements 4b

Hi Leonardo,

It was really nice to see you again after so many years – and great to catch up on all your news. Thanks again for a lovely dinner. And thank you for the flowers – they're beautiful!

I hope you had a good flight home and are not too tired. Keep in touch – and see you in May!

Min

Unit 2, p24, Explore speaking 5a (Student B)

Role card 2

You are Jake Sanders and you work for Findajob.

Call CSP and:

- say you want to talk to Sara Moore. You want to find out about an ex-employee, Megan Simmons.
- leave your contact details and a message.

Your phone number: 0443 657 234

Your email address: j.sanders@findajob.com.au

Unit 5, p43, How would you like to pay? 6a (Student B)

CONVERSATION 1

You're an assistant in a small shop.

You sell:
postcards of Glasgow 80p each
books of 12 stamps £3.50 each
local newspaper £1.20 each
phone cards £5 or £10 each

You don't have:
drinks
sandwiches

You don't take cards, only cash.
You don't want any big notes.

CONVERSATION 2

You're a visitor to a museum.

Choose the kind of ticket you want.
an adult ticket, a child ticket (under 18),
a student ticket, a senior citizen ticket (over 65)

Tick (✓) three more things you'd like to buy.
a museum guidebook
a guided tour of the museum
a map of Glasgow
a book about Glasgow's history
postcards
stamps

You'd like to pay by card.
You'd like a bag.

Unit 8, p69, It was made in ... 3 (Group B)

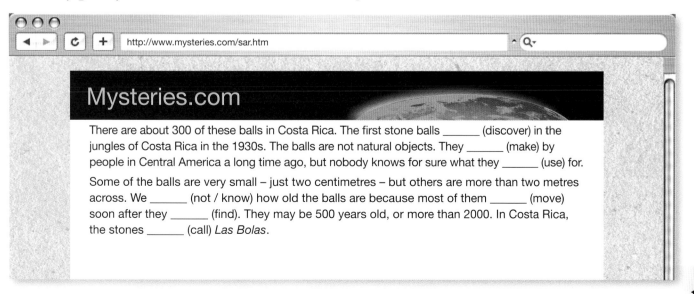

Mysteries.com

http://www.mysteries.com/sar.htm

There are about 300 of these balls in Costa Rica. The first stone balls _____ (discover) in the jungles of Costa Rica in the 1930s. The balls are not natural objects. They _____ (make) by people in Central America a long time ago, but nobody knows for sure what they _____ (use) for.

Some of the balls are very small – just two centimetres – but others are more than two metres across. We _____ (not / know) how old the balls are because most of them _____ (move) soon after they _____ (find). They may be 500 years old, or more than 2000. In Costa Rica, the stones _____ (call) Las Bolas.

Unit 9, p74, Why do we do it? 3b (Student C)

Why do people cry?

The human eye produces three kinds of tears. Basal tears are produced all the time to keep our eyes wet and help us to see. Reflex tears clean our eyes when we get dirt in them or, for example, chop onions. Emotional tears are produced when we're very sad or happy, or in great pain. Interestingly, emotional tears contain a lot of chemicals and hormones which we don't find in the other kinds of tear.

Basal and reflex tears are certainly useful, but why do we produce emotional tears?

Why do emotional tears have a different chemistry from other tears? Why do we cry at all? There seem to be two answers to these questions.

First, when we feel very strong emotions like extreme sadness or happiness, our bodies make a lot of extra chemicals and hormones. Then, when we cry, our emotional tears take these chemicals and hormones out of our bodies. This may be why people sometimes say that they 'feel better' after crying. One of the hormones in emotional tears is prolactin.

Women usually have about twice as much prolactin in their bodies as men, and this may explain why women cry more often than men.

The second reason for crying is to communicate with other people. Babies can't speak, so they use crying to tell people when they're hungry, frightened, and so on. As adults, we cry less often but we probably cry for the same reasons: to show people that we're in physical or emotional pain, and that we need help.

Unit 12, p103, Independent learning 4

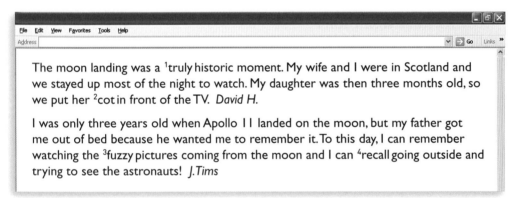

The moon landing was a [1]truly historic moment. My wife and I were in Scotland and we stayed up most of the night to watch. My daughter was then three months old, so we put her [2]cot in front of the TV. *David H.*

I was only three years old when Apollo 11 landed on the moon, but my father got me out of bed because he wanted me to remember it. To this day, I can remember watching the [3]fuzzy pictures coming from the moon and I can [4]recall going outside and trying to see the astronauts! *J.Tims*

Unit 14 Target activity 3 (Group D)

You work for the government, at the Department of Transport. You live and work hundreds of kilometres from Sandstown, but it's your job to decide what to do about the airport.

You go to Sandstown to meet people and hear their opinions. You organise a meeting with three people:
- someone who lives near the airport in Sandstown.
- someone who lives in the village of Sibley.
- someone who works at the Nature Reserve.

Discuss these questions.
1 At the moment, do you have an opinion about which solution is best?
2 What will you say at the meeting? What questions will you ask?

Unit 2, p24, Explore speaking 5b (Student B)

Role card 4
You work for CSP.
Answer the phone and:
- explain that the person is not there
- take the caller's contact details and a message.

Unit 3, p27, Food and you 5

basil cheese chicken cream curry fruit herbs lasagne

mushrooms salad sauces spices strawberries vegetables

Unit 3, p28, Eating out 4

bread cake cucumber ice cream oil olives pasta a pear

potatoes prawns rice salmon soup steak tomatoes

Unit 3, p32, Explore writing 2

Verbs for preparing

chop cut pour serve shake stir

Verbs for cooking

bake boil fry grill roast toast

Grammar reference and practice

1 PRESENT SIMPLE, PAST SIMPLE, PRESENT PROGRESSIVE

MEANING

You can vhappen all the time.
I live in Frankfurt in Germany.
I play tennis with my sister every weekend.

You can use the past simple to talk about things that are in the past and finished.
When I was fifteen, I decided to be a doctor.
I studied for seven years.

You can use the present progressive to talk about things happening now, or around now.
Sorry, I can't go out now. I'm waiting for a phone call.
I'm reading a really interesting book about the history of Turkey.

FORM

	present simple	past simple	present progressive
❓	Where do you live?	What did you study?	What are you waiting for?
➕	I live in Frankfurt.	I studied medicine.	I'm waiting for a phone call.
➖	I don't live in Berlin.	I didn't study languages.	I'm not waiting for you.
❓	Do you play tennis?	Did you have a good weekend?	Are you listening to me?
✔	Yes, I do.	Yes, I did.	Yes, I am.
✘	No, I don't.	No, I didn't.	No, I'm not.

Remember...
(1) In the present simple, verbs with *he / she / it* have s or es.
Where does he live? He lives in Frankfurt. He doesn't live in Berlin. Does he play tennis? Yes, he does. No, he doesn't.

(2) In the past simple, some verbs are regular and others are irregular.
Regular: *play > played   decide > decided   study > studied*
Irregular: *be > was / were   have > had   go > went*

(3) In the present progressive, you can make negatives in two ways.
You aren't listening to me. You're not listening to me.
No, you aren't. No, you're not.

But there's only one kind of negative with *I*.
I'm not talking to you.
No, I'm not.

PRONUNCIATION

Question words and main verbs usually have stress.
Where do you live?   I live in Frankfurt.

But in negative sentences and short answers, do / did / be or not also have stress.
I didn't study languages.   You aren't listening to me.
Yes, he does.   No, I'm not.

PRACTICE

1 Complete the sentences with the correct form of the verb.
1 Why don't you call Alain now? He usually __*finishes*__ (finish) work early on Fridays.
2 It (rain) _____ all day yesterday so we _____ (decide) to stay at home.
3 Ahmed _____ (not work) today. He's ill.
4 I _____ (not drive), so I usually walk to places when I can, or get buses.
5 I _____ (see) Helena in town yesterday. And guess what? She _____ (get) married last month.
6 Can we make something vegetarian? Pam _____ (not eat) meat.
7 Sorry, Petra _____ (talk) to a client at the moment. Can you phone back later?
8 When I _____ (be) a child, we _____ (not have) a lot of money, so we _____ (not go) to restaurants.

2 **a** Complete the questions with do, does, did or are.
1 How often __*do*__ you cook for more than two people?
2 When _____ you have your first English lesson?
3 What time _____ you usually go to bed?
4 What _____ you doing at work these days?
5 Where _____ you get your watch?
6 How _____ you meet your oldest friend?
7 How often _____ it snow in your home town?
8 How many books _____ you reading at the moment?

b Ask and answer the questions.

2 PRESENT PERFECT 1 – FOR EXPERIENCE

MEANING

You can use the present perfect to talk about experiences up to now, from past to present.

I've seen all Almodóvar's films.
Oh really? I haven't seen any of them.

Don't use the present perfect with finished times in the past.
~~I've been to Tokyo four years ago.~~ I went to Tokyo four years ago.
~~I've seen Jane last week.~~ I saw Jane last week.

You can use ever in questions and negatives. Ever means 'in my / your whole life'.
Have you ever been to Japan?
I haven't ever been to Germany.

FORM

have / has + past participle.

I, you, we, they	he, she, it
➕ I've seen all Almodóvar's films.	➕ She's visited more than twenty countries.
➖ We haven't met Jane's husband. We've never met Jane's husband.	➖ He hasn't done a computer course. He's never used a computer.
❓ Have they been to Japan? Yes, they have. No, they haven't.	❓ Has he taken his driving test? Yes, he has. No, he hasn't.

Contractions:
➕ I've = I have   you've = you have   we've = we have
they've = they have
he's = he has   she's = she has   it's = it has

➖ haven't = have not
hasn't = has not

Some past participles are regular and end in -ed. They're the same as the past simple.
like > liked   smoke > smoked   visit > visited

Some past participles are irregular but the same as the past simple.
buy > bought   have > had   meet > met

Some past participles are irregular and different from the past simple. They often end with *n*.
eat > ate > eaten   do > did > done   see > saw > seen

See *Irregular verbs* on p160.

PRONUNCIATION

You usually stress the past participle.

You don't usually stress have / has in positive sentences and questions.

I've seen all Almodóvar's films.   Has he met Jane?

But you usually stress have / has in negative sentences and short answers.

We haven't met Jane's husband.   Yes, they have.   No, she hasn't.

You often say *been* as /bɪn/.

PRACTICE

1 a Complete these sentences with the verbs in (brackets) in the present perfect or past simple.
1 A Have you ever _been_ to India?
   B Yes, I _went_ there in 2006. (go)
2 A Have you _____ any Brazilian films?
   B Yes, I've _____ City of God. (see)
3 A Have you ever _____ anything creative?
   B Well, I _____ some short stories a few years ago. (write)
4 A Have you _____ any computer courses?
   B Yes, I _____ one on web design when I was a student. (do)
5 A What languages have you _____ ?
   B Well, I _____ English and German at school. (study)
6 A Have you ever _____ a politician?
   B Yes, I _____ my local politician last year. (meet)

b Ask the questions and give your own answers.

PRESENT PERFECT 2 – WITH *FOR* AND *SINCE*

MEANING

You can also use the present perfect to talk about situations which began in the past and continue in the present.
I've lived here for ten years.
I haven't eaten since breakfast.

FORM AND PRONUNCIATION

See *present perfect 1* – for experience.

PRACTICE

1 a Add for or since to these sentences.

1 My parents have lived in the same house *since* they got married.
2 My mum's had the same hairstyle about fifteen years.
3 I've had the same computer five years.
4 There hasn't been any snow in my country 2008.
5 I've known my best friend school.
6 My brother's worked at the same company he left university.

b Make the sentences true for you. Then compare with a partner.

3 NOUNS WITH PREPOSITIONAL PHRASES

MEANING

You can use prepositional phrases to give extra information about nouns.

Let's go to the restaurant. Which restaurant? *The restaurant in the town centre.*

I'd like the salad. Which salad? *The salad with blue cheese.*

Can you give me my book? Which book? *The book on the table.*

FORM

Prepositional phrases can go *after a noun*.

      noun   prepositional phrase

Let's go to the restaurant in the town centre.

Adjectives usually go *before a noun*.

      adjective   noun

Let's go to the Italian restaurant.

You can use adjectives and prepositional phrases together.

    adjective   noun   prepositional phrase

Let's go to the Italian restaurant in the town centre

prepositional phrase

next to the cinema.

PRONUNCIATION

You usually stress the nouns, not the prepositions.

The restaurant in the town centre.

The salad with blue cheese.

The book on the table.

You usually say the prepositions of, for and to as /əv/, /fə/ and /tə/ in sentences.

PRACTICE

1 **Complete the sentences with from, in, on or with.**

1 *Churrasco* is grilled meat _*with*_ salt and garlic.
2 This is Rajeev, my friend _____ work.
3 Let's go to the coffee shop _____ the corner.
4 I usually have my tea _____ milk.
5 The food _____ that supermarket is cheap.
6 The girl _____ blonde hair is my sister.
7 Do you know the man _____ the grey suit?
8 He has a house _____ a small garden.
9 The hotel _____ the hill has a great view.
10 The market _____ the town centre is good for fresh fruit.

2 - from
3 - on
4 - with
5 - from
6 - with
7 - in
8 - with
9 - on
10 - in

2 **a Put the words in order to make sentences.**

1 in red wine sauce / sounds nice / Steak. *Steak in red wine sauce sounds nice.*
2 with potatoes / is / Grilled salmon / my favourite dish .
3 today / the cheese plate / Do you have / with fruit bread ?
4 tomato / is / The soup of the day / with basil .
5 fresh fruit salad / I'd like the / for dessert, please / with cream .
6 with milk and sugar / please / two coffees / Can we have ?

b What do you think of the dishes and drinks in 2a? Would you order them in a restaurant?

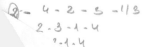

2 - 4 - 2 - 5 - 1/3
2 - 3 - 1 - 4
3 - 1 - 4

⑤ 2 - 1 - 4 - 3
⑥ - 3 - 4 - 2 - 1

4 PAST PROGRESSIVE

MEANING

You can use the past progressive to talk about an action that was in progress at a time in the past.

I started making the dinner at 5.30 pm.
At 6.00 pm I was making the dinner. (point in time = 6.00 pm)
The dinner was ready at 7.00 pm

I left work at 4.00 pm.
When you phoned me, I was driving home. (point in time = when you phoned me)
I got home at 4.20 pm.

6.00 pm   you phoned me   NOW

making the dinner   driving home

Compare the past simple and the past progressive:
I made the dinner yesterday. (talking about a finished action)
At 6 pm yesterday, I was making the dinner. (saying an action was in progress at a time in the past)

When she phoned me, I drove home. (She phoned me, and then I drove home.)
When she phoned me, I was driving home. (She phoned me in the middle of my journey home.)

FORM

was / were + -ing	
❓ What were you doing at 6 pm yesterday?	❓ Were you driving home when I called?
➕ I was making the dinner.	➕ Yes, I was.
➖ I wasn't watching TV.	➖ No, I wasn't.

Remember:
I / he / she / it was
you / we / they were

PRONUNCIATION

In positive sentences and questions, you don't usually stress was and were. We say /wəz/ and /wə/.
In negative sentences and short answers, you usually stress was and were. We say /wɒz/ and /wɜː/.

Who was making the dinner?   I was making the dinner.

You weren't making the dinner.

Yes, I was.

PRACTICE

1 **Complete the sentences with the verbs in brackets in the past progressive.**

1 We first met Jim and Esin when we _*were travelling*_ in Turkey. (travel)
2 What _____ you _____ when I called you? There was no answer. (do)
3 It _____ when I left my flat this morning. Now it's hot and sunny. (rain)
4 My brother _____ the computer so I used it to check my email. (not use)
5 "Where's Ben?" "He _____ in the garden about an hour ago." (play)
6 I saw an accident when I _____ to work this morning. (drive)

2 - were / doing
3 - was raining
4 - wasn't using
5 - was playing   8 - wasn't falli
6 - was driving
7 - was / doing

7 _____ Pedro _____ his homework when you saw him? (do)

8 I went home at about two o'clock yesterday. I _____ well. (not feel)

2 (Circle) the best verb form in each sentence.

1 I (went) / was going to bed at two in the morning but …

2 … I couldn't sleep. My neighbours had / were having a party.

3 Sorry, can you say that again? I didn't listen / wasn't listening.

4 When I was younger, my family lived / was living in Berlin for three years.

5 The family had / were having lunch when the police arrived / were arriving.

6 The last time I saw / was seeing Joanna, she lived / was living in Paris.

7 I first met / was meeting my husband when I stood / was standing at a bus stop.

8 We worked / were working abroad when we had / were having our first child.

5 HAVE TO, CAN

MEANING

Use have to to say that something is necessary (now, in the future or in general).
Sorry, but I have to go now. My taxi's waiting for me. (now)
I have to get up at five o'clock tomorrow morning. My train leaves at ten past six. (in the future)
On a normal working day I have to be at the office before nine-thirty. (in general)

Use don't / doesn't have to to say something is not necessary.
Please start eating. You don't have to wait for me.

Use can to say that something is possible (now, in the future or in general).
You can use my phone if you want. (now)
We can meet again next weekend if you have time. (in the future)
You can pay your phone bill at the post office or on the Internet. (in general)

Use can't to say something is not possible.
I'd like to buy a flat but I can't get a loan from the bank.

FORM

I, you, we, they	he, she, it
➊ I have to go now.	Alain has to get up early tomorrow.
➋ I don't have to go until ten.	Rebecca doesn't have to get up until nine.
➌ Do you have to go so soon?	Does Rebecca have to work tomorrow?
✔ Yes, I do.	Yes, she does.
✘ No, I don't.	No, she doesn't.

I, you, he, she, it, we, they
➊ You can get married when you're 18.
➋ You can't get married when you're 16.
➌ Can you get married when you're 16?
✔ Yes, you can.
✘ No, you can't.

PRONUNCIATION

You usually stress have / has but not to. Have to and has to are often pronounced /ˈhæftə/ and /ˈhæstə/.
I have to go.

You don't usually stress can in positive sentences and questions. You say /kən/.
You can use my phone.   Can you smoke when you're sixteen?

You usually stress can in negative sentences and short answers. You say /kæn/ and /kɑːnt/.
Yes, you can. /kæn/

You can't drive when you're fourteen.   No, you can't. /kɑːnt/

PRACTICE

1 Complete the sentences with the correct form of can or have to, positive or negative.

1 Is there a cash machine near here? I _____ get some money.

2 "Can I make myself a cup of coffee?" "Of course you can. You _____ ask."

3 Where I live, you _____ buy anything after five p.m. All the shops are closed.

4 Carlo's not coming to work this morning. He _____ go to the doctor's.

5 OK, I can hear you! You _____ shout!

6 People think Poland's a cold country, but summers in Poland _____ be really hot.

7 Our company likes its employees to dress smartly. You _____ wear jeans, and men _____ wear a tie.

8 Sorry, I _____ meet you for lunch tomorrow. I _____ go to work.

2 a Order the words to make questions.

1 do get up have to on a typical day What time you ?
What time do you have to get up on a typical day?

2 Can manage online you your bank account ?

3 at weekends do have to How often work or study you ?

4 children in your country do go have to How many years to school ?

5 join people in your country Can the army when they're 16 ?

6 Do English ever have to for your work or studies use you ?

7 do do have to tomorrow What things you ?

8 go students in your country to university without paying Can ?

b Discuss the questions.

[handwritten notes:]
2 (8 - were having
5 - wasn't listening
4 - lived
5 - were having / arrived
6 - saw / was living
7 - met / was standing
8 - were working / had .

6 COMPARING THINGS

MEANING

Monday	Tuesday	Wednesday	Thursday
28°C	24°C	24°C	19°C

Comparatives
Monday was sunnier than Tuesday.
Thursday's weather was much cooler than Monday's.

Superlatives
Monday's weather was the hottest and sunniest.
Thursday's was the coldest and wettest.

as ... as
Tuesday was as warm as Wednesday.
Tuesday wasn't as warm as Monday.

FORM

Spelling rules	Adjective	Comparative	Superlative
most one-syllable adjectives	fast	faster	the fastest
one-syllable adjectives ending in one short vowel + a consonant	big	bigger	the biggest
most two-syllable adjectives	careful	more careful	the most careful
two-syllable adjectives ending in –y	happy	happier	the happiest
adjectives with three syllables or more	comfortable	more comfortable	the most comfortable

Some common irregular comparatives and superlatives are:
good – better – best
bad – worse – worst
far – further – furthest

PRONUNCIATION

You usually stress more and adjectives. You don't stress than and -er. You say /ðən/ and /ə/.

This camera's more expensive than my old one.

It's harder working at home than in an office.

You usually stress most and adjectives. You don't stress the and –est. You say /ðə/ and /ɪst/.

This is the most comfortable room in my flat.

I'm the tallest in my family.

But when *the* is in front of a word starting with a vowel, we pronounce it with an /iː/.

the earliest   the oldest

You don't usually stress *as*. You say /əz/.

I don't think you're as tall as me.

PRACTICE

1 Complete the sentences with the correct form of the adjectives.

1 It's much _____ (wet) in the north of the country than in the south.
2 He's _____ (relaxed) person I know.
3 Amie is much _____ (happy) now than she was.
4 Jaynie is as _____ (good) at her job as Matt is.
5 He's much _____ (energetic) than I am.
6 That's the _____ (bad) meal I've ever had here.
7 This report isn't as _____ (interesting) as the last one.
8 Is this the _____ (good) hotel you could find?

2 Order the words to make sentences.

1 the / Running the marathon / is / difficult thing / I've ever done / most .
2 cheerful / when it's sunny / I'm usually / more .
3 getting a taxi / Getting a bus / is / easy / as / as .
4 frozen vegetables / good / I think / as / fresh ones / are / as .
5 intelligent / person I know / My brother / most / is / the .
6 worst / way to travel / Organised holidays / the / are .
7 to get fit / than / Doing exercise / a healthier way / is / dieting .
8 as / last summer / isn't / This summer / nice / as .

7 *WILL, MIGHT, MAY*

MEANING

You can use will to say you are sure about something in the future.
In 2050, 70% of people around the world will live in cities. (future)

But you can also use will to talk about now, or about things in general.
A Shall I phone Irina?
B No, call her later. She'll be at work now. (now)

I work with a really good team. If you have a problem, they'll always try to help. (in general)

You can use will with other words to show that you are more or less sure.
+++ *Brazil will definitely win the next World Cup.*
 ++ *Brazil will win.*
  + *Brazil will probably win.*
  ? *Maybe / Perhaps Brazil will win.*

You can use both might and may to say you're not sure about something.
A Shall we have a barbecue tomorrow?
B I'm not sure. It might / may rain. (future)

A Where's Irina?
B I don't know. She might / may be in a meeting. (now)

A Where's Lagos?
B I don't know. I think it might / may be in Nigeria. (in general)

May is a little more formal than might. May is more common in formal kinds of writing, but might is more common in everyday speech.

There is an important difference between might / may and can.
The supermarket might / may be crowded on Saturday. (I'm not sure if it will be crowded on Saturday.)
The supermarket can be crowded on Saturday. (I'm sure it is sometimes crowded on Saturday.)

FORM

will / might / may + infinitive without to

➕	➖	❓	✅/❌
It'll / It will rain.	*It won't / will not rain.*	*Will it rain?*	*Yes, it will. / No, it won't.*
It might rain.	*It might not rain.*	-	*It might. / It might not.*
It may rain.	*It may not rain.*	-	*It may. / It may not.*

PRONUNCIATION

You usually contract will like this: 'll /əl/ and won't /wəʊn(t)/.

You don't usually stress will / might / may.

Will Amy pass her exam next week?   I think she'll try her best.

They might cancel the party.

But you stress won't, not and short answers.

She won't pass.   She might not pass.   She might.

PRACTICE

Complete the sentences with will or might in the positive or negative.

1 A What are you doing tonight?
   B Nothing. I'm really tired so I __'ll__ just stay in.
2 A Where are you going?
   B Sorry, I just have to go to the bank. I _____ be long.
3 A Are Penny and Alex here yet?
   B No, they said they _____ be late. It depends on the traffic.
4 A Will you finish painting the kitchen today?
   B No, I'm tired. I _____ probably do it in the morning.
5 A Why isn't Jacob at work today?
   B I don't know. He hasn't called. He _____ be ill.
6 A Do you know where Ahmed is?
   B Yes, he _____ be in the café next door. He always has lunch there.
7 A Shall I give Lucy a call?
   B OK, but call her on her mobile. She _____ be at home until six.
8 A Can we meet again tomorrow?
   B I'm not sure. I'm pretty busy tomorrow so I _____ be able to see you.

(handwritten answers:)
2- won't
3- may
4- will
5- may
6- will
7- won't
8- may not

REAL CONDITIONALS

MEANING

You can use real conditionals to do a lot of different things. For example:
If you want to visit this country, you have to get a visa.
(giving information)
If you're interested in ballet, you must see Carlos Acosta.
(recommending something)
If you're not feeling well, you can go home. (giving permission)
If you've worked here for five years, you should ask for a pay rise.
(giving advice / your opinion)
If I see Jeff tomorrow, I'll give him your phone number.
(making a promise)

In all these sentences, the speaker feels that the situation in the *if* part of the sentence (*If you want to visit this country...*, etc.) is real or possible.

FORM

Conditional sentences have two parts:

if-clause   main clause
***If** it rains tomorrow, **we**'ll stay at home.*

You can reverse the two parts. In this case you don't usually write a comma (,).

main clause   *if*-clause
***We**'ll stay at home **if** it rains tomorrow.*

PRONUNCIATION

The pronunciation of real conditionals is the same as in other sentences. For example, we usually stress verbs and nouns but not modal verbs or prepositions.

If it rains tomorrow, we'll stay at home.

PRACTICE

Circle the correct form of the verb.

1 Can you give me your mobile number? I call / 'll call you if I need / 'll need some help.
2 Don't worry if I 'm / 'll be late home tonight. I've got loads of work at the office.
3 You've worked really hard. I 'll be / 'm very surprised if you don't / won't pass the exam.
4 If you come / 'll come to Sao Paulo again, you come / must come and see us.
5 If you 're / 'll be interested in antiques, you love / 'll love this museum.
6 If there 's / 'll be a lot of traffic tomorrow , we leave / 'll leave home early.
7 If you go / 'll go to the shops later, do / will you get me a paper?
8 You leave / should leave now if you don't / won't want to be late.

8 SOME AND ANY

MEANING

You use some and any with plural nouns when you don't need to say exactly how many.
I need to buy some apples. (= more than one apple)
I don't need to buy any apples. (= more than one apple)
I'd like an apple, please. (= one apple)
I don't like apples. (= apples in general)

You also use some and any with non-count nouns when you don't need to say exactly how much.
We have to get some milk.
Can you give me some help?
We haven't got any tea.
Do you need any help?

FORM

You usually use some in positive sentences and any in negative sentences.
I'd like some coffee, please.
Sorry, we don't have any coffee.

In questions we often use any.
Do you have any milk?

But you use some in questions when you expect the answer "yes", or when you'd like the answer to be "yes".
Would you like some milk? (= an offer)
Can I have some milk? (= a request)

PRONUNCIATION

You don't usually stress some and any. You usually say some with a schwa (ə) /səm/.
I'd like some coffee.

But at the end of a sentence you stress some and any. You say /sʌm/ and /ˈeniː/.
I have some. I don't have any.

PRACTICE

1 Complete the sentences with some or any and one of these words.

cash   emails   hotels   information   ~~milk~~
old friends   rice   help

1 Is black coffee OK? I'm afraid we don't have **any milk**.
2 I'm really sorry, I didn't buy _____. Can we have pasta?
3 Is there a bank near here? I need to get _____.
4 I spent last weekend with _____. We had a great time.
5 Can you help me? I'd like _____ about flights to Paris.
6 I'm looking for somewhere to stay in the city. Do you know _____ near here?
7 I haven't written to my friends for a while. I really need to write _____.
8 I don't need _____ with my suitcase, thanks.

2 Circle the best word in the questions.

1 Do you have some / any brothers or sisters?
2 Have you done some / any exercise this week?
3 Could I have some / any orange juice, please?
4 Do you speak some / any foreign languages?
5 Can you give me some / any time to think about it?
6 Can I have some / any more paper, please?

PASSIVES

MEANING

1 Compare:
Alessandro Volta invented the electric battery in 1800. (ACTIVE)
In this sentence, the writer is most interested in Alessandro Volta. The sentence could be from an article about Volta's life.

The electric battery was invented in 1800. (PASSIVE)
In this sentence, the writer is most interested in the electric battery. The sentence could be from an article about the history of the battery.

2 You can use by to say who does / did the action in a passive sentence.
The electric battery was invented by Alessandro Volta in 1800.

But often you don't use by because you don't know who did the action, or it's not important.
Two hundred bikes are stolen in this city every week.
Did you hear? Mike was offered a job yesterday.

FORM

You always make passives with be + past participle.

	Present simple passive am / is / are + past participle	Past simple passive was / were + past participle
➕	They're made of glass.	It was invented in 1820.
➖	They aren't made of plastic.	It wasn't invented in the 18th century.
❓	Are they made of glass?	Was it invented in the 19th century?
✔	Yes, they are.	Yes, it was.
✘	No, they aren't.	No, it wasn't.

PRONUNCIATION

You usually stress the past participle.

You don't usually stress be in positive sentences and questions.

It was made in China.   Was it made in China?

But you usually stress be in negative sentences and short answers.

It wasn't made in China.   Yes, it was.

PRACTICE

1   Put the words in order to make passive sentences.

1   ago   this bill   sent   two weeks   was .
2   in   the Great Wall of China   the 6th century BC   started   was .
3   are   these offices   every morning   cleaned   ?
4   invented   Alexander Bell   the telephone   by   was .
5   lost   my sister's   books   in the post   were .
6   radium   Maria Skłodowska-Curie   discovered   was   by .
7   two-thirds   with water   covered   of the Earth   is .
8   John F. Kennedy   killed   in Dallas   was   in 1963 .

2   Complete the sentences with the active or passive, present or past. Use these verbs.

build   give   include   drink

1   a   This house _____ by my grandparents.
    b   My grandparents _____ this house.
2   a   Where I live, the rent _____ gas and electricity.
    b   Where I live, gas and electricity _____ in the rent.
3   a   This necklace _____ to me by my husband.
    b   My husband _____ me this necklace.
4   a   About a billion cans of Coca-Cola _____ every day.
    b   People _____ about a billion cans of Coca-Cola every day.

⑨ PRESENT PERFECT 3 – GIVING NEWS

MEANING

You can use the present perfect to talk about actions which:
- are in the past and finished, but
- have a result in the present.
I've passed my driving test. (present result: Now I have a driving licence.)
She's lost her keys. (present result: Now she doesn't have her keys.)
They've moved home. (present result: now they're looking for a new home.)

You can use the present perfect in this way to give news.
Have you heard? Howard and Jola have had a baby!
Germany have won the World Cup.
There's been an earthquake in the north.

Note: speakers of American English often use the past simple for giving news.
I lost Jane's keys.
Did you hear? Howard and Jola had a baby!

Remember that you use the past simple, not the present perfect, if you say when something happened.
Howard and Jola had a baby yesterday! ~~have had~~
There was an earthquake in the north this morning. There~~'s been~~.

With go there are two forms of the present perfect. They have different meanings.
Sorry, Rachel isn't here. She's gone to the dentist. (She went to the dentist and now she isn't here.)
I'm sorry I'm late. I've been to the dentist. (I went to the dentist and came back.)

FORM

Look at the grammar reference for unit 2 on p133.

PRONUNCIATION

Look at the grammar reference for unit 2 on p133.

PRACTICE

1   Complete the sentences with these verbs in the present perfect.

~~do~~   fail   leave   die   make   write   see   win

1   Ah, you *'ve done* the washing up. Thanks very much.
2   Congratulations! You _____ a two-week holiday in Kyoto.   *have won*
3   Jitka's a bit sad today. Her cat _____ just _____.   *have died*
4   Happy birthday! We _____ you a cake.   *4) had made*
5   I can't find my keys. I'm sure I _____ them today, but I don't know where!   *5- have been*
6   Oh no! I _____ my economics exam. I'll have to do it again in January.   *6- have failed*
7   The police are looking for Greg, but I think he _____ the country.   *7- had left*
8   I _____ about 40 emails today. I never want to see a computer again!   *8- have written*

2   Make questions with the present perfect.

1   The Internet's not working. we / pay / the last bill?
    Have we paid the last bill?
2   I thought we could go to Stefan's party together.
    you / decide / to go?   *Have you decided to go*
3   That letter from the bank might be important.
    you / open / it?   *Have you open it yet?*
4   I keep calling you but there's no answer.
    you / change / your phone number?   *have you change y ph*
5   Do you know where Fernanda is?
    anyone / see / her today?   *Has anyone seen today*
6   Ms Wilden wants that report this afternoon.
    the marketing team / finish / it?   *Have the marketing finished it?*
7   Your parents'll be here in half an hour!
    you / start / making the dinner?   *Have you started making-*
8   I sent Shelley's birthday present two weeks ago.
    she / receive it?   *Has she received it yet*

3   Complete these sentences with been or gone.

1   Donna's *gone* to see her grandmother. She'll be back on Friday.
2   I'm sorry I didn't call you. I've *been* on holiday for a week.
3   We've *been* to that new restaurant a couple of times. It's great.
4   I don't believe it! My car's *gone*! I can't see it anywhere.

gone -> is still there

been -> is back you return

(handwritten at top: I finish NUNCS / I'm going to go on to cou... / NUNC)

10 FUTURE PLANS AND ARRANGEMENTS

MEANING

be going to and the present progressive
You can use be going to to talk about people's personal ideas and plans for the future.
I'm going to have a day off tomorrow.
He's going to start his own company next year.

You can use the present progressive to talk about future arrangements that have been made with other people or with organisations (companies, schools, airlines, clubs …).
I'm meeting Leonardo Barreiros at 2 pm tomorrow afternoon.
We're going to Greece in May.

Sometimes the difference between be going to and the present progressive is important.
~~*I'm going to get married next week.*~~ (it's not just my idea)
I'm getting married next week. (it's an arrangement with someone else)

But often the difference is very small.
I'm going to visit my sister next month. (it's my plan …)
I'm visiting my sister next month. (… and I've arranged it with my sister)

present simple
You use the present simple for fixed events in the future: timetables (bus, train, etc.) and schedules (flights, classes, etc.).
My flight leaves at 3.45 tomorrow afternoon.
Tonight's class starts at 7.00 and ends at 8.30.

am / is / are
You can also talk about the future in simple sentences with am / is / are and:
– adjectives like *free, busy, home, away, back. I'm away next week.*
– expressions with *in, on, at,* etc. *I'm at a conference.*

You usually use time expressions with all the above forms. For example: *tomorrow afternoon, at 7.00, next month …*

FORM

be going to
Use be going to with the infinitive.

❓ Are you going to see her again?	➕ I'm going to see her on my next trip to Malaysia.
✔ Yes, I am. ✖ No, I'm not.	➖ I'm not going to see her this month.

The present progressive, the present simple
See *Grammar reference* for unit 1, p132.

PRONUNCIATION

be going to
You usually stress going and the infinitive. You say to with a schwa, /tə/
I'm going to see a film with Leonardo on Saturday.

In negative sentences and short answers, you also stress be.
We aren't going to have a holiday this year.
Yes, I am. (but notice: No, I'm not.)

In fast speech you often say going to without stress, as /gənə/.
We're gonna watch a film tonight.

The present progressive, the present simple
See *Grammar reference* for unit 1, p132.

PRACTICE

1 Complete the sentences with the verbs in brackets. Use be going to or the present simple. *Personal*
1 When _does_ your train _arrive_ (arrive)
2 What _are_ you _doing_ this summer? (do)
— 3 I _____ my essay this weekend. (finish) *am going to*
4 I think the last bus _____ at 11.30pm. (leave) *leaves*
5 We _____ friends of ours in Bombay this summer. (visit) *are going to visit / are visiting*
6 The meeting _____ at 2.30 as usual. (start) *starts*

2 Complete the sentences with the present progressive or be. Use these verbs: *Personal / Ady*

go	phone	be away	get	have	be in

1 We _'re having_ a party for Margaret next Wednesday.
2 I*'m going* to the hairdresser this afternoon at 3.00.
3 We _____ a cat this weekend. The children are really excited. *are getting*
4 We _____ from home next week. *are*
5 I _____ her this evening around 6.00. *'m phoning*
6 I checked his schedule. He _____ Paris tomorrow. *is*

11 WOULD

MEANING

You can use would ('d) to talk about situations which:
- are in the present or future.
- you feel aren't real or won't happen.
I live in a small flat, but my dream home would have a big garden and a swimming pool.
It wouldn't be difficult for me to find a new job, but I haven't got time to look for one.

FORM

Use would with the infinitive.
➕ It would have a big garden.
➖ It wouldn't be in a big city.
❓ Would it have a swimming pool?
✔ Yes, it would.
✖ No, it wouldn't.

Contractions:
I'd   you'd   he'd   she'd   it'd   we'd   they'd

PRONUNCIATION

You usually stress the infinitive. You don't usually stress would in positive sentences and questions.
How would you find a new job?
I'd have to move to a new city.

But you stress *would* in negative sentences and short answers.
It wouldn't be easy.
Yes, it would. No, it wouldn't.

PRACTICE

1 Complete the conversations with would or wouldn't. Use contractions where possible.
1 A I_'d_ love to apply for that new job in the IT department.
  B So, why don't you?
  A Well, I don't think the boss _would_ be very happy about it. What _would_ you do?
  B I _wouldn't_ worry about the boss. If you want the job, go for it.

2 A We're thinking about moving to Hampden.
   B Really? I'm surprised. I _would_ want to be so far
      from the town centre. [handwritten: n't]
   A Well, I've got a car.
   B Yeah, but _Would_ you want to drive everywhere? I
      know I _wouldn't_

2 **Complete the sentences with would or wouldn't and one of these verbs.**

   be   help   invite   look   ~~play~~   spend   want

   1 I _'d play_ football this weekend but I've got a problem
      with my knee.
   2 If you're busy tomorrow, we can meet another time. It
      _____ a problem. _wouldn't be_
   3 I _____ for a new flat but I'm working so hard I
      haven't got the time. _would look_
   4 I _____ to work in another country. All my family and
      friends are here. _wouldn't want_
   5 We _'d_ _____ Jules and Rachel for dinner too, but we've
      only got four chairs. _would invite_
   6 Maybe you should get a flat in the centre. Then you
      _____ so much on transport. _wouldn't spend_
   7 Why don't you ask your parents for the money? I'm
      sure they _____ you. _would help_

12 INFINITIVES AND GERUNDS

MEANING and FORM

A You can use infinitives with to (to go, to have, etc.):

1 after adjectives
   I'm happy to say you've passed the test.
   Are you ready to go?
   Common adjectives with the infinitive: *difficult, easy, free,
   hard, ready, (un)able, sorry*

2 after some verbs
   I want to go home now.
   We've decided to move house.
   Some common verbs with the infinitive are: *agree, decide,
   hope, learn, need, offer, plan, promise, want, would like.*

B You can use gerunds (*going, having*, etc.):

1 after prepositions
   You can start by doing some light exercises.
   You can learn a lot from watching television.

2 after some verbs
   I practised playing the piano every day when I was a kid.
   Have you finished painting the wall yet?
   Some common verbs with the gerund are:
   *can't stand, dislike, don't mind, enjoy, finish, miss, practise,
   suggest.*

You can use a dictionary to check whether verbs are followed
by an infinitive with to or a gerund.

PRONUNCIATION

A In infinitives, you usually stress the verb but not to. You can
say *to* /tə/.

I want to go home now.

B In gerunds, you usually stress the first part of the verb but
not -ing.

You can learn a lot from watching television.

PRACTICE

1 **Circle the correct form, the gerund or infinitive with to.**

   1 I promise being / to be on time tomorrow.
   2 You can memorise the words by repeating / to repeat
      them.
   3 The police asked seeing / to see my passport.
   4 I have to go to the dentist's getting / to get my teeth
      checked.
   5 I really want passing / to pass my driving test.
   6 You should always get insurance before going / to go
      on holiday.
   7 I can't stand driving / to drive to work when there's a
      lot of traffic.
   8 Are you ready going / to go?

2 a **Complete the sentences with the correct form, the
   gerund or the infinitive with to.**

   1 Do you ever practise _____ (speak) English when
      you're alone?
   2 Is it easy _____ (find) a job where you live at the
      moment?
   3 Have you ever thought about _____ (learn) another
      language?
   4 What do you do _____ (relax) after work?
   5 Are you good at _____ (cook)?
   6 Do you think people learn a lot from _____ (visit)
      other countries?
   7 What do you plan _____ (do) in the next five years?
   8 Do you enjoy _____ (go) to football matches and
      other sports events?

   b **Ask and answer the questions.**

13 USED TO, WOULD

MEANING

You use used to and would to talk about past habits and
routines.
I used to play football on Saturdays when I was a kid.
I'd play football on Saturdays when I was a kid.

You use used to, but not would, to talk about past states.
I used to be a lawyer. ~~I would be a lawyer.~~
I used to live abroad. ~~I would live abroad.~~

Common state verbs are: *be, have, like, love, think, know,
believe, understand, seem, feel, smell, taste.*

                                              NOW
   ✗ ✗ ✗ ✗ ✗
   ───┼──────▶

I used to play computer games when I was young. ✓
I'd play computer games when I was young. ✓

                                              NOW
   ▬▬▬▬▬
   ───┼──────▶

I used to believe that monsters lived under my bed. ✓
I'd believe that monsters lived under my bed. ✗

FORM

used to / would + infinitive

❓ What did you use to do?	❓ What would you do
➕ I used to play football.	on Saturdays?
➖ I didn't use to play football. /	➕ We'd play football.
I never used to play football.	➖ We wouldn't play
(never is often used as the	football.
negative)	Would you play
Did you use to play football?	football?
✅ Yes, I did.	✅ Yes, I would.
❌ No, I didn't.	❌ No, I wouldn't.

PRONUNCIATION

You don't normally stress would in sentences. You usually stress used in used to.

I used to play football. used to = /juːstə/

I'd play football.

In negative sentences and short answers, you stress did and would.

I didn't use to play football.

We wouldn't play on Sundays.

Yes, I did.

No I wouldn't.

PRACTICE

1 a Complete the sentences with used to or would and these verbs.

| buy live not / like play believe |
| think get up work |

1 I _____ in ghosts.
2 I _____ ice cream, but now I love it!
3 She _____ work was boring until she became a nurse.
4 They _____ in a flat in New York.
5 We _____ together in a fast food restaurant.
6 We _____ chess when we were at university.
7 I _____ chocolate once or twice a day.
8 I _____ at five in the morning.

b In which sentences can you use:
a used to or would?   b only used to?

2 a Put the words in the correct order to make questions.

1 of clothes / did / What kind / you / to wear / use ?
2 How / to travel / people / did / before planes / use ?
3 did / Where / to play / you / use / as a child ?
4 to eat / What food / use / at college / did / you ?
5 on holiday / you / Where / use / to go / did ?
6 use / people / What / to do / before electricity / did?

b Ask and answer the questions.

14 UNREAL CONDITIONALS

MEANING

You can use unreal conditionals to talk about situations which are imaginary and probably won't happen.

Real situation
Not many people drive electric cars.
I don't have a lot of money.

Imaginary situation
If everyone drove electric cars, the air would be cleaner.
If I had a lot of money, I'd buy a big house in the country.

These sentences use past verbs (*drove*, *had*, etc.) but they are not about the past. They're about the present or the future.

FORM

If + past simple, would + infinitive
If everyone drove electric cars, the air would be cleaner.
If everyone drove electric cars, the air wouldn't be so polluted.

You can change the order. When the if clause comes second, you don't need a comma.
would + infinitive if + past simple
The air would be cleaner if everyone drove electric cars.
The air wouldn't be so polluted if everyone drove electric cars.

In unreal conditionals, you can use was or were after *I*, *he*, *she* or *it*.
If it was / were warmer, we'd have the party in our garden.
If I was / were a university student, I'd study business or law.

PRONUNCIATION

The pronunciation of real conditionals is the same as in other sentences. For example, you usually stress verbs and nouns but not modal verbs or prepositions.

If everyone drove electric cars, the air would be cleaner.

PRACTICE

1 Complete the sentences with the verbs in brackets to make unreal conditional sentences.

1 If we *used* solar power, it *would save* a lot of money. (use, save)
2 If I _____ a bit of money, I _____ a second-hand car. (have, buy)
3 If she _____ John, I'm sure she _____ him. (meet, like)
4 I _____ for a new flat if I _____ more time. (look, have)
5 If I _____ go back to university, I _____ a degree in economics. (can, do)
6 I _____ walking in the mountains if I _____ work tomorrow. (go, not have to)
7 It _____ easier to pay our bills if we _____ internet banking. (be, use)
8 If I _____ the chance, I _____ to a different country. (have, move)
9 If I _____ closer to my office, my life _____ a lot easier. (live, be)
10 I _____ a lot healthier if I _____ so many sweets and biscuits. (be, not eat)

1.1

Hi, my name's Kate Mori and I'm from Ottawa in Canada. I live with my husband, Masao, and, er, we have a cat. I'm a teacher. I work in a kindergarten. I speak English and French, and right now I'm studying Japanese, and slowly making progress! Er, I also study art history at night school once a week. Erm, I'm really interested in art, especially certain Canadian artists like Frank Johnston, so when I have the time, I like visiting the art galleries we have round here. Erm, Masao's interested in art too so we usually go together. What else? Well, sometimes I play tennis with my brother. He lives near me. And in the winter I go skating on the canal, which is a typical Ottawa thing to do!

1.2

INTERVIEWER So Kate, why are you learning Japanese?

KATE Well, last year I got married to Masao. He's from Japan.

I Congratulations.

K Thanks. So now I'm learning because I really want to talk with my husband's family, his parents and so on. They don't speak English …

I And you don't speak Japanese?

K Well, I can say 'hello' and 'goodbye', but I'd like to have a real conversation with them.

I Hm, so, does Masao teach you?

K No. He tried to give me some lessons but I just can't study at home. I can't concentrate.

I OK, so what do you do?

K Well, I didn't want to stop studying, so I started going to classes.

1.3

INTERVIEWER So Kemal, you're at university?

KEMAL Er, yes, I'm studying chemistry, but I also have Spanish lessons twice a week.

I Spanish?

K Yeah.

I And why is that?

K Because I like it.

I OK.

K You know, I've always liked learning languages. I sometimes need English for my studies but Spanish is my hobby, I guess. I like reading in Spanish.

I You mean books?

K Not books, no, but er, you know, things on the Internet, sometimes magazines. And I love Spanish cinema. One day I want to watch Spanish films without the subtitles.

I Have you ever been to Spain?

K Actually, no.

I Ah.

K I'd really like to go to Spain, of course, but maybe after I finish my studies here.

I So Sun-Hi, you're learning English.

SUN-HI Yes, I have a job with a large international company in Seoul, so I need English for my work.

I Hm, do you travel a lot?

S No, I don't need English for travel so much but, er, we have a lot of English-speaking visitors from other countries, especially Australia.

I Ah, I see.

S So I always talk to them in English. Of course we have a lot of visitors from other places too.

I Sure.

S Europe, other countries in Asia, but we usually speak in English.

I What about writing?

S Well, yes, my speaking's OK but I need to practise my writing. I read and write a lot of emails in English but it takes me a long time.

1.4

INTERVIEWER Erm, Natalie, did you have a lot of experience of music when you were little?

NATALIE I think I was very lucky, in that I came from Trinidad and Tobago, so when I was younger there was a lot of music around me all the time. Lots of different types of music. We did have music from the rest of the world but our local music is very special.

I Was that in your home, or just generally in the streets and … ?

N It's everywhere. You cannot get away from music in Trinidad. We have … we've created our own instrument called the steel drum. And you put … you take an oil drum and you hammer it and you get notes out of it. And they make huge orchestras … and I learned how to play the steel drum when I was a little girl.

I Do you have one?

N I have one in Trinidad, but they're very difficult to travel with.

I I low, how big is it?

N Erm, I would say it's about – what's this? – half a metre wide, maybe, and probably a metre high.

I Right.

N And you play it with sticks, so I couldn't really travel with it. But Trinidad definitely has a lot of variety. We have a local music called calypso, which is similar to music from Latin America, er, sort of a merengue beat. And we have a lot of reggae, which probably you would have heard of, from Jamaica.

I What's your personal favourite?

N Erm, well I play classical piano. I was brought up to play classical piano, but nowadays I play more Cuban music on piano. Son, salsa, things like that, rumba.

I And do you still play the steel drum?

N I have forgotten some. I would love to

be able to play it again because I think it's very original and it has a lovely sound, but unfortunately I don't have it with me.

1.5

JOHN So, have you got any plans for the weekend?

CAMERON No, not really. You?

J Well, I was thinking about going to the festival, you know?

C WOMADelaide?

J Yeah, it starts on Friday. Do you want to go?

C Sure, if we can get tickets for a day or a night. I couldn't do the whole weekend.

J Me neither, it's too expensive. So when's best for you?

C Sunday probably. It doesn't really matter – it depends what's on.

J Yeah, and if there are any tickets left. Why don't we have a look online?

C OK, hang on a minute. Right. Sunday. Ah, Cesaria Evora's playing. She's amazing.

J Yeah, I'd love to see her. Or Mista Savona looks interesting.

C Hm, I'm not really into reggae.

J OK, well … er, erm … What do you think about this? The Terem Quartet?

C The folk? Yeah, that sounds good.

J Well, there's plenty of good stuff on Sunday. Do you want me to see if there are any tickets?

C Good idea. And do you want to ask anyone else? Maybe Jen?

J Yes, and Sally would probably like to come too. Maybe we could get a group together.

C Yeah, it would be a good laugh.

1.6

1 hockey, running, skiing, swimming, tennis, yoga
2 volleyball
3 aerobics, karate

1.7

INTERVIEWER So, how did you get into biking?

LI Well, it started when I was a kid. Er, my dad had a motorbike and I thought it looked like fun. Then I really got into motorbikes when I was a teenager. My first boyfriend also had a really nice bike, so we went riding in the countryside a lot and, yeah, it was great, er, but really I wanted to ride the bike, not sit on the back!

I OK, and what about now?

L Well, last year I wrote a book for children. Er, it was about a mother who rode a motorbike, a Harley-Davidson in fact, so I just had this motorbike idea in my head. Then I decided that I really wanted to learn something new. It didn't really matter what but I wanted to learn a new skill, you know, and the great thing about it is, it doesn't take very long to learn. So I saved up some money and I started having lessons.

I   And how did that go?

L   Well, it was a fascinating experience. It was very difficult at first, er, much harder than I expected, but I enjoyed it too. At times it was quite frightening – terrifying in fact! Er, I passed my test a few months ago and I'm much more relaxed now, but I still need to get a lot more experience.

I   So, what is it that you like about being on a bike? Do you like going fast?

L   No. I'm not interested in going fast. I love it because I feel free. I can go wherever I want to go, any time. So, no, for me, speed isn't important.

I   Do you use your bike for getting around, getting to work … ?

L   No, it's too dangerous. I've been into the town centre on my bike one or two times and there are so many cars, people, it's terrible. I really like riding in the countryside on big, empty roads where there are no cars. And as you ride along you can smell things – not, you know, cars, but the trees, flowers, the rain. That's what I really like about it.

1.8

Write the name of a sport you're interested in, but don't play.
Write the name of a sport you did when you were younger, but don't do now.
Write the name of a sport you really don't like.
Write the name of a sport you like to watch on TV.
Write the name of a group or singer you'd like to see in concert.
Write the name of a group or singer you loved when you were younger.
Write the name of a group or singer you listen to a lot at the moment.
Write the name of a group or singer you really don't like.

1.9

sport born motorbike doctor work

1.10

1 normal	6 world
2 work	7 motorway
3 important	8 word
4 information	9 doctor
5 forty	10 orchestra

1.11

1

INTERVIEWER   Luis, you're twenty-nine …

LUIS   Right.

I   … and you're a student?

L   Well, I work as an archaeologist but, yeah, I'm also a student, I guess.

I   Right. What kind of archaeology do you do?

L   I do a lot of work in the rainforest, in the Central Amazon.

I   But right now you're doing a degree, aren't you?

L   Yes, I'm doing a doctorate in archaeology. Actually, I'm writing a thesis on my work in the Amazon.

I   And when do you finish?

L   I've got just one more year to go – I hope!

I   And will you stop then?

L   Stop studying?

I   Yes.

L   Well, I think an archaeologist is always studying, so, no, I'll never stop. It's a way of life for me.

2

I   Pierre, you didn't like school much. Why was that?

PIERRE   Well, I didn't like a lot of subjects at school, like maths and science. I just wasn't very good at them, and I hated doing exams and tests and so on.

I   Hm. But you were interested in art?

P   Yes, I've always enjoyed art.

I   So, you left school when you were … ?

P   I left school when I was eighteen. I passed my exams – just! – and then I got a job. Then, er, about twenty years later, I decided I wanted to do a degree in art. So I applied to some colleges and I got into the School of Art and Design in Limoges.

I   Oh, and how is it?

P   It's a great experience, completely different from school.

I   How exactly?

P   Well, I'm studying something I really want to study, you know?

I   Right.

P   And I'm a lot older and more confident, so it's easier to ask questions, talk to the teachers, things like that.

3

I   Margaret, you're a student at the University of the Third Age?

MARGARET   Yes, we call it the U3A.

I   U3A. And what is that exactly?

M   Well, 'the third age' means it's for people over fifty. Anyone over fifty can join. We have meetings and talks in members' homes, and we don't do exams or get degrees. So, you see, it's not a typical university!

I   And why did you join?

M   Well, I retired three years ago. I had a lot of free time, and nothing to do. It wasn't a very happy time, to be honest. Then I read something about the U3A and went to a talk and it was great.

I   Hm. What kind of courses have you done?

M   Oh, there are so many interesting things. I've done courses in music, erm, local history and Spanish. I choose things I haven't studied before.

I   And what's next?

M   Well, I've never been very good with computers, so, er, last week I signed up for an IT skills course.

1.12

What kind of courses have you done?
I've done courses in music, er, local history and Spanish.
I choose things I haven't studied before.
I've never been very good with computers.

Has she ever studied Spanish?
Yes, she has.
No, she hasn't.

1.13

1 What subjects have you always enjoyed?
2 What subjects have you always been good at?

1.14

3 What's the most useful subject you've ever studied?
4 Who's the best teacher you've ever had?
5 Have you ever done a course in your free time?
6 Have you ever written a thesis or a very long essay?
7 Have you done a lot of exams in your life?
8 What's the most difficult exam you've ever passed?

1.15

INTERVIEWER   OK, right. So, it's Lauren, isn't it?

LAUREN   Yes, that's right.

I   Great. Have you got your form there?

L   Yes, here you go.

I   And did you bring a copy of your CV?

L   Yes.

I   OK. Er, let's just have a look. So, you've done lots of different things! Sales … administration … and you've worked in a restaurant.

L   Yes, that's right. Last summer.

I   OK. And you're looking for work in … ?

L   Well, yes, as you can see, I've got experience in sales, administration and catering, so I'm looking for work in any of those areas really.

I   Right. Er, let's start with catering. You worked for Café Concerto last summer. What qualifications do you have? Do you have any kind of food safety or hygiene certificate?

L   Yes, I've got a certificate in Food Safety for Catering. It's level two.

I   Ah, that's excellent. Have you got a copy of that with you?

L   Er, no, sorry.

I   Oh, that's no problem. Could you fax it over later today? Or bring it in?

L   Sure.

I   Great. Now, administration … How are you with computers?

L   Well, I have experience working with Word and Excel, so quite good, I think.

I   OK, good, and more generally ... it doesn't say here, no ... do you have a driving licence?

L   Yes, I do.

I   Good. And what languages do you speak?

L   Erm, a little French and Spanish.

I   OK. And more recently you worked in sales for CSP. Did you enjoy that?

L   Yes, I've been in sales for a year now and I worked for CSP for six months. It was a nice company.

I   So why did you decide to leave?

L   Well ... it's quite a small company, you know. I've always wanted to work for a big company. I think that would be a good experience for me.

I   OK. Now ... what would you say are your strengths and weaknesses?

L   Hm, that's a difficult question. Well, I'm good at talking to people, I think. And I really enjoy working in a team. But maybe I'm not very good at working on my own? I prefer working with people.

I   OK, great. Well, I'm sure we'll have something for you. We'll put your details on our system and see what we have. And I'll need to contact your references.

🔊 1.16

CLARE   Hello, CSP, Clare speaking. How can I help you?

YUSUF   Oh, hello, my name's Yusuf Karim. I'm from the job agency, Findajob. Could I speak to Lisa Moore, please?

C   Certainly. Can I ask you the reason for the call?

Y   Of course. I'm calling about an ex-CSP employee, Lauren Gordon. Lisa Moore was her manager.

C   Thank you. Let me just see if Lisa's available. Hello? I'm afraid she's in a meeting. Can I take a message?

Y   I'm sorry, this line's not very good. Could you say that again, please?

C   Yes, of course, I'm sorry. Would you like me to take a message?

Y   Yes, please.

C   Er, what was your name again, please?

Y   Yes, it's Yusuf Karim.

C   Could you spell that for me?

Y   Yes, it's Yusuf with a Y, Y-U-S-U-F, and Karim is K-A-R-I-M.

C   OK. And what's your telephone number?

Y   I'll give you my mobile number. It's oh four one two, double five six, two oh seven.

C   Sorry, can you speak more slowly, please?

Y   Yes, it's oh four one two, double five six, two oh seven.

C   Right. And has Lisa got your email address?

Y   Er, no. It's y dot karim at findajob dot com dot au.

C   Sorry, y dot karim at ... ?

Y   Findajob – that's one word – dot com dot au.

C   OK, so that's y dot karim at findajob dot com dot au. And what would you like me to tell her?

Y   Well, I'd like to ask her some questions about Lauren Gordon, what was she like as an employee and things. It would be great if she could phone me.

C   OK, I'll give her the message and ask her to contact you.

Y   Thank you. That's very helpful.

C   No problem. Goodbye.

🔊 1.17

1   Can you speak more slowly, please?
2   What was your name again, please?
    Could you say that again, please?
    Sorry, y dot karim at ... ?
3   Could you spell that for me?
4   OK.
    Right.
    OK, so that's ...

🔊 1.18

lawyer   visitor   grammar   neighbour

🔊 1.19

1   dollar
2   winter
3   computer
4   singer
5   doctor
6   colour
7   composer
8   footballer
9   calendar
10 teenager

🔊 1.20

unfriendly, friendly
expensive, cheap
relaxing, stressful
inconvenient, convenient
quiet, noisy
boring, interesting
empty, crowded
old-fashioned, modern

🔊 1.21

LYNN   So, where are you taking me?

BRYAN   Well, I've had a look in this guide and, er, I think these three look quite good. Have a look.

L   Hmm.

B   What do you think?

L   Well, they all look nice ... but I went to Bopha Devi recently.

B   OK, then, uh, what about this one?

L   Abla's?

B   Yeah, I've heard the food there's very good.

L   I don't know ... it's a long way from here.

B   OK, er ... how about The Bridge?

L   Yeah, we could sit outside. Ah, but do you think they do vegetarian food?

B   I'm sure they do.

L   OK, let's go to The Bridge. Is that OK with you?

B   Sure, it's your birthday.

L   Great.

B   I'll call and book a table for, say, seven thirty?

L   Fine.

B   Right, what's the number?

🔊 1.22

WAITER   Hi, are you ready to order?

LYNN   Yes, I think so. Erm ... what's the soup of the day?

W   Er, today it's, er, cream of mushroom soup.

L   OK, so I'll have that ... and, er, the pasta, please.

W   OK. And for you, sir?

BRYAN   Yeah, could I have the cheese salad to start ...

W   Cheese salad ...

B   ... and then the steak?

W   Fine, and how would you like your steak?

B   Er, medium, please.

W   All right. Can I get you something to drink?

B   Do you want some wine?

L   Not right now actually, maybe later.

B   OK.

L   Can we have a bottle of water?

W   Sure. Sparkling or still?

L   Er, still.

B   Yep.

L   Still, please.

W   OK, thanks very much.

🔊 1.23

Can we have a bottle of water?

🔊 1.24

1   Could I have the cheese salad to start ... and then the steak?
2   OK, so I'll have that and the pasta, please.
3   Medium, please.
4   Still, please.
5   Yes, I think so. What's the soup of the day?

🔊 1.25

1   I'd like to book a table for two, please.
2   My parents cook a big meal for nine or ten people every weekend.
3   Could I have the chicken in garlic sauce, please?
4   That table in the corner's free. Why don't we sit there?
5   Would you like a bottle of water with your meal?
6   The weather was great, so we sat at a table on the terrace.
7   There's a good menu with lots of vegetarian dishes and the staff are very friendly.
8   I'll have the salmon with rice, please.

🔊 1.26

MANUEL   So how about we organise a barbecue?

EREN   Barbecues can be tricky because that means that we have to cook meat and quite a few people are vegetarian.

M   Mmm. That's a thought.

SARAH We could do some pasta alternative, maybe?

SUSANNE No, we can put veggies on the barbecue as well.

E Yeah, that could be ... but then some people are really strict that they don't want, like, any kind of meat, fat and stuff being mixed with ...

SA Yes, that's true as well.

M But we could have a barbie, we could have like mushrooms and things like this on one burner and another ... and meat and sausages on another place.

SU Separated, yeah.

E I think that would work if you have like, yeah ...

M Different grills.

E Yes, that would work.

M So what should we buy?

E Well, sausages are nice.

1.27

MANUEL What about salads?

EREN Greek salad I can do.

M Okay, okay. We need to buy some feta cheese then.

E Yeah, feta cheese and some black olives and, erm, olive oil.

M Very important. What about dessert?

SUSANNE Now this is getting too much now.

M Well, it depends. A lot of people are going to come.

SU Well, then keep it easy and simple. Ice cream?

M What about fruit? Melons?

1.28

MATT Well, in my family we usually eat together in the evening, erm, maybe pasta, salad, chicken. Everyone sits around the table and eats and talks about everything – what we did that day, how we feel ... erm, our plans for the next day, the food ... whatever. I don't know what other people do but I send my kids to wash their hands before dinner. Er, Friday evenings are a bit more relaxed. If we're at home, we usually have a quick meal in front of the TV ... pizza or Chinese food or something. No one really talks. Everyone's a bit tired by Friday.

CARLOS Er, in my family we all have breakfast at different times because we all get up at different times. Later in the day, if we have guests, we usually have a ... you know, a buffet-style dinner ... and everyone chooses things from a side table and then takes their food to the main table. My mum says *bon appétit* before we start eating but that's all. And during the meal, we talk about work and family and football and different things but we don't usually talk about the food.

1.29

enjoy   employee   noisy   boil

1.30

1	oil	5	toilet
2	join	6	boyfriend
3	self-employed	7	employ
4	appointment	8	choice

1.31

A	meter	D	passenger
B	fare	E	taxi rank
C	receipt	F	change

1.32

1

NICOLA Hi. Er, how much is it to the city centre?

TONY Er, that depends on the traffic. It's usually about thirty, thirty-five dollars.

N OK. Can I put my case in the back?

T I'll do that for you. So, where are we headed?

N Erm, can you take me to the Park Inn?

T The Park Inn on Broadway, right?

N Um, yes, that's the one.

T All right ... So, is this your first time in Canada?

N Well, no. I came here with my parents, like, fifteen years ago but I don't remember much.

T Right, so what brings you back here?

T Here we are. The Park Inn.

N Thanks. Er, how much is it?

T Thirty-one fifty, please.

N Just make it thirty-five dollars.

T Thanks very much ... And here's your change, fifteen dollars.

N OK. Thanks.

T Now, let's get your case.

2

DAN Hello. The Royal Bank on Howe Street, please.

TONY OK.

T OK, that'll be eight dollars and fifty cents.

D Actually, could you wait here for five minutes? I just have to get some papers.

T Well, OK, but can you pay me first?

D Of course ... here's ten. I'll be back in five minutes.

T OK.

D Thanks for waiting. OK, I'd like to go to the airport, please.

T OK. Which terminal?

D Domestic, please.

T All right, the domestic terminal ... So you're going somewhere on business, right?

D Yeah, I've got some meetings in Calgary.

T So do you work for the bank?

T OK, that's thirty-five dollars and 75 cents.

D And can I have a receipt, please?

T Sure ... here you are. Have a safe trip now.

D Thanks, bye.

1.33

1 How much is it to the city centre?
2 Can you take me to the Park Inn?
3 I'd like to go to the airport, please.
4 Can I put my case in the back?
5 And can I have a receipt, please?

1.34

What was he doing?
He was standing outside the terminal.
He wasn't looking very happy.

Were they going back to Canada?
Yes, they were.
No, they weren't.

1.35

The Ten-Dollar Bill
One sunny morning a man was walking through the city on his way to work. He was wearing a smart suit and tie and talking on his phone. Suddenly, the sun went in and it started raining heavily. The man saw a taxi and started running towards it. As he was running, a ten-dollar bill fell from his pocket onto the ground, but he didn't notice. He got into the cab, shut the door, and the cab drove away.

1.36

OSMAN Well, er, I was travelling to the USA on business and, uh, I got a plane from Germany, from Frankfurt. Anyway I was just reading the airline magazine and relaxing, when suddenly some late passengers arrived. A few of them came into Business Class, where I was sitting. One of them was this really big guy with a huge beard and sunglasses. He was wearing a black biker jacket, black leather trousers and he had a lot of tattoos. He looked kind of scary, actually. Anyway, he sat down next to me and before I could pretend to fall asleep, he introduced himself and we had a good chat. He was a nice guy. Interesting. His name was Bernd, I think, but it was a long time ago. Then, recently, I was in Germany again and, er, I turned on the television and there he was, on a news programme. He's a top manager for the Harley-Davidson clothing company in Germany, and he was speaking at some big conference. And he was still wearing his biker clothes, so I recognised him immediately.

ANNIE I went to Montpellier, er, one or two years ago. I was looking for a little restaurant to eat on my own. It was in February but in Montpellier it was really nice weather so you could eat outside. So I sat at a table for two. At one point a man arrived and there was only one table for five available, so he asked me if he could sit at my table, erm, and we started having a chat. He was a really nice person. He was from Switzerland and he was studying, er, French, erm, in Montpellier, so I started teaching him a bit. We met several times when I was there and, erm, next to Montpellier there is a nice town, next to the sea, erm, so we, we had a day trip there and, and that's it really. We became pen friends but of course I have my boyfriend at home so, erm, that's it.

1.37

ASTRID   When I was learning French, once I knew a few basic words, I liked reading children's books. I found it very useful, because the sentences are very simple.

TOM   When I was learning German, I used to change the language on my computer games to German. Then I could pretend to my parents that I was learning, instead of playing. But it really did help me learn.

MASHA   When I learn a foreign language, I like watching DVDs in that language, er, with subtitles on so I can, er, pause and look in a dictionary what the word means and see how it's spelt. And also when I was in Germany learning German I changed the menu of my mobile phone into German, so that helped.

1.38

VALÉRIE   Good morning, can you take me to the Holiday Inn, please?

TONY   Sure. Which one?

V   Er, the one on Broadway, please.

T   So, what brings you to Vancouver?

V   I have some old friends here. Actually, we were at university together.

T   So it's not your first time here?

V   Oh, no. I visit every three or four months.

T   Right. So you like it here?

V   Yes. In fact, I'd really like to live here.

T   Oh, yeah? Where do you live?

V   In Montreal. Well, actually, I've got a small business there.

T   Really? What do you do?

V   I own a couple of restaurants.

1.39

right	neighbours
night	bought
frightening	through
eight	straight

1.40

enough   laugh   yoghurt   spaghetti

1.41

1	light	6	flight
2	thought	7	spaghetti
3	eighteen	8	daughter
4	neighbourhood	9	frightening
5	enough	10	tonight

2.1

A	a cash machine	D	notes
B	bills	E	coins
C	cash	F	a card

2.2

THIAGO   Hello. Do you have Scottish pounds?

ASSISTANT   Er, no, we don't, but English pounds are OK in Scotland.

T   Oh, OK. Can I change these euros, please?

A   Of course. That's fifty, a hundred, and fifty, sixty, seventy, eighty. That's a hundred and eighty euros, yes?

T   Yes, that's right.

A   Right, that's ... a hundred and fifty pounds. Here you are.

T   Sorry, do you have any smaller notes?

A   No problem. Are twenties OK?

T   That's great, thanks.

2.3

1

ASSISTANT   Hello, can I help?

THIAGO   Yes, I'll take these postcards, please.

A   OK.

T   And, er, do you have any maps?

A   I'm sorry, we don't have any maps at the moment. You could try next door.

T   OK.

A   Anything else?

T   No, that's all, thanks. How much is that?

A   Eight postcards. That comes to six pounds forty, please.

T   Can I pay by card?

A   I'm afraid not, no. There's a cash machine just around—

T   No, it's OK, I've got some cash, I think.

A   Thank you. And that's 60 pence change.

T   Thanks.

A   Would you like a bag?

T   Er, yes, please.

A   There you are. Bye now.

T   Goodbye.

2

WAITRESS   How was your meal? Everything OK?

THIAGO   It was very nice, thank you.

W   Would you like to see the dessert menu?

T   No, thanks.

W   Maybe some coffee?

T   Er, no, that's OK. Could I have the bill?

W   Certainly. How would you like to pay?

T   Do you take cards?

W   Yes, of course. Just one moment.

W   Can you type in your PIN and press 'ENTER', please.

T   Er, right.

W   And there's your receipt. Thanks very much.

T   Thanks.

3

ASSISTANT   Good morning.

THIAGO   Hi. One student, please.

A   Can I see your student card?

T   Sure. Here you are.

A   That's fine. That's two fifty, please.

T   OK.

A   Sorry, do you have anything smaller?

T   I'm sorry, no, that's all I've got.

A   That's OK. That's three, four, five, ten, thirty, fifty pounds. And here's your ticket and a guide to the museum exhibits.

T   Thanks very much.

2.4

1   Anything else?
2   How much is that?
3   Can I pay by card?
4   Would you like a bag?
5   Could I have the bill?
6   How would you like to pay?
7   Do you take cards?
8   Can I see your student card?
9   Do you have anything smaller?

2.5

1   Grameen's customers have to make groups of five people.
2   They don't have to be women.
3   They can't usually get credit from normal banks.
4   They can get bigger loans if they make all their repayments.

2.6

MEGAN   When you go over to someone's house for dinner in Canada, you should probably ask ahead of time if you can bring something with you, just to be nice. Erm, and you should probably show up with a gift. Maybe you can bring a bottle of wine, or maybe some flowers, something like that. The other thing to remember is that you have to take your shoes off when you get to the house. Don't wear your shoes inside.

YUKIO   OK, when you go to a Japanese hot spring, there are a few rules. Women go to the women's area and men to the men's area. First, you go into the washing room. Here you wash yourself with a towel and lots of soap. Then you have to wash off all the soap so you are really clean. After that, you can get into the hot spring. The water's quite hot, so you shouldn't stay in it too long. You can get out and rest for a while and then go back in. What else? Well, you can't make a lot of noise. The spring should be a quiet place where people can just relax.

2.7

1

A   When can we meet? Tomorrow? Sunday?

B   It doesn't really matter. I'm free all weekend.

2

A   I'm sorry I'm late! Where's the meeting?

147

B Don't worry about it. The meeting hasn't started yet.

3

A Do you like parties?

B It depends. Generally yes, but not when there are too many people.

4

A Do you want to come to the cinema tonight?

B Mm, I'm not sure I have time. I'll think about it, OK?

5

A Have we got any food at home?

B Not really ... we've got some milk in the fridge. That's it.

6

A What time do I have to start work?

B It's up to you. But you have to be here eight hours a day.

2.8

JOHN What do you think about this article? I think I agree. You shouldn't tell people how much you earn.

HAYLEY Why not? I tell people how much I earn!

J Really?

H Yeah, sure. Why not?

J It just seems really ... I don't know.

H I mean, I don't tell people when I first meet them. I don't say, 'Hi, my name's Hayley and I earn fifty thousand dollars a year.' But if it's part of the conversation, then, sure. It's part of my life, it's part of who I am.

J Really? In the UK, in general, I don't think people like to say how much they earn. It's just more private, maybe.

2.9

conversation   expression   musician

2.10

1 education   6 action
2 discussion   7 electrician
3 information   8 promotion
4 expression   9 organisation
5 politician   10 introduction

2.11

1 How many books do you have at home?
2 How many hours a week do you work or study?
3 How many emails do you get every day?
4 How many cups of coffee or tea do you drink a day?
5 How many kilometres do you drive in a typical month?
6 How many minutes does it take you to get to this class?
7 How many times have you travelled by aeroplane?
8 How many people live in your home town?

———— UNIT 6

2.12

A doing the vacuuming
B cleaning the windows
C doing the dusting
D doing the ironing

E doing the cooking
F making the bed

2.13

JEEVAN The summer months in India can actually be quite dangerous; it's so hot before the rains come. The most important thing is to drink a lot, to cover up when you go outside, to cover your head. You'll see Indian men and women wearing long clothes which cover everything, including their arms and legs. Only tourists wear shorts and T-shirts in the hot sun. On summer afternoons in Kolkata, where I live, the streets are empty because it's too hot to go out, so most people are either at work or at home, asleep. A lot of people use air conditioning but it's expensive. Not everyone can afford it. Cold drinks like *mango panna* are really popular. This is a drink made from unripe mangoes; it really helps to cool your body.

VASILY I live in Moscow, in Russia. Our winters last from, er, about November to March and we get quite a lot of snow. In January and February, it's usually minus five to minus ten degrees Celsius but it can get a lot colder, even down to minus thirty. OK, maybe it isn't as cold as Siberia, but it's cold enough! You have to wear lots of big, heavy clothes and boots and, er, everything takes longer ... putting clothes on to go out, taking them off when you get inside. And you have to be more careful on the roads too because they can be icy. Everyone has to carry an emergency kit in the car, so if the car stops you'll be OK. These days a lot of young people prefer to escape the winter and go to much hotter countries like Egypt and Turkey; but most people I know spend half the winter at home watching TV. Me? I like to get out of the city and go skiing. But I think we all look forward to the New Year celebrations, which are really fun and help us to get through our long winters.

2.14

You have to be more careful on the roads.
That's hotter than the surface of the sun.
The heaviest hailstone fell in Bangladesh in 1986.
The most important thing is to drink a lot.
It weighed one kilogram and was as large as a melon.
It isn't as cold as Siberia.

2.15

INTERVIEWER Excuse me, do you have a few minutes?

SALLY Well ...

I We're opening a new fitness centre and we'd like to find out what local

people really need. Could I ask you some questions? We'd really value your opinion.

S Er, yes, OK.

I Thank you. It'll only take a few minutes.

S No problem.

I Right. So, erm, do you use a fitness centre at the moment?

S Er, yes, sometimes.

I Where is that, if you don't mind me asking?

S That's OK, I go to the Meanwood Fitness Centre in Kent Town.

I Right, and what do you think of it?

S Well, to be honest, it's not that good.

I Yes? Why is that?

S Well, the pool's OK, but it could be bigger. And there should be time for adults only. I'd prefer women-only classes as well.

I OK, I'll make a note of that. Ah, what about the facilities?

S Well, the facilities could definitely be better too. I don't mind the changing rooms but I'd much rather have private showers.

I Private showers. Right. Now, we're planning to have a sauna. Are you interested in using a sauna?

S Er, well, maybe. But I think I'd rather have a nicer pool than a sauna.

I OK. Erm, how often do you go to the fitness centre?

S Well, I try to go once a week, but I'd like to go more often.

I Uh-huh. And how long do you usually spend there?

S Erm, about an hour and a half, I suppose. I usually swim for half an hour, then go to the gym for a bit.

I OK. And which machines do you prefer using in the gym?

S Well, I generally use the running and rowing machines.

2.16

1 h free   5 g hair
2 c shopping   6 f energy
3 d current   7 b stay
4 e best   8 a her

2.17

1 gym   6 cleaning
2 thunderstorm   7 rainbow
3 cycling   8 vacuuming
4 chores   9 tornado
5 clouds   10 working

2.18

1

BILL Would you mind answering a few questions, please? It won't take long.

SHEILA Er, yes, that's OK.

B Thank you. Are you happy with the fitness centre generally?

S Erm, well, it could be better.

B Oh. I see. Do you think you could tell me a bit more?

s Well, to be honest, the pool isn't always very clean. And the staff don't seem very interested.

B Oh dear. Well, I'll definitely tell the manager.

2

BEN Hi. I wonder if you could change this ten for me. I need some coins for the ticket machine.

CLODAGH Sorry, but I'd rather not. People are always asking me for change.

B Oh.

C Perhaps you'd like to buy something?

B Erm, no, not really.

3

PHIL Here's your drink. Sorry it took so long.

CATHERINE So, what do you think of the game?

P Erm, it's a bit boring.

C Boring?

P Well, you know I'm not really interested in football.

C So should we go? The second half starts in two minutes.

P No, you stay here. I'll do some shopping, then come back in an hour, OK?

C Well, OK. See you later.

2.19

1 Can you answer a few questions? Would you mind answering a few questions, please?

2 Can you change this ten for me? I wonder if you could change this ten for me.

3 Can you tell me a bit more? Do you think you could tell me a bit more?

4 No, I don't want to. Sorry, but I'd rather not.

5 No, I don't need anything. No, not really.

6 The pool is dirty. The pool isn't always very clean.

7 The staff aren't interested. The staff don't seem very interested.

8 It's boring. It's a bit boring.

9 I'm not interested in football. I'm not really interested in football.

2.20

SUE Yes?

ANDRE It's André. I want to talk to Sue.

S This is Sue, but I'm busy. Call me later.

A Tomorrow?

S No. I don't work on Sundays.

A Monday afternoon?

S OK. Call me at the office. The mobile's expensive.

A OK. Bye.

2.21

comfortable   available   possible
sensible

2.22

1	fashionable	6	sensible
2	memorable	7	enjoyable
3	available	8	comfortable
4	terrible	9	horrible
5	possible	10	impossible

UNIT 2

2.23

TOURIST OFFICER Can I help you?

LIZZY Oh, yes, please. How can I get to Anne Frank's house?

T Oh, you can walk from here. It's very easy. Let me show you on the map.

L OK.

T We're next to the main train station.

L Yeah.

T Go out of here and turn left. Go down the big street. It's called Damrak.

L OK.

T You'll go past a big building on your left, the Beurs.

L OK.

T If you continue along Damrak, you'll come to the Dam.

L That's the big square, right?

T That's right. You'll see the National Monument on your left, and the Royal Palace on your right.

L Right.

T So, turn right and go past the palace. Then go along Raadhuisstraat, here, for about five hundred metres.

L OK.

T When you get to the canal called Prinsengracht, turn right. The house is by the canal, just here.

L That sounds pretty easy. Is it far?

T No, two kilometres, maybe a bit less. It's a nice walk.

L That's great. Thanks for all your help.

T You're welcome. Is there anything else I can help you with?

L No thanks, that's fine.

2.24

Go out_of here_and turn left.

2.25

1 Turn right_and go past the palace.
2 You'll go past_a big building_on your left, the Beurs.
3 You'll see the National Monument_on your left_and the Royal Palace_on your right.

2.26

TOURIST OFFICER Hello, can I help you?

SERGEI Yes. Erm, I've only got one free day to see the sights in Amsterdam, and I was wondering, do you organise tours of the city?

T Er, yeah, we can, but it's quite easy to get around the city on your own.

S OK.

T But, erm, you've only got one day? That's not enough!

S Yes, I know, I have to leave first thing tomorrow, so ...

T OK, well, er, what would you like to do?

S Erm, I don't know. Have you got a map or something?

T Yes, we have. Here you are. Er, it has all the sights on it ...

S Ah. Thanks. Can you recommend some things to see?

T Well, one of the most popular things to see is Anne Frank's house. That's here.

S Ah, of course. I've heard of her.

T Yes, this is the house where she wrote the famous diary. Erm, there are often long queues, unfortunately, so the best time to go is early evening.

S Well, that should be OK. It sounds interesting.

T Yes, if you're interested in history, it's definitely a good place to visit. OK, er, we have a lot of museums. So, if you like art, there's the Van Gogh museum here.

S Ah, right. Er, do you sell tickets?

T I'm afraid we don't, no. Er, there's also a science museum – NEMO. That's here.

S Hm, maybe not this time, but the Van Gogh museum sounds good. Erm ... what about this? I don't know how to say it. The Gardens?

T Ah, yes, The Keukenhof Gardens. They're very nice but they're not actually in Amsterdam.

S Ah.

T You have to get a train and then a bus, it takes about an hour.

S Hm, OK. I think that's too far.

T Right, what else? Erm ...

S Actually, I think that's, er, probably enough. Thanks very much.

T No problem. Have a nice day.

S Thanks.

2.27

A Rob! Can you answer the door? I'm doing the washing up.

B Yeah, OK. Who is it?

A It'll be Leona. I invited her for a coffee.

A Don't forget, it's Deiter's birthday on Monday.

B Ah, yes. How old is he?

A He'll be twenty-five, I think.

2.28

1

A I'll have the pasta, please.

B Fine. And would you like something to drink?

2

A Are you OK? You don't look well.

B Hm, it's very hot in here!

3

A Hello?

B Hi, Jan. It's Laurence.

A Sorry, I can't talk now. I'm in a meeting.

● 2.29

NATALIE   When I go travelling, which I really like to do a lot, I think it's very important to try to speak the language of the people of the country you're visiting. I think it's a good way of getting to know people and understanding a bit more.

PAULA   Yeah, but sometimes don't you think that makes conversation a bit slow, like if you're walking around with a little dictionary and you have to sort of look up words every time you want to say something and if the other person speaks your language then maybe it's just easier to, you know, speak the language that you both share.

N   Yeah, I think you're right in that way. I know when I go to France even if I speak French the people reply to me in English because I don't speak French well enough, but I think it's wrong to go to a country and expect people to speak to you in your language. I think if they are willing, then it's OK.

P   Yeah, probably. You're probably right, yeah.

● 2.30

OK, you go out of here and turn left and you'll see a coffee machine in the corner. Turn right and continue along the corridor. Turn right again and pass the teachers' room. The room you want is on your right, after the library.

● 2.31

build   buy   fruit

● 2.32

1	biscuit	6	fruit
2	build	7	guide
3	buy	8	guy
4	guitar	9	juice
5	suit		

● 2.33

STALLHOLDER 1   Hi, can I help you?

CAROLINA   Yes, can I see the big rug at the top?

S   The orange one?

C   Erm, no, the white one, next to the orange one.

S   OK, I'll get it for you.

C   Thanks a lot.

S   There you are.

C   How much is it?

S   It's a hundred.

C   Hm. How about seventy-five?

S   I can't take less than ninety.

C   Really? I could give you eighty.

S   I'll do it for eighty-five.

C   Well … OK, I'll take it.

STALLHOLDER 2   Do you need any help?

C   No, thanks, I'm just looking.

S   They're nice candlesticks, aren't they?

C   They're nice, but do you have any silver ones?

S   Er, yeah, there are some here.

C   Oh, yes. Can I have a look at those ones there?

S   These big ones?

C   No, the smaller ones, just there … That's right.

C   How much do you want for them?

S   Ah, these ones are thirty-five.

C   Would you take twenty?

S   I can take thirty.

C   Erm … thanks, but I'll leave them.

C   Excuse me?

STALLHOLDER 3   Yeah, do you need some help?

C   Yes, how much is that leather jacket?

S   The red one?

C   Yeah.

S   Ah, it's seventy-five.

C   Is it second-hand or … ?

S   No, we don't have any second-hand clothes. All our stuff's new.

C   OK.

S   But there are some second-hand stalls just over there, if that's what you're looking for.

C   No, no, it's OK. Erm, so what size is it?

S   I'll have a look for you. Erm, it's a medium, but I might have some other sizes.

C   Can I try it on?

S   Yes, of course. There's a mirror just here.

C   Oh, right.

S   What do you think?

C   It's nice, but do you have any other colours?

S   That jacket, I'm afraid not, no. Just the red.

C   Mm, OK … I think I'll take it. Can I pay by credit card?

S   No problem.

C   OK. It was seventy-five, right?

● 2.34

CAROLINA   Can I have a look at those ones there?

STALLHOLDER   These big ones?

C   No, the smaller ones.

C   I could give you eighty.

S   I'll do it for eighty-five.

C   Well, OK … I'll take it.

● 2.35

CAROLINA   Can I see the big rug at the top?

STALLHOLDER   The orange one?

C   No, the white one.

C   Would you take twenty?

S   I can take thirty.

C   Thanks, but I'll leave them.

● 2.36

STALLHOLDER   Hello. Do you need any help?

CAROLINA   Yes. Do you have any bookcases?

S   Yes, we do. We've got some nice bookcases over here.

C   Oh, right. How much is the big one?

S   It's 110, but we've got some cheaper ones. This black one's just 80.

C   Hm. Do you think you'll get any more?

S   Yes, I get them in quite often, so you could try again in a few weeks.

● 2.37

ANNA   I think my favourite thing is my TV, because I watch TV every day for one hour or two hours. I like to watch my favourite programmes. And it helps me relax after a long day at work.

ALBA   My most treasured possessions are my books. I've had some of them since I was five. They were given to me by my mother and they've travelled with me from Venezuela to Scotland, then to Italy, then to Austria, then to the UK. Wherever I go, the longer I live, the more books I buy and they just pile up. I have boxes upon boxes and they will go with me everywhere I go. I love my books.

CLAUDIA   Erm, one of my favourite things I own is my passport. It, erm, I use it a lot and it has a lot of stamps from different countries in it because I travel a lot. I need it for work but I also need it every time I go on holidays and I just like it because it means I can do a lot of different things in lots of different countries.

EREN   One of my most treasured possessions is a perfectly round pebble. It's a pebble that I found when I was little. I think I was about ten years old and I was playing on the beach, and it just reminds me of those days, the, erm, sunny summer days and long evenings and, erm, it's so round that people just can't believe that it's completely natural. And I absolutely love it because it is, erm, like a mosaic. It has some white bits and grey bits, different colours.

● 2.38

1

AGNIESZKA   So, what are we having to eat?

BRENDA   I don't know. Is there a menu in English?

A   I don't think so. Can I help?

B   Yeah … *barszcz* I know, *placek* I know … what's '*kluski*'?

A   *Kluski*. They're made of potato.

B   Potato?

A   Yeah, they're like little balls. Sometimes they have meat inside them.

B   OK. What about this?

2

NAZIF   Hi, Helen.

HELEN   Afternoon. Have you lost something?

N   Yes, I'm looking for my blue … erm … What's it called?

H   Your pen?

N   No. I don't remember the word in English. It's a kind of book. You write in it, you know, times, things to do …

H You mean your diary?
N That's it, a diary.
H Is that it over there?
3
HAE-WON Manuel, what's a 'kettle'?
MANUEL A what?
H A 'kettle'.
M Where's that?
H Um ... it's in paragraph two.
M Hang on. Oh, it's a ... you usually find it in the kitchen.
H OK ...
M You use it to make water hot.
H Right ...
M When you make tea or coffee, for example.
H Oh, I see. Thanks.

2.39
SANDRA OK, it's dark blue with silver numbers and it's made of metal. It's quite thin. It's about ten by four centimetres and weighs about eighty grams. It has a camera.

2.40
1 Farsi is spoken in Iran.
2 The first colour photographs were taken in the 1860s.
3 The Yellow River is located in China.
4 In 1867, Alaska was sold to the USA by Russia.
5 *Ulysses*, by James Joyce, was written in the 20th century.
6 The 2005 Nobel Prize for Literature was given to Harold Pinter.
7 In English, baby elephants are called 'calves'.
8 The first football World Cup was won in 1930 by Uruguay.

2.41
now   down   shower   show   yellow   known

2.42
1	known	6	follow
2	flown	7	borrow
3	brown	8	tomorrow
4	yellow	9	crowded
5	shower	10	flower

2.43
1 Babies start to yawn six months before they're born.
2 Adults laugh, on average, seventeen times a day.
3 The average baby cries for two or three hours a day.
4 You use 12 muscles to smile; you use about 70 muscles to speak.
5 When you sneeze, air leaves your nose at one hundred and fifty kilometres per hour.

2.44
1
A I'm very hungry. Shall we make some dinner?
B Good idea. I'm absolutely starving.
2
A Are you sure the shops will be open tomorrow?
B Yes, I'm positive. Don't worry.
3
A You look really tired. Have you had a long day?
B Yeah, I'm exhausted. I'm going to bed.
4
A It's very hot in here, isn't it?
B Hot? It's boiling! Can we open a window?
5
A How could you do that parachute jump? Weren't you frightened?
B Yeah, I was absolutely terrified, but it was fun!
6
A I heard Kirsten found a job. She must be really pleased.
B Oh, yes, she's delighted.
7
A Will Ron be angry if we don't go to the meeting?
B I think he'll be absolutely furious!
8
A Is it cold there at the moment? Should I bring a winter coat?
B Yes. It's freezing.
9
A Were you surprised you passed the exam?
B I was really amazed. I don't know how I did it.

2.45
1
RACHEL Hi, Jean-Paul.
JEAN-PAUL Morning, Rachel. Happy birthday!
R Oh, cheers. How did you know?
J Oh, you know. Somebody told me. Er ... I've just bought you a present.
R Is it for me? Ah, that's very kind of you.
J You're welcome. Be careful!
R Ouch!
J I said be careful!
R What is it?
J It's a cactus. You said your flat needed some plants, so ...
R Well, yes, it does. Yes. Thanks very much, Jean-Paul.
J Don't mention it. Are you doing anything exciting tonight?
R Oh, you know, just going out with some friends. Why don't you come along?
J I'd love to, thanks.
2
J Hi, Rachel. What are you reading?
R Oh, hi. I got a letter from NBS this morning.
J Who?
R NBS? I applied for a job there.

J Yeah?
R Well, they've given the job to someone else.
J Oh, that's not good.
R They said I don't have enough experience.
J Well ...
R I've been here for almost five years, Jean-Paul!
J I'm really sorry, Rach.
R Me too.
J So, does that mean you're staying here?
3
R Hi, Jean-Paul. How are you?
J I'm OK.
R Look, Jean-Paul, about last night ... I'm really sorry. My sister called, the one who lives in New Zealand, she's just had a baby, her second. She called me and we ended up talking on the phone all evening!
J That's OK.
R So did you go to the cinema?
J Well, we said we'd meet outside the cinema at seven-thirty, so, yes, I did.
R So who did you go with?
J What? I didn't go with anyone.
R Sorry!
J Don't worry about it. It was a good film, anyway.
4
R Good morning, Jean-Paul!
J Oh, hello. You look happy this morning.
R Yes, I've done it!
J Done what?
R I've found a new job!
J Oh, right, congratulations! Well done!
R Thanks!
J So, where are you going?
R Cool Net.
J What?
R Cool Net.
J But that's not in New York. It's miles away!
R Yeah, about two hundred miles. Actually, I should start looking for a place to live there ...
J That's a long way to go for a new job.
R Not really, I've been here for almost five years.
J Me too.
R So – time for a change, I think!

2.46
Good news
That's great! You did well.
Congratulations.
Well done.

Bad news
I'm sorry to hear that.
I'm really sorry.
That's not good.

Thanking
Thanks very much.
Cheers.
That's very kind of you.

Apologising
I'd like to apologise.
I'm really sorry.
Sorry.

2.47
A
1 Thanks very much.
2 That's great!
B
3 I'd like to apologise.
4 I'm sorry to hear that.

2.48
SHARMILA   It's great to see you, Jenny.
JENNY   Yeah, you too. So, what have you been up to?
S   Erm, things are very busy right now.
J   Really?
S   Yeah, everything seems to be happening at once. Erm … remember I told you we were planning to move?
J   Yeah.
S   Well, we've moved now …
J   Oh, right.
S   … and it's fantastic! We just love the house. There's loads of room and the street is quiet. And I've just started a new job!
J   Oh, great! So what are you doing?
S   I'm still teaching maths. But I'm at a different school.
J   And how is it?
S   Well, it's close to our new house, so that's nice, but some of the kids are difficult!
J   Hm, that's not good.
S   No. Well.
J   And how's Mani?
S   He's changed jobs as well, actually. He's getting more money now. He's really happy.
J   Oh, that's good.
S   Yeah. Anyway, what's new with you?
J   Not much.
S   No? How are things at work?
J   The same, really. Same job, same boyfriend, but, yeah, we're OK. We went to this great concert last weekend.
S   Oh, what did you see?
J   We saw this great band …

2.49
BEN   Hi, Rosy, it's Ben. Look, would you like to come out to dinner tonight?
ROSY   Maybe. I've just got back from a hard day at work. Who's going?
B   Well, just me actually.
R   Oh, right. You know, I think I'm just going to stay in.
B   That's OK, don't worry. By the way, do you think Jen'll be at home?
R   Actually, I've just seen her at the bus stop.
B   Really? What's her mobile number? I just have her home number.
R   Oh, just a second. Here you are. It's 077 145 96 70.
B   Thanks, Rosy. You're a star. Well, have a nice evening.

2.50
Well, I lived in Cairo, in Egypt, for a year and they used a lot of gestures there that I didn't know. Erm, I remember when I first got a taxi, I asked to go to the centre – in my terrible Arabic – and the driver pointed at his eyes with his finger. And I really didn't understand this. I thought he meant, er, "Be careful" or something like that. Anyway, the rest of the journey was, you know, fine and then a few days later I asked an Egyptian friend about the gesture. He explained that it means "of course, no problem". Taxi drivers often do it when you've told them where you want to go. So that was interesting, yeah.

2.51
age   huge   bridge   judge   average
language

2.52
1 bridge   6 village
2 message   7 fridge
3 luggage   8 page
4 change   9 average
5 orange   10 arrange

3.1
1 business centre   6 single room
2 parking   7 double room
3 air conditioning 8 twin room
4 laundry   9 buffet breakfast
5 health club

3.2
RECEPTIONIST   The Sun Hotel. How may I help you?
LEONARDO   Hello, is that reception?
R   Yes, it is. Can I help you?
L   Yes. I've seen your website and I'd like to just check a couple of things.
R   Yes. Go ahead.
L   Erm, your website says you have internet access in each room. Is it wireless?
R   Yes, it is.
L   And is internet access included? Or is there an extra charge for that?
R   No. It's included in the room rate.
L   OK, and, erm, I'll probably arrive quite late, around 10 pm. Is that all right?
R   Yes. We have twenty-four hour reception.
L   That's good. And another thing, er, does the hotel have a swimming pool?
R   Yes, and we also have a fitness room.
L   OK, well, that sounds fine. Erm, could I book a room then, please?
R   Yes, just a moment … For what dates, please?
L   I'd like to book a single room for three nights, from the tenth of November.
R   Certainly. And what's your name, please?
L   It's Leonardo Barreiros, B-A-double R-E-I-R-O-S.
R   Thank you, Mr Barreiros, and can I take your credit card number?
L   Er, yes, it's a Visa card, number four one three nine, one one …

3.3
RECEPTIONIST   Good evening.
LEONARDO   Hello. I have a reservation. My name's Leonardo Barreiros.
R   Sorry, could you spell your surname, please?
L   B-A-double R-E-I-R-O-S.
R   Thank you. Yes, that's fine, Mr Barreiros. Three nights, yes?
L   That's right. I'm leaving on the 13th, Saturday.
R   Can I see your passport, please?
L   Here you go.
R   And could you fill in this registration card?
L   Right … Here you are.
R   Thank you. Here's your passport and the key to your room. It's room number fourteen oh six, on the fourteenth floor.
L   Thanks, and, uh, do you have a map of the city?
R   Yes, here you are. There's also an information folder in your room.
L   Thanks. Oh, ah, what time is breakfast?
R   It's from 6.30 to 10 am, in the dining room.
L   And what's the check-out time?
R   It's eleven am.
L   Right.
R   Would you like some help with your suitcase?
L   No, thanks. That's fine.
R   All right, Mr Barreiros. The lift is over there. Enjoy your stay.

3.4
Checking and booking
1 Your website says you have internet access. Is it wireless?
2 And is internet access included? Or is there an extra charge for that?
3 Does the hotel have a swimming pool?
4 I'd like to book a room for three nights, from the tenth of November.
Checking in
5 I have a reservation. My name's Leonardo Barreiros.
6 What time is breakfast?
7 What's the check-out time?

3.5
MIN   Hello? Min Ang here.
LEONARDO   Hello, Min. It's Leonardo.
M   Leonardo, hi! How are you feeling? Did you have a good flight?
L   Yes, it wasn't bad, thanks. Listen, Min, when are you free? What are you doing on Friday evening? Are you free then?
M   Er, Friday's difficult. I've got to work late. But, erm … I'm free on Wednesday evening.
L   Sorry, but I don't get there till about ten, so …
M   OK, well, what about lunch on Thursday … or Friday?
L   I can't on Friday, but Thursday … hmm, well, I'm meeting a colleague at one but I can rearrange it, no problem. So, could we meet at one o'clock?

M Yes, one o'clock's fine.
L And where should we meet?
M Well, how about at Petronas Towers? My office is near there. Let's meet by the main entrance of Tower Two.
L OK, that sounds good. I'll see you on Thursday then.
M Great. There's so much to talk about …

🌐 3.6

LEONARDO Hello.
MIN Hello, Leonardo. It's Min. I'm really sorry but I can't make it tomorrow. I've got meetings all day now.
L Oh … OK.
M But I'm free in the evening.
L Ah … I'm busy tomorrow evening.
M Oh, no! When exactly do you leave Kuala Lumpur?
L My flight leaves on Saturday morning at 11.15. You're working late on Friday, right?
M Yes, but … well, I guess I can take some work home … Yes, OK, let's meet on Friday evening.
L Are you sure? Great! And let's have dinner.
M That would be lovely.
L So, we're still meeting at Petronas Towers, right? Let's say at 6.30.
M OK, 6.30, Tower Two, main entrance. See you then.

🌐 3.7

1 What are you doing after class? / What are you going to do after class?
2 What time does this class finish?
3 Are you going anywhere on your next holiday? / Are you going to go anywhere on your next holiday?
4 What are you having for dinner tonight? / What are you going to have for dinner tonight?
5 Are you busy tomorrow evening?
6 What time do the shops close tonight?
7 Are you meeting any friends this weekend? / Are you going to meet any friends this weekend?
8 Are you working tomorrow afternoon?

🌐 3.8

JASON Are you doing anything this week?
AKIO Not much. Why?
J Well, it's the festival and there's a group I'd really like to see. My friend can get me free tickets.
A Yeah? Which group?
J Ladysmith Black Mambazo. You know, from South Africa. Do you fancy going too?
A Yeah, I'd love to. They're fantastic. When is it?
J Well, it's most of the week. I can do Thursday or Friday evening. What about you?
A Oh, sorry. I can't make it on Thursday or Friday. I'm working both nights.
J Can you make Saturday?
A Yeah, yeah. I'm off on Saturday.

J Me too. OK, they're performing twice on Saturday, at 3.30 and 8.00.
A Ah, can you do 3.30? The afternoon's best for me.
J Yeah, and we could have lunch first at Hana's Café at 12.30. It's close to the festival hall.
A Hana's Café? Nice place. OK, I'll see you there.

🌐 3.9

AKIO Jason, listen. I'm sorry but I can't make it on Saturday. Marianne just asked me to work from 2.00 till 10.00.
JASON That's too bad.
A Yeah, I'm really sorry. Can we postpone?
J Well, the thing is, Sunday's the last day.
A Well, can you do Sunday afternoon?
J No, I can't, actually. I'm seeing my mum. I'm free in the evening, though. Hold on, I'll just check the programme … Where is it? … Ah, here it is. Oh, no! Sunday afternoon's their last performance!
A Really? Well, I'll have to go then. Can I still have one of your free tickets?
J Well … yeah, I suppose so. I'm going to go tomorrow then … by myself.

🌐 3.10

MARTIN Erm, I'm a student at Université Bordeaux but every summer I go to England and get a job in, uh, a café or a pub, or something … and I need English for these jobs. My speaking's OK but, uh, I find listening kind of difficult so I try to listen to other people's conversations … and, yeah, I chat with the people I work with, usually after work, and when they say something I can't understand, I say, 'Wait! What did you say? Say it again. What does it mean?' and I try to use the expression myself. And then the next time I hear that expression, I know it.

ALEXEI I travel to the States a few times a year, so it's important for me to understand English well … especially, like, restaurant conversations or hotel conversations – checking in, room service and, erm, what else … oh, buying tickets. You know, things like that. So before I go to a restaurant or station, I think about what I want to say, what they'll probably say and … sometimes I check a phrase book. You know, I plan everything and then when I get there, I can understand things better and answer better. It usually works quite well.

AE-YOUNG Well, I use the Internet for listening practice. I like to know what's happening in other countries, so I listen to the news in English on my computer – the BBC World Service or CNN or something – and write down useful and

important words just for one news story … one's enough. Then I listen again and I write more words, then I listen again. Each time it gets easier to hear.

🌐 3.11

1
ANNA Did I tell you? I'm going to the cinema next week with some friends.
ROSE Oh, yeah? What are you going to see?
A 'Metropolis'. It's on at the Roxy.
R Oh, right. That's a good film.
A Are you free on Thursday evening?
R Erm, yes, I am, actually.
A Well, would you like to come with us?
R That would be really nice, Anna.
A What time?
2
LEO Hello.
JO Hi, Leo. It's Jo. How are you?
L Not bad. Is everything OK with you?
J Yeah, fine. Erm, what are you doing tomorrow?
L I'm working all day … from twelve to eleven. Why, Jo?
J Do you want to meet up for a coffee in the morning?
L Sorry, I'll be too tired. I never get up in the morning.
J Oh, OK. Well, maybe next time …
3
ANNA Sorry to bother you, Rose. Have you got a moment?
ROSE Yes. Go ahead.
A Sorry, but could you help me with my computer?
R I can try. What's the problem?
A I need to print something but it's not working.
R Again? OK. Let's have a look.

🌐 3.12

laundry   sauna   saw   awful

🌐 3.13

laugh   aunt   Australia   sausage

🌐 3.14

1 awful	6 sauce
2 daughter	7 strawberry
3 sauna	8 yawn
4 laundry	9 saw
5 lawyer	10 autumn

🌐 3.15

1 barbecue	9 comfortable
2 swimming pool	10 spacious
3 garden	11 modern
4 balcony	12 traditional
5 parking	13 large
6 fireplace	14 warm
7 air conditioning	15 cool
8 wooden floors	

🌐 3.16

DONNA José, come over here. Let's have a look at these homes.
JOSÉ Why? We can't move. We don't have enough money.

D Can we just have a look in the window? We can look, can't we?

J I suppose so.

D It'd be really nice to get out of the city.

J Hmmm, would it?

D Look at this one ... a house with two bedrooms, a large kitchen, a swimming pool! Imagine it, we'd come home from work, go for a swim to cool off, have a barbecue ...

J That would be nice, yeah.

D Sure it would!

J But it's three hundred and eighty dollars a week. We'd never be able to afford it.

D You never know. Maybe one day. What about this one near the beach? You could go surfing after work.

J It's three and a half hours from Sydney! I'd be too tired to go surfing after commuting for three and a half hours.

D You'd move schools, I guess. I bet you'd find a nice little school nearby.

J Yeah, but I love my job, the kids, all my friends at work. I wouldn't want to move schools.

D Well, you might change your mind. Can you imagine? Working in a small friendly school, rather than one with thousands of kids, cycling to work. Life would be so much easier.

J Well, sorry, but it sounds boring to me! You know I love the city. What would I do in the middle of nowhere?

D OK, OK. But one day, you know, if we have kids, maybe we'd want to get out of Sydney.

J Hmmm. Would you change your job? Would you leave IT?

D Yes, I think I would, actually.

J Oh, yeah? And what would you do? It's not easy to change jobs like that.

🔊 3.17

What would I do in the middle of nowhere?
I bet you'd find a nice little school nearby.
I wouldn't want to move schools.

Would you change your job?
Yes, I think I would, actually.
No, I wouldn't.

🔊 3.18

NATALIE My ideal home would be pretty much like the place I live in now but I would like it to be fifteen degrees warmer, so instead of growing lettuce and spinach I could grow things like mangoes and oranges and tomatoes. That would be really perfect.

EDUARDO Right now I live in a very small apartment, so I think my ideal home would have a lot more space. It would have a big living room, a big kitchen, big everything. I'd like to have maybe two bedrooms, one for me and one for guests. Also there would be really big windows with views of the mountains, like my old home in Brazil.

🔊 3.19

1 The worst thing about Chandigarh is, it's too quiet.
2 The best thing about the college is, it's so green.
3 The thing is, Chandigarh is too popular.
4 The trouble is, concrete is not beautiful to look at.

🔊 3.20

DONNA How's your daughter getting on? She's moved to Canberra, hasn't she?

MARISA Yeah, that's right. She's very happy, she loves it there and loves her job, but there are some problems with her flat.

D Oh, no. What sort of problems?

M Well, she lives with a family, Mr and Mrs Pierce, and they're really nice, but Eva doesn't get on well with their daughter!

D Ah, that sounds really awkward. Why don't they get along?

M Well, I think she's always complaining about Eva, saying she doesn't clean enough, her music's too loud, things like that. Eva doesn't really know what to do.

D Could she organise her day so she doesn't see the daughter?

M Eva says she's there all the time! Apparently, she even goes in her room. Sounds really annoying!

D Wow. Well, maybe she should talk to her, tell her how she feels.

M Yeah, she did that, but Eva says she's not interested. Maybe she should try again.

D I think so, yeah.

M I've never really been in that situation, so I don't know what to suggest. What would you do?

D What, if I was Eva? I'd probably talk to the parents, actually.

M Hm, I think she'd find that difficult. The problem is, they're really nice.

D Well yeah, so they'll probably listen.

M Yes, I think you're right. She'll have to think carefully about what to say.

D Would it be possible to write to them?

M A letter? No ... I don't think she'd want to do that. I'll tell her to talk to the parents.

D Yes, and I'd tell her to move if that doesn't work!

M Well, you know, it's not so easy. At least she's close to her college.

D I bet you miss her.

M Yes, it's hard, but she's fine really. She's enjoying her independence!

🔊 3.21

PAULA I have a big problem with my housemate. He loves cooking. He cooks almost every day, he uses every pan in the kitchen, every pot, every fork and knife, and he never, ever does the dishes.

LEONARDO Really? Have you tried leaving a note in the kitchen saying, Please wash all the pots and ... ?

P I've left notes, I've sent text messages, emails, everything. And he always says, 'Oh, sorry, I promise to do it next time, I forgot, I'm really busy,' and then, every time I wake up because he leaves most of the time earlier than me, like, the kitchen is a mess. It's really, really bad.

L Well, I also have problems with my neighbour. He sings very loudly in the morning and it's not that bad but he tries to imitate an opera singer.

P That's really bad.

L It is really bad but there's nothing I can do about it, like leaving a note or sending text messages or emails because I don't even know him.

🔊 3.22

ELA Well, in our flat there are five rooms. There's a living room and a bedroom – they're quite big – and we also have a study, a kitchen and a bathroom. I suppose my favourite room is the study. It's also the smallest room but it's the room that I really feel is mine. I don't just work in the study; I also like to lie on the sofa and read a good book.

🔊 3.23

NATALIE So, Megan, I know you've lived in a few different countries. I was just wondering how you felt when you moved into a new place. How did you get on with your neighbours?

MEGAN Erm, now that I live in the UK, I don't know any of my neighbours at all. I think that might be also because I live in an apartment block and you just never have any contact with anybody. When I was living in Costa Rica we lived in a house, erm, but also, it was much more common to talk to your neighbours. Very quickly, as soon as we moved in, all the ladies on the street came by, knocked on the door, introduced themselves.

N That's really nice.

M It was really nice. It was much easier to get to know people in the community.

N Uh huh.

🔊 3.24

block	school
back	architect
fork	quiet
broken	question

🔊 3.25

1	back	7	square
2	technology	8	headache
3	parking	9	quick
4	quiet	10	stomach
5	ticket	11	thick
6	market	12	think

● 3.26

a The Vatican City is in Rome, Italy.
b San Marino is in the east of Italy.
c Nauru is an island in the South Pacific.
d The Marshall Islands and Tuvalu are groups of islands in the Pacific Ocean.
e Saint Kitts and Nevis is a two-island nation in the Caribbean Sea.
f The Maldives are in the Indian Ocean, south-west of Sri Lanka.
g Malta is in the Mediterranean Sea, to the south of Sicily.
h Liechtenstein is between Austria and Switzerland.
i Monaco is in the south of Europe, on the Mediterranean coast, and it borders France.

● 3.27

PRESENTER In the studio with me today is Hiroto Saitou, the author of a fascinating new book about sumo wrestling called *Yokozuna*, published by Newman Press. Hiroto Saitou, welcome.
HIROTO Thank you.
P What exactly does the title of your book, *Yokozuna*, mean?
H Well, *yokozuna* is the very highest rank in sumo. If you're a *yokozuna*, you're a top champion. Sometimes there are no *yokozuna*, and at other times there have been three or four at the same time. The name comes from the rope – called a *tsuna* – that the *yokozuna* wears. The rope can weigh up to 20 kilos but it's not used during matches. It's only worn before matches, during a special ceremony.
P I see. Now, I always thought sumo wrestlers had to be Japanese, but that's not true, is it?
H That's right. Traditionally, sumo is very much a Japanese sport and, for foreigners, it was very difficult to become a *yokozuna*. But in 1993, Akebono Taro was the first foreigner to become a *yokozuna* in 1500 years. He was the first non-Japanese to reach the highest rank.
P So is that why he's such an important person in sumo?
H Yes, because, erm, before Akebono, nobody believed that foreigners could become *yokozuna*.
P So, where's he from?
H Well, he was born in Hawaii. His real name is Chad Haaheo Rowan. He changed his name when he went to Japan.
P Now, there seem to be a number of Hawaiians who are good at sumo. Why is that?
H Well, some Hawaiians make excellent sumo wrestlers because they are big and heavy. They can put on weight quite easily. Konishiki, for example, was another successful Hawaiian wrestler, though he never became a *yokozuna*. The two men actually fought each other in March 1991. It was the first sumo match between two non-Japanese wrestlers and Akebono defeated Konishiki.
P Oh. So, what was special about Akebono?
H Well, he was an unusual success story. As a young man, he enjoyed playing basketball and he won a basketball scholarship. He also wanted to study hotel management, but then he became interested in sumo from watching it on TV. A family friend introduced him to Azumazeki Oyakata, who was also from Hawaii. Azumazeki had his own group of sumo wrestlers, which we call a 'stable'. So in 1988, Rowan flew to Japan to join Azumazeki's stable. There, he was given his professional name, Akebono, which means 'new dawn'.
P And he was extremely successful in his career, wasn't he?
H Yes, that's right. His first professional appearance was in March 1988 and during his thirteen years of sumo wrestling, he won the Emperor's Cup a total of eleven times. He retired in 2001.
P That's fascinating. Thank you very much for giving us an insight into this extraordinary sport.

● 3.28

1 He was born in Hawaii.
2 He won a basketball scholarship.
3 He wanted to study hotel management.
4 He became interested in sumo from watching it on TV.
5 He flew to Japan to join Azumazeki's stable.
6 Akebono defeated Konishiki.
7 He was the first foreigner to become a *yokozuna* in 1500 years.
8 He retired in 2001.

● 3.29

agree	finish
become	practise
decide	retire
defeat	study
enjoy	suggest

● 3.30

decide – decided   practise – practises
buy – buying   speak – spoken

● 3.31

RENATA I think one of the most important people in Polish history, I mean recent history, is Lech Wałęsa …
INTERVIEWER Right.
R … who was the first president of Poland after communism. As far as I know, he was an ordinary worker, but he had a very strong character and he wanted to change the country. He became leader of a kind of workers' organisation, I mean *Solidarność*.
I That was Solidarity? The union?
R Solidarity, yes. So he was a real leader and people followed him.
I Do you know anything about his life?
R Not very much. I think he was an electrician and I know that he worked in Gdańsk. I remember him from that time, but I don't know what he did before that.
I OK. And then he became the president?
R Yes. Communism ended in Poland in 1989 and Wałęsa won the election for president.
I And how long was he president?
R Five years? Yes, five years. And then he lost the next election in 1995.
I Right.

● 3.32

RENATA When it comes to places, I think that Kraków is very important.
INTERVIEWER Yeah, of course.
R You probably know it was the capital of Poland in the past. It's a very nice city, an old city and it has a very rich history. It gets a lot of tourists but it's also a place where artists live and that creates a special atmosphere.
I Right. Do you mean it's an artistic place?
R Well, yes, there's a lot of beautiful architecture, galleries and music as well. Especially if you're around in the evening, and you go to clubs and pubs. It's the place to go to hear jazz.
I Is Kraków well known for jazz?
R Yes, you can find a lot of jazz clubs in the city centre. If you enjoy listening to music and stuff, you should definitely go.
I It must have a very interesting history.
R Yes … I don't know much about its history. It was the capital of Poland but then the capital was moved to Warszawa, to Warsaw … but Kraków is still the art capital of Poland.
I Is it near Warsaw?
R No. No, Warsaw is more or less in the centre of the country but Kraków is in the south.
I Ah. And how big is it?
R It's not very big, maybe the fourth or fifth biggest city in Poland? I don't really know for sure, but I think the population is less than a million.
I Right.

● 3.33

1
PAT I'm so looking forward to seeing you, Helen, and meeting your new boyfriend … Luis, right? But what clothes should I bring? Is it warm?
HELEN Yes, it's warm in the day but bring some jumpers or a jacket or something for the evenings.
P Jumpers? Thick ones, woolly ones, you mean?

H Er, yes, maybe.

P Like my blue one? You know the one?

H Yes, the blue one or your red one or whatever. It doesn't matter.

2

P So, what are we having for lunch, darling?

H Er, I'm not sure yet. Maybe some soup? (later)

P Mmmm, this soup's absolutely delicious. Your cooking has got much better, Helen. What's in it?

H Oh, er, vegetables mainly. Onions, peppers, potatoes and stuff like that.

P Right. So, you, er, chop the veg, and then what?

H Well, I think you add water and some herbs and things ... Sorry, I didn't actually make it. Luis did.

P Ah, OK. Well, tell him it was lovely, and I'd like the recipe! When are we seeing him again?

H This afternoon, at three.

P Ah.

3

P So, Luis, you were born in Spain, right?

LUIS Yes, that's right. In Galicia.

P Oh, yes. Where exactly?

L Well, actually, in a farmhouse in the middle of nowhere! It was sort of surrounded by mountains. The nearest town was Ortigueira, which is on the, er, the north-west coast.

P Oh, right. And did you stay there throughout your childhood?

L No. We moved to Argentina, to Buenos Aires, when I was three, so I don't really remember it at all. But I've always had a, a kind of special feeling about the mountains. It's difficult to explain, but I love being able to see the mountains. It gives me a sense of space, I guess.

🔊 3.34

student   president   parliament
government   important   elephant

🔊 3.35

1 student	6 accountant
2 moment	7 apartment
3 different	8 excellent
4 important	9 independent
5 president	10 elephant

🔊 3.36

NATALIE It's really strange about mobile phones these days. I know I have a funny relationship with mine because sometimes I will use it every day and then I'll go for three weeks when I just leave it at home and I don't bother with it. What about you?

PAULA How, how do you communicate with people when you, er, leave your mobile behind?

N The funny thing is, I don't. I quite like just to leave it in the house and have nobody call me.

P I think, I don't know, I think I would die without my mobile phone.

N Really?

P If I, the, the few times that I, I, forget it I just feel naked without it. I, I become desperate. I need to have my mobile phone with me ... erm ...

N Is that for someone to contact you or for you to send messages?

P I don't know. It's just the fact that I need it with me all the time.

METIN I have an old iPod which I only use for music. I always leave it in my coat pocket so when I go out, I know I have it. I use it all the time ... on the way to work, on the bus, when I go shopping ... The other day it was hot so I left my coat at home and forgot my iPod. I was so bored ... and also kind of nervous. I really need my music to relax.

FABIO Wow, interesting! I have an iPod, too, but I hardly ever use it. It was just a waste of money.

M Really? I couldn't live without mine.

F Well, to be honest, I'm just not interested in electronic gadgets, machines and stuff. I don't even have a computer at home. I don't know how to use them.

M You're joking!

F No. It makes life easier, not having that stuff.

M No way! It would make life more difficult for me. I mean, how do you live without the Internet?

F It's easy ... Actually, I have a mobile phone. My company gave it to me and I use it for my job. Well ... and to call friends, sometimes. And check the football scores. But that's it!

M Hm.

🔊 3.37

Call 1

BANK ASSISTANT You're through to Alan at Interbank. How can I help you?

CHRISTINE Oh, hello. Can I check how much is in my account, please?

B Of course. I'll just have to ask you a few questions, for security. ...

B OK, that's fine. Erm, your bank balance is two thousand, two hundred and twenty-five dollars and fifty-three cents.

C How much?

B Two thousand, two hundred and twenty-five dollars and fifty-three cents.

C I don't understand. I thought I only had about two hundred. Was a large amount paid in recently?

B Er ... Yes, two thousand dollars was paid in yesterday.

C Really? That's odd. It must be my annual bonus. I was expecting it ... but not that much.

B Er ... is there anything else I can help you with today?

C No, no. Thanks very much. You've made my day!

Call 2

RECEPTIONIST Good morning, ABC Investments. How can I help you?

C Can I speak to John Andrews, please?

R Yes, who's calling?

C It's Christine, his wife.

R Just a moment, please.

R Hello, Christine? I'm sorry, but John isn't here at the moment. I think he's at lunch.

C Oh. Do you know when he'll be back?

R No, sorry, but he shouldn't be too long. Do you want me to take a message?

C Er, yes, please. When he comes back, could you ask him to call me? Tell him I've got some good news!

R All right, I will. Bye.

Call 3

JOHN Hello?

C Hello, John? It's Christine.

J Hi. Listen, the reception's really bad here. I'll call you back in a second. OK?

C Yeah, OK.

J Christine? Can you hear me now?

C Yeah, that's better. Listen, I've got some great news. I've got my bonus!

J Oh, really? How much is it this time? 200? 300?

C No. That's what's so amazing! It's 2,000!

J 2,000! You're joking! Are you sure they haven't made a mistake?

C Thanks a lot!

J No, I'm sure you've earned every cent. Wow! We could book that holiday in Norway!

C That's why I'm calling. I checked flights to Norway in May and they're a really good price. Shall I book them?

J Er, well ... maybe we should talk about it tonight ...

C Come on, John. We've thought about it for years! We'll never get another chance like this.

J OK, OK. Go ahead and book. Listen, I've got to go but I'll call you back later, OK?

C OK. Speak to you later.

🔊 3.38

Call 4

CHRISTINE Hello?

BANK MANAGER Oh, hello. Is that Christine Andrews?

C Yes.

B Oh, hello. This is Paul Jennings from Interbank. Is this a good time to talk?

C Yes, it's fine.

B I'm afraid we've made a mistake on your account, number 12807747.

C Oh, no. What's happened?

B Unfortunately, a cheque for a different C Andrews was paid into your account by mistake. The person has the same name and almost the same account number. Only one number is different.

We're very sorry but I'm afraid this was a computer error.

c Ah. Well, that explains it.

b So, we'll make the necessary arrangements and the money will leave your account today.

c Erm, well, hold on minute. Unfortunately, I've booked a holiday with the money, so I'll, er, need to call the holiday company to cancel. I don't …

🔊 3.39

1 Can I speak to John Andrews, please?
2 It's Christine, his wife.
3 I'm sorry, but John isn't here.
4 Listen, the reception's really bad here.
5 Just a moment, please.

🔊 3.40

I used to believe that monsters lived under my bed.

I used to jump out of bed so they couldn't get me.

I'd jump out of bed so they couldn't get me.

🔊 3.41

LEONARDO In Costa Rica, if you have a meeting, er, people always ask you, OK, is it going to be Costa Rican time or regular time, 'cos if it is Costa Rican time, you're supposed to get there like maybe thirty or forty minutes later. I think that Costa Rican time exists because people are never in a hurry, people take their time having their breakfast, erm, and you take your time having your lunch and maybe you go to work and you start talking with friends and colleagues and there's never a hurry for anything.

MEGAN I also find that because I'm in a hurry to get where I'm going I'm usually right on time and I have to get used to the fact that, erm, everybody else is going to be getting to the meeting a little bit more slowly and that things will probably start after we've had a coffee and a chat as opposed to right on time.

🔊 3.42

receive   money   eight   they

🔊 3.43

group A	group B
ceiling	grey
journey	neighbour
key	weigh
receipt	
Turkey	

🔊 3.44

1 neighbour   6 ceiling
2 receipt   7 eight
3 key   8 money
4 grey   9 weigh
5 journey   10 receive

🔊 3.45

LEWIS Do we have to watch this?

AMELIA What?

L This boxing match. Can't we watch something else?

A No, I want to see it.

L But you don't like boxing.

A I do. I've always liked it.

L But why? I think it's awful.

A Really? I find it quite exciting.

🔊 3.46

AMELIA Really? I find it quite exciting.

LEWIS But it's very violent. I mean, a lot of boxers get injured. Some even die.

A Sorry, but more people die in football matches, you know – from heart attacks and stuff. Lots of sports can be dangerous.

L Yes, but in football, you're not trying to hurt someone, are you? In boxing, the idea is to hit the other guy until he can't stand up.

A We all know that people are aggressive. Naturally. It's silly to say they're not—

L Well, not really. I think it depends on their environment.

A Hmm … anyway, boxers don't just hit each other, you know. They train for thousands of hours. The best boxers are great athletes – like Mohammed Ali. And anyway, nobody has to box. They have a choice. I really feel that if people want to box, we shouldn't stop them.

L And what about children – like under sixteen – they shouldn't box. They're too young. And it teaches them to be violent and—

A No, no. It's a sport, like any other sport, and it actually trains them to defend themselves. And it's perfectly safe … they wear helmets and all the protective gear.

L But what if people want to fight in the streets, or in the park?

A Of course that's not the same. In a proper boxing match, they have rules to protect the boxers—

L Yeah, but—

A Just a second. The thing is, they have rules and there's a referee. The boxers wear gloves, there are doctors near the ring. If you ban boxing, people will just start boxing illegally and that'll be a lot more dangerous.

L OK, that's a good point.

A Another thing is, being a boxer is a job, you know. Some people box to make money, to live.

L But you said boxers are great athletes, right?

A Yes, exactly.

L So they don't have to box. They could do another sport … Oh, look, it's finished.

A What, already? Oh, thanks a lot.

L Sorry. Erm … would you like some more coffee?

🔊 3.47

1 I think it's awful.
2 I find it quite exciting.
3 We all know that people are aggressive.
4 And anyway, nobody has to box.
5 I really feel that if people want to box, we shouldn't stop them.
6 Of course that's not the same.
7 The thing is, they have rules and there's a referee.
8 Another thing is, being a boxer is a job, you know.

🔊 3.48

1 Sorry, but more people die in football matches, you know.
2 Yes, but in football, you're not trying to hurt someone, are you?
3 Well, not really. I think it depends on their environment.
4 Just a second. The thing is, they have rules and there's a referee.
5 OK, that's a good point.
6 Yes, exactly.

🔊 3.49

1 If I <u>see</u> Susan, <u>I'll</u> give her your message.
2 If I <u>had</u> a bike, <u>I'd</u> use it to get to work.
3 <u>He'd</u> be a lot healthier if he <u>did</u> some exercise.
4 If we <u>go</u> to Spain, <u>we'll</u> visit Andalusia first.
5 If you <u>had</u> a computer, your life <u>would</u> be a lot easier.
6 If she <u>works</u> late, <u>she'll</u> get a taxi home.

🔊 3.50

1
A Can I take you out for dinner?
B That would be lovely!
2
A Would you close the window, please?
B Yes, it is rather cold.
3
A Let's eat and then go to the cinema.
B I'd prefer to go to the cinema first.
4
A Brandon Hotel. Can I help you?
B Yes. I'd like to book a room, please.
5
A We're going for a drink. Can you come too?
B I'd love to. I'll just get my jacket.
6
A Would it be possible to meet up tomorrow?
B I'd rather meet today if we can.
7
A Would you mind lending me your dictionary?
B Sorry, but I'd rather not. I'm using it now.
8
A How about coffee at three o'clock?
B Four would be better for me.

● 3.51

MIGUELA   A couple of years ago, I planned a holiday to Australia and I really wanted to, er, improve my speaking before I went, so I went back through my coursebook CD and listened to all the conversations in shops and restaurants and things like that again.

ASLAN   OK.

M   And then I read the scripts, and I tried to speak at the same time as the recording.

A   You mean you repeated each line after the recording?

M   You can do that at first, yes. But after a while, you can actually try to speak at the same time as the person on the recording.

A   Wow! And did it work?

M   Yeah, it gets easier the more times you do it, of course. You can do it with songs too, but that's more difficult.

A   Mm. Well, I had one teacher who told us to use dictaphones, you know? Voice recorders?

M   Yeah, I know. And you can use your computer for that too.

A   That's right, yeah. Well, we all had to prepare a talk about something – I think I did a talk about Istanbul, actually. So I planned and recorded it.

M   OK.

A   Then I listened to my talk, and I wrote down what I said.

M   That's interesting. And then …

A   Then I tried to, er, improve the text, you know, to make it better.

M   How did you do that?

A   Well, I checked my grammar, I looked up some new words in a dictionary, checked some pronunciation, things like that. Then I practised my talk again, and recorded it again. I remember I recorded my talk three or four times.

M   Wow!

A   Yeah. By the end it was brilliant. No, really, it was. It was much better. So I do this sometimes when I know I have to give a talk in English. It's quite hard work, but it really helps.

● 3.52

1

LEONA   Excuse me, I'm Leona Cook from UPC news. Can you tell us, what do you think about Sandstown airport?

KARL   Well, I haven't thought about it a lot, but I suppose it should be moved. It's very old. I remember when it was built … thirty-five, forty years ago?

L   Forty-two years. What do you think about the idea of simply extending the airport by building another terminal? Wouldn't that be better?

K   Well, I'm not sure about that. There isn't room, unless they build over the North Park, and I wouldn't want that. I don't think there are enough green spaces in the town as it is.

2

LEONA   Excuse me. Can I ask you, what's your opinion about the airport? Where do you think it should be?

CAROLE   I know some people think we should move it, but I don't really agree. I use the airport quite a lot and it's good to have the airport near the town. It's true we need a bigger airport, but the location isn't a problem.

L   But if they made the airport bigger, they'd have to build over the North Park, wouldn't they? Surely that wouldn't be a good thing?

C   Actually, I'm not so sure. I grew up near that park and I don't think it's anything special, and it's already very noisy because of all the planes. But there's lots of lovely countryside outside the town, and we don't want to lose that.

3

LEONA   Excuse me, Leona Cook, UPC news. There's a lot of discussion at the moment about the airport here and where it should be. Do you have any thoughts on that?

ABBAS   Well, I might be wrong, but I think they should build the airport near Sibley. But not in the Nature Reserve.

L   But Sandstown already has an airport. Wouldn't it be cheaper just to make that airport bigger?

A   That's a good point, but I think they could sell the land in Sandstown. I guess it's worth a lot of money. Then they could use that money to pay for the new airport. Yeah.

● 3.53

1   I haven't thought about it a lot, but I suppose it should be moved.

2   Well, I'm not sure about that.

3   I don't really agree.

4   It's true we need a bigger airport, but the location isn't a problem.

5   I'm not so sure.

6   I might be wrong, but I think they should build the airport near Sibley.

7   That's a good point, but I think they could sell the land in Sandstown.

8   I guess it's worth a lot of money.

● 3.54

people   channel   usual   awful

● 3.55

1 skilful		7 travel
2 simple		8 possible
3 people		9 useful
4 hospital		10 vowel
5 vegetable		11 usual
6 national		12 awful

Vowels

Short vowels

/ə/	/æ/	/ʊ/	/ɒ/	/ɪ/	/i/	/e/	/ʌ/
teacher ago	married am	book could	on got	in swim	happy easy	wet any	cup under

Long vowels

/ɜː/	/ɑː/	/uː/	/ɔː/	/iː/
her shirt	arm car	blue too	or walk	eat meet

Dipthongs

/eə/	/ɪə/	/ʊə/	/ɔɪ/	/aɪ/	/eɪ/	/əʊ/	/aʊ/
chair where	near we're	tour	boy noisy	nine eye	eight day	go over	out brown

Consonants   voiced   unvoiced

/b/	/ð/	/v/	/dʒ/	/d/	/z/	/g/	/ʒ/
be bit	mother the	very live	job page	down red	magazine	girl bag	television

/p/	/θ/	/f/	/tʃ/	/t/	/s/	/k/	/ʃ/
park shop	think both	face laugh	chips teach	time white	see rice	cold look	shoe fish

/m/	/n/	/ŋ/	/l/	/r/	/w/	/j/	/h/
me name	now rain	thing drink	late hello	carry write	we white	you yes	hot hand

Irregular verbs

Infinitive	Past simple	Part participle
All forms are the same		
		bet
		cost
		cut
		hit
		let
		put
		set

Past simple and past participle are the same

bring	brought
build	built
burn	burned
buy	bought
catch	caught
feed	fed
feel	felt
fight	fought
find	found
get	got
have	had
hear	heard
hold	held
keep	kept
leave	left
lend	lent
lose	lost
make	made
mean	meant
meet	met
pay	paid
read /riːd/	read /red/
say	said
sell	sold
send	sent
shoot	shot
sit	sat
sleep	slept
spend	spent
stand	stood
teach	taught
tell	told
think	thought
understand	understood
win	won

Infinitive	Past simple	Past participle
All forms are different		
be	was / were	been
begin	began	begun
blow	blew	blown
break	broke	broken
can	could	been able to
choose	chose	chosen
do	did	done
draw	drew	drawn
drink	drank	drunk
drive	drove	driven
eat	ate	eaten
fall	fall	fallen
fly	flew	flown
forget	forgot	forgotten
freeze	froze	frozen
give	gave	given
go	went	been / gone
grow	grew	grown
hide	hid	hidden
know	knew	known
ride	rode	ridden
ring	rang	rung
rise	rose	risen
see	saw	seen
shake	shook	shaken
show	showed	shown
sing	sang	sung
speak	spoke	spoken
steal	stole	stolen
swim	swam	swum
take	took	taken
throw	threw	thrown
wake	woke	woken
wear	wore	worn
write	wrote	written
Infinitive and past participle are the same		
become	became	become
come	came	come
run	ran	run
Infinitive and past simple are the same		
	beat	beaten